Dickens and Christmas

Lucinda Hawksley

PEN & SWORD
HISTORY

First published in Great Britain in 2017
and republished in this format in 2021 by
PEN & SWORD HISTORY
an imprint of
Pen and Sword Books Ltd
Yorkshire – Philadelphia

ISBN 978 1 52678 037 9

Typeset in Times New Roman by CHIC GRAPHICS
Printed in the UK by CPI Group (UK) Ltd, Croydon, CR0 4YY

Pen & Sword Books Limited incorporates the imprints of Atlas,
Archaeology, Aviation, Discovery, Family History, Fiction, History,
Maritime, Military, Military Classics, Politics, Select, Transport, True
Crime, Air World, Frontline Publishing, Leo Cooper, Remember When,
Seaforth Publishing, The Praetorian Press, Wharncliffe Local History,
Wharncliffe Transport, Wharncliffe True Crime and White Owl.

For a complete list of Pen & Sword titles please contact

PEN & SWORD BOOKS LIMITED
47 Church Street, Barnsley, South Yorkshire, S70 2AS, England
E-mail: enquiries@pen-and-sword.co.uk
Website: www.pen-and-sword.co.uk

Or
PEN AND SWORD BOOKS
1950 Lawrence Rd, Havertown, PA 19083, USA
E-mail: Uspen-and-sword@casematepublishers.com
Website: www.penandswordbooks.com

Contents

Dedication

This book is dedicated to my cousins (and godsons) Georgina, Harriet, Theo and Monty – whose great grandfather, Cedric Dickens, loved Christmas as much as their great great great great grandfather, Charles Dickens.

In memory of Bishop Michael Whinney.

Acknowledgements

For help with researching this book my thanks to the director of the Charles Dickens Museum and all the excellent staff and volunteers. Many thanks also to Emma Sharples from the Met Office, Beverley Cook at the Museum of London, Professor Michael Slater, and Dr Tony Williams (current President of the Dickens Fellowship); as well as the staff at the British Library and the London Library.

CHAPTER ONE

Charles Dickens's First Christmas

"'A merry Christmas, uncle! God save you!" cried a cheerful voice. It was the voice of Scrooge's nephew, who came upon him so quickly that this was the first intimation he had of his approach.

"Bah!" said Scrooge, "Humbug!"

He had so heated himself with rapid walking in the fog and frost, this nephew of Scrooge's, that he was all in a glow; his face was ruddy and handsome; his eyes sparkled, and his breath smoked again. "Christmas a humbug, uncle!" said Scrooge's nephew. "You don't mean that, I am sure?"

"I do," said Scrooge. "Merry Christmas! What right have you to be merry? What reason have you to be merry? You're poor enough."

"Come, then," returned the nephew gaily. "What right have you to be dismal? What reason have you to be morose? You're rich enough."

Scrooge having no better answer ready on the spur of the moment, said "Bah!" again; and followed it up with "Humbug."

"Don't be cross, uncle!" said the nephew.

"What else can I be," returned the uncle, "when I live in such a world of fools as this? Merry Christmas! Out upon merry Christmas! What's Christmas time to you but a time for paying bills without money; a time for finding yourself a year older, but not an hour richer; a time for balancing your books and having every item in 'em through a round dozen of months presented dead against you? If I could work my will," said Scrooge indignantly, "every idiot who goes about with 'Merry Christmas' on his lips, should be boiled with his own pudding, and buried with a stake of holly through his heart.'"

Charles Dickens, *A Christmas Carol* (1843)

DICKENS AND CHRISTMAS

In December of 1812, John and Elizabeth Dickens, who lived in the town of Portsmouth on the south coast of England, celebrated Christmas with their young family. They had a two-year-old daughter Frances (known in the family as Fanny) and a 10-month-old baby, named Charles. John Dickens was a clerk in the Navy's Payroll Office – an ironic job for a man who was renowned for being terrible at controlling his own finances.

For many in Britain, Christmas of 1812 was not a happy time. It was an era of austerity, while the country fought two wars, against the French army of Napoleon Bonaparte, and against the United States of America. To add to the heavy costs of wartime, the country also had to contend with the profligate spending of the Prince Regent, son of the incapacitated monarch King George III and heir to the throne.

In 1812, while the Dickens family would have been celebrating a lower-middle-class Christmas at their modest home in Portsmouth, the newspapers were regaling the general public with stories of how the aristocracy spent Christmas:

'At Chatsworth, the princely seat of the head of the Cavendishes, open house was kept on Christmas Day to all comers. Old English hospitality will preside there until the close of Twelfth Night.' (*The Globe*, Monday 28 December 1812)

'The Marquis and Marchioness Camden gave a magnificent ball and supper at their seat in Kent … The preparations displayed uncommon taste, and consisted of the usual brilliancy of light, and unique table decorations, for which that distinguished family is remarkable. The dancing commenced at ten o'clock, with the favourite tune of *Salamanca* … About thirty couples danced. About one o'clock the company supt; at half-past four the party broke up.' (The *Morning Post*, Monday 11 January 1813)

'On Christmas Eve ... the Duchess of York gave, as usual, her annual splendid fête at Oatlands, to a number of the Nobility and Gentry as well as to the tradespeople and her charity children … At one o'clock an elegant and substantial dinner was served up in the Steward's room for the tradespeople, and at two o'clock an elegant dinner was served up in the anti-chamber adjoining the Great Hall for the children, who were visited while at dinner by their Royal Highnesses the Duke and Duchess, the Duke of Cambridge, and all the company present; and they were waited upon by their Royal Highnesses's domestics; at six o'clock a sumptuous dinner was served up in the principal dining room, after which the company retired to one of the principal drawing rooms, where tables were placed all round, decorated in a manner similar to a Dutch Fair, and containing a variety of valuable trinkets, & c., the whole of which were ticketed with the names of all the company, including tradespeople, children & c., all of whom received, with grateful pleasure, their separate allotments.' (The *Ipswich Journal*, Saturday 2 January 1813)

Despite these glowing reports of grand parties and wealthy revellers, Christmas of 1812 was not a time of unmitigated harmony and happiness. Many felt that the season was changing beyond recognition, and not for the better. It was considered that a new spirit of selfishness was taking hold of the country. Several newspapers reported the most prominent criticism; that the season had lost its earlier significance of being a time when the poor were given alms and the rich were expected to share their wealth. In this still new century, it was felt by many critics that there was too much emphasis on money and possessions at Christmas time. Newspaper editors made much of the fact that the poor were being forgotten and left to go hungry while the rich enjoyed their parties and banquets. As the wars of 1812 pinched the finances of families all over Britain, a profligate celebration of Christmas by the rich was seen by many observers as unfeeling, when considering how many people were struggling to buy basic necessities.

For many centuries, Christmas Day in England was not the celebration it became by the end of the Victorian era. For the majority of the population it was a working day as usual and for all but the most privileged it was not a time of great feasting or parties. By the start of the nineteenth century, it was starting to gain more popularity as a feast day than in previous years, but the main celebration of the year was still that of Twelfth Night.

Christmas advertising of that time was prevalent, but they were advertising goods to be enjoyed throughout the Twelve Days of Christmas. It was not yet common for presents to be exchanged just on 25 December, but families often bought new toys and books for the children to enjoy over the festive season. Charles and Fanny Dickens would have been too young to appreciate what the newspapers of the day were advertising as 'Christmas Presents Conveying Instruction and Amusement', but the list of presents deemed indispensable in the winter of 1812 included the following books:

Gay's Fables, embellished with 100 beautiful woodcuts by Branston
(3s 6d)

The Book of Trades, in which every Trade is illustrated with separate
Engravings, and its history, utility, present state, advantages and
disadvantages are fully and accurately described. (10s 6d)

Advice to Youth, a Compendium of the Duties of Human Life by Dr
Hugh Blair [no price given]

The Magic Lantern, an amusing and instructive Exhibition for Young
People, with eleven coloured Engravings. By the Authoress of
Short Stories, Summer Rambles & c. & c. (6s)

*The Accomplished Youth; or the true Principles of Morality and
Politeness* (2s 6d)

The History of British Birds (5s)

The History of British Domestic Quadrupeds (2s 6d)

The Daisy, or Cautionary Stories in Verse, adapted to the ideas of
Children, from four to eight years old (1s or 2s coloured)

Another popular Christmas present at this time was the annual, a book
containing snippets of information, such as poems, excerpts from books,
household tips and activities and ideas for games to play. These annuals
were beautifully illustrated and lavishly decorated, intended to be given as
a high-status gift. They did not, at this date, concentrate on the theme of
Christmas. Although they were usually published for the Christmas market,
the publishers continued to sell them throughout the coming year, so an
annual released, for example, for Christmas 1812, would be titled *The 1813
Annual*.

A popular carol often sung during the Christmas of 1812 was a reminder
that the charitable giving that had characterised past Christmases needed to
be renewed. It is a very old Christmas song, most commonly known as *The
Ditchling Carol*, and its verses have varied over the centuries. Below is the
version that was printed in a number of newspapers in the year of Charles's
birth:

> Be merry all, be merry all,
> With holly dress the festive hall,
> Prepare the song, the feast, the ball,
> To welcome merry Christmas.

And, oh!, remember, gentles gay,
For you who bask in fortune's ray,
The year is all a holiday.
The poor have only Christmas.
When you, with velvets mantled o'er,
Briefly December's tempests frore,
Oh! spare one garment from your store
To clothe the poor at Christmas.

From blazing loads of fuel, while
Your homes with indoor summer smile,
Oh! spare one fagot from your pile
To warm the poor at Christmas.

When you the costly banquet deal
To guests who never famine feel,
Oh! spare one morsel from your meal
To feed the poor at Christmas.

When gen'rous wine your care controls,
And gives new joy to happpiest souls,
Oh! spare one goblet from your bowls
To cheer the poor at Christmas.

So shall each note of mirth appear
More sweet to heav'n than praise or prayer,
And angels in their carols there
Shall bless the Rich at Christmas.

By the year of Charles's second Christmas, London was about to witness an historic event. The winter of 1813 to 1814 went down in British history as one of the coldest in living memory. By the start of the new year, the River Thames in London had frozen so solid that it was possible to walk right across the river. Soon the frozen water had become a new byway, with resourceful traders setting up stalls on the thick floor of ice. These stalls soon grew into the now-famous Frost Fair of 1814.

There is a history of Frost Fairs taking place on London's frozen river since the 'mini ice age' of the seventeenth century. The first recorded fair took place in the winter of 1607 to 1608, but the most famous was in the winter of 1683-1684, when King Charles II visited the fair and ate ox meat roasted on a spit in the middle of the river. John Evelyn wrote in his diary for January 1684:

The weather continuing intolerably severe, streets of booths were set upon the Thames; the air was so very cold and thick, as of many years, there had not been the like … *Coaches plied from Westminster to the Temple, and from several other staires to and fro, as in the streetes, sliding with skeetes, a bull-baiting, horse and coach races, puppet plays and interludes, cookes, tipling and other lewd places, so that it seemed a bacchanalian triumph or carnival on the water, whilst it was a severe judgement on the land, the trees not onely splitting as if lightning-struck, but men and cattle perishing in divers[e] places, and the very seas so lock'd up with ice, that no vessels could stir out or come in.'*

The great freeze of 1813-1814 led to what was to be the very last Frost Fair. On Charles Dickens's second birthday, Monday 7 February 1814, the *Sussex Advertiser* printed the following account of frozen revelries on the Thames:

'The icy surface between the bridges, now called Frost Fair, was on Friday visited by thousands, drawn by curiosity from all parts of London, & c … The foot-path in the centre of the river was hard and secure, and among the pedestrians we observed four donkies, which trotted a nimble pace, and produced considerable merriment. At every glance, the spectator met with some pleasing novelty – Gaming, in all its branches, through out different allurements, while honesty was out of the question. Many of the itinerant admirers of the profits gained by E. O. Tables, Rouge et Noir, Tetotum, Wheel of Fortune, the Garter & c., were industrious in their avocations, leaving their kind customers without a penny to pay for the passage over a plank to the shore. Skittles was played by several parties, and the drinking tents filled by females and their companions, dancing reels to the sound of fiddle, while others sat round large fires, drinking rum, grog and other spirits. Tea, coffee, and eatables were provided in ample order.... The scene presented a perfect representation of a Dutch fair. Several tradesmen attended with their wares, selling books, toys, and trinkets of every description. Those who made purchases were presented with a label setting forth that the article was bought on the Thames frozen over.

Kitchen fires and furnaces were blazing in every direction, and animals from a sheep to a rabbit, and a goose to a lark, were turning on numberless spits.'

The Dickens family may well have attended the Frost Fair, as by the time of Charles's second birthday they had left Portsmouth, had moved briefly to London and finally settled in Kent. The family stayed in Kent for several years, although John's inability to manage their finances, meant they often had to move house with very little warning. Wherever they lived, and no matter how difficult the circumstances, books were a constant companion for Charles, and a means of escape. John Dickens loved collecting books, and his son read them avidly. In the 1880s, the Dickens family's nursemaid was interviewed by Robert Langton for his book *The Childhood and Youth of Charles Dickens* (1883). As a young woman, her name had been Mary Weller (a name which Dickens used in *The Pickwick Papers*). In the interview, Mary commented:

'Little Charles was a terrible boy to read, and his custom was to sit with his book in his left hand, holding his wrist with his right hand, and constantly moving it up and down, and at the same time sucking his tongue.'

In his unfinished autobiography, Dickens wrote about hiding himself away with his father's books and reading stories that fired his imagination:

'My father had left a small collection of books in a little room upstairs to which I had access (for it adjoined my own), and which nobody else in our house ever troubled. From that blessed little room, *Roderick Random, Peregrine Pickle, Humphrey Clinker, Tom Jones, The Vicar of Wakefield, Don Quixote, Gil Blas* and *Robinson Crusoe* came out, a glorious host, to keep me company. They kept alive my fancy, and my hope of something beyond that place and time – they, and the *Arabian Nights*, and the *Tales of the Genii* – and did me no harm; for, whatever harm was in some of them, was not there for me; *I* knew nothing of it. It is astonishing to me now, how I found time, in the midst of my porings and blunderings over heavier themes, to read those books as I did. It is curious to me how I could ever have consoled myself under my small troubles (which were great troubles to me), by impersonating my favourite characters in them … I have been Tom

7

Jones (a child's Tom Jones, a harmless creature) for a week together. I have sustained my own idea of Roderick Random for a month at a stretch, I verily believe. I had a greedy relish for a few volumes of voyages and travels – I forget what, now – that were on those shelves; and for days and days I can remember to have gone about my region of our house, armed with the centre-piece out of an old set of boot-trees: the perfect realisation of Captain Somebody, of the Royal British Navy, in danger of being beset by savages, and resolved to sell his life at a great price ... When I think of it, the picture always rises in my mind, of a summer evening, the boys at play in the churchyard, and I sitting on my bed reading as if for life. Every barn in the neighbourhood, every stone in the church, and every foot of the churchyard, had some association of its own, in my mind, connected with these books, and stood for some locality made famous in them. I have seen Tom Pipes go climbing up the church steeple; I have watched Strap, with the knapsack on his back, stopping to rest himself upon the wicket-gate; and I *know* that Commodore Trunnion held that club with Mr. Pickle in the parlour of our little village alehouse.'

Mary Weller also reminisced about Charles and Fanny performing together with 'Fanny accompanying the Pianoforte ... A rather favourite piece for recitation by Charles at this time [around 1819] was "The Voice of the Sluggard" from Dr. Watts, and the little boy used to give it with such great effect, and with *such* action and *such attitudes*.' The Dickens family was very fond of music, and Christmases in their household centred around music, singing and dancing.

When the family lived in Chatham, in Kent, John and Elizabeth Dickens became friendly with Mr Tribe, the landlord of the Mitre pub. Many years later, Mr Tribe remembered the children dancing together and singing sea shanties. Charles Dickens had recollections of he and Fanny being lifted onto one of the tables in the middle of the pub, to use as their stage, and of singing a song called 'The Cat's Meat Man'. When Dickens became famous, regulars to the Mitre often boasted of having witnessed the Dickens children perform. As an adult, Dickens commented to his friend John Forster that he must have seemed annoyingly precocious to those adults expected to watch him, although Mary Weller described him as having been 'a lively boy of a good, genial, open disposition, and not quarrelsome as most children are at times'.

In his 1858 Christmas story, *The Holly Tree*, Dickens drew upon these childhood memories, writing:

'There was an inn in the Cathedral Town where I went to school, that had pleasanter recollections about it ... It has an ecclesiastical sign ... the Mitre, ... and a bar, that seemed to be the next best thing to a bishopric, it was so snug. I loved the landlord's youngest daughter to distraction, – but let that pass. It was in this inn that I was cried over by my rosy little sister, because I had acquired a black eye in a fight. And though she had been, that holly-tree night, for many a long year where all tears are dried, the Mitre softened me yet.'

"Many of the hearts that throbbed so gaily then have ceased to beat; many of the looks that shone so brightly then, have ceased to glow; the hands we have grasped have grown cold; the eyes we sought have hid their lustre in the grave; and yet the old house, the room, the merry voices and smiling faces, the jest, the laugh, the most minute and trivial circumstances connected with those happy meetings, crowd upon our mind at each recurrence of the season, as if the last assemblage had been but yesterday! Happy happy Christmas, that can win us back to the delusions of our childish days; that can recall to the old man the pleasures of his youth; that can transport the sailor and the traveller, thousands of miles away, back to his own fireside and his quiet home!

Charles Dickens, *The Pickwick Papers* (1837)

CHAPTER TWO

Deck the Halls

"Would that Christmas lasted the whole year through, and that the prejudices and passions which deform our better nature, were never called into action among those to whom, at least, they should ever be strangers."

Charles Dickens, *Christmas Festivities* (1835)

There is a strangely prevalent belief that the British did not celebrate Christmas in any memorable way until after the marriage of Queen Victoria and Prince Albert (who is usually credited with bringing Germanic Christmas traditions to Britain), and the arrival of Charles Dickens's Christmas Books in particular. Contemporary accounts from centuries before Dickens was born show this to be untrue, such as this account from a Swiss traveller, living in England in the 1720s:

'Christmas day is the great festival of all Christian nations but on that day the English have many customs we do not know of. They wish each other a Merry Christmas and A Happy new Year; presents are given and no man may dispense with this custom. On this festival day churches, the entrances of houses, rooms, kitchens and halls are decked with laurels, rosemary and other greenery. Everyone from the King to the artisan eats soups and Christmas pies. The soup is called Christmas porridge and is a dish few foreigners find to their taste... as to Christmas pies everyone likes them and they are made with chopped meat, currants, beef suet and other good things. You never taste these dishes except for two or three days before and after Christmas and I cannot tell you the reason why.'

In Regency England, the celebrating of Christmas included decorating the house with greenery, playing games, singing, dancing, eating special Christmas foods and giving gifts if the family could afford to do so. The Dickens family would not, however, have had a Christmas tree, nor would they have expected a visit from Father Christmas. The first known British Christmas tree is attributed to Queen Charlotte, the German wife of King George III, who is said to have brought a Christmas tree from Germany after her marriage in 1761. In 1800, the elderly queen held a party for the children of her court at the Queen's Lodge, in Windsor. The tree she decorated for the children was a yew tree, onto which was attached lighted candles, and bundles of sweets, almonds and fruit. During Charles Dickens's childhood, Christmas trees were barely known in Britain, outside the royal court.

The figure of Father Christmas was little known in Britain before the Victorian age. A Father Christmas character could be seen in traditional mummers' folk dances and he makes an appearance in Ben Jonson's comedy 'masque' written for King James I, but he was not the same benign Father Christmas who grew out of the legend of St Nicholas and Santa Claus. Although Clement Clarke Moore's poem 'A Visit from St Nicholas' (better known today as ''Twas the Night Before Christmas') was published in America 1822, when Charles was ten years old, it was almost unknown in Britain. The image of a jolly, round old man with a beaming smile and thick white beard who brings presents to children on Christmas Eve did not become popular in Britain until the second half of the nineteenth century.

During Charles's childhood, the Christmas season lasted from Christmas Eve (24 December) until Twelfth Night (6 January). In the Christian church, 6 January is commemorated as the feast of Epiphany, the day on which the three wise men, or three kings, arrived at the stable in Bethlehem to visit the newborn baby Jesus. In 1756, during the reign of King George II, *The Gentleman's Magazine* reported that 'His Majesty, attended by the principal officers at Court ... went to the Chapel Royal at St James' and offered gold, myrrh and frankincense.' By the nineteenth century, however, these religious celebrations on 6 January had become almost forgotten, outside of the church itself. By the time of Charles Dickens's birth, the celebration of Twelfth Night in Britain was much more closely associated with parties and drinking, than with the original religious holiday.

There is often debate about when Twelfth Night should fall, as the twelfth evening after Christmas Day is actually 5 January. The diaries of the seventeenth century courtier Samuel Pepys, however, show that he celebrated it on 6 January, except for in those years when it fell on a Sunday, when celebrations were deferred until the Monday. Dickens's letters also show that his family celebrated on 6 January.

For many centuries, it was traditional for leaders of the Twelfth Night revels to be chosen and named as the 'King' and 'Queen; as such, it was in their power to dictate what the rest of the gathered party should do. Traditionally, these monarchs were chosen by chance; everyone present at a party would be given a slice of what was known as Twelfth Cake, inside which had been baked a dried bean and a dried pea. Whoever discovered these in their slice of cake became a monarch: getting the dried bean meant being the king and the dried pea meant being the queen. This quotation from Robert Herricke's poem *Twelfe Night, or King and Queene* (c.1630s) shows that this was common in the seventeenth century:

> "Now, now the mirth comes
> With the cake full of plums,
> Where Beane's the *King* of the sport here;
> Besides we must know,
> The Pea also
> Must revell, as *Queene*, in the Court here."

A seventeenth century recipe book, *A True Gentlewoman's Delight* (1653) by Elizabeth Grey, the Countess of Kent, includes a recipe for a 'spice cake', the type of cake used to create a Twelfth Cake:

> 'Take one bushel of Flower, six pound of Butter, eight pound of Currans, two pints of Cream, a pottle of Milk, half a pint of good Sack, two pound of Sugar, two ounces of Mace, one ounce of Nutmegs, one ounce of Ginger, twelve yolkes, two whites, take the Milk and Cream, and stirre it all the time that it boyles, put your Butter into a bason, and put your hot seething Milk to it, and melt all the Butter in it, and when it is bloud-warm temper the Cake, put not your Currans in till you have made the paste, you must have some Ale yest and forget not Salt.'

Samuel Pepys, a contemporary of the culinary countess, also wrote about Twelfth Night. On 6 January 1663, he recorded:

> '6th (Twelfth Day). Up and Mr. Creed brought a pot of chocolate ready made for our morning draft, and then he and I to the Duke's, but I was not very willing to be seen at this end of the town, and so returned to our lodgings, and took my wife by coach to my brother's,

where I set her down, and Creed and I to St. Paul's Church-yard, to my bookseller's, and looked over several books with good discourse, and then into St. Paul's Church ... So to my brother's, where Creed and I and my wife dined with Tom, and after dinner to the Duke's house, and there saw "Twelfth Night" acted well, though it be but a silly play, and not related at all to the name or day.... This night making an end wholly of Christmas, with a mind fully satisfied with the great pleasures we have had by being abroad from home, and I do find my mind so apt to run to its old want of pleasures, that it is high time to betake myself to my late vows, which I will to-morrow, God willing, perfect and bind myself to, that so I may, for a great while, do my duty, as I have well begun, and increase my good name and esteem in the world, and get money, which sweetens all things, and whereof I have much need. So home to supper and to bed, blessing God for his mercy to bring me home, after much pleasure, to my house and business with health and resolution to fall hard to work again.'

In 1665, Pepys wrote rather irritably in his diary that his wife and her friends had continued the Twelfth Night party long after he had decided to go to bed and that his wife didn't go 'to bed at all'. In 1669, Pepys wrote with relish about their Twelfth Cake and his family's Twelfth Night revels:

'... very merry we were at dinner, and so all the afternoon, talking, and looking up and down my house; and in the evening I did bring out my cake – a noble cake, and there cut it into pieces, with wine and good drink: and after a new fashion, to prevent spoiling the cake, did put so many titles into a hat, and so drew cuts; and I was the Queene; and The. Turner, King – Creed, Sir Martin Marr-all; and Betty, Mirs Millicent: and so we were mighty merry till it was night; and then, being moonshone and fine frost, they went home, I lending some of them my coach to help carry them, and so my wife and I spent the rest of the evening in talk and reading, and so with great pleasure to bed.'

By the time of Charles's first Christmas, in 1812, the dried bean and pea tradition had, mostly, been phased out and instead the Twelfth Night king and queen were chosen by a variety of different methods, including a lottery during which names would be chosen from a hat, or by the monarchs being voted in by their friends. Twelfth Night parties had also expanded so that everyone present had a role to play, not just the king and queen. Guests would be allotted characters and would have to dress up and act out their role, letting the other guests guess whom they were supposed to be. Entrepreneurial printers were quick to capitalise on this and posters, pamphlets and packs of cards were available to buy, often from bakers' shops, which detailed the types of characters that could be allotted to Twelfth Night revellers.

A description of a Twelfth Night party written by Jane Austen's niece, Fanny Austen Knight, dates from 1809, the year in which John and Elizabeth Dickens were married:

> '[Aunt Louisa] who was the only person to know the characters ... took [them] one by one out of the room, & having equipped them, put them into separate rooms, and lastly dressed herself. We were all conducted into the library and performed our different parts. Papa & the little ones from Lizzy downwards knew nothing of it & it was so well managed that none of the characters knew one another ... we had such frightful masks, that it was enough to kill one with laughing at putting them on & altogether it went off very well.'

Jane Austen's novels were published during the first years of Dickens' life and, although Christmas does not feature strongly in her books, there is a general impression of the Christmas season in the 1810s being one of parties and feasting. In *Emma*, published in 1815, when Charles was three years old, Mr Elton comments:

> 'Christmas weather ... Quite seasonable; and extremely fortunate we may think ourselves that it did not begin yesterday, and prevent this day's party, which it might very possibly have done ... This is quite the season indeed for friendly meetings. At Christmas every body invites their friends about them, and people think little of even the worst weather. I was snowed up at a friend's house once for a week. Nothing could be pleasanter. I went for only one night, and could not get away till that very day se'nnight.'

Such a snowy scene would have been reminiscent of Dickens's own childhood Christmases, as the 1810s was the coldest decade recorded in England since the 1690s. Between 1812 and 1820 six 'white Christmases' were recorded (with either snow or a thick frost on the ground). This may be one reason why Dickens was so fond of writing snowy Christmassy scenes in his fiction.

14

DECK THE HALLS

As Charles was one of eight children (two of whom died in infancy), the Christmas scenes at the Dickens family home would have been similar to a scene in Jane Austen's *Persuasion* (1817), published when he was five:

> 'On one side was a table occupied by some chattering girls, cutting up silk and gold paper; and on the other were tressels and trays, bending under the weight of brawn and cold pies, where riotous boys were holding high revel; the whole completed by a roaring Christmas fire, which seemed determined to be heard, in spite of all the noise of the others.'

The celebrating of a festival in the middle of winter dates back millennia and has mutated, grown and shrunk, according to governments, religions and social pressures. The tradition of British people decorating their homes with greenery dates back to pagan times, the pre-Christian celebrations of the Winter Solstice and the Roman festival of Saturnalia. Long before Christianity came to Britain, it was common practice to bring greenery into the home and to burn yule logs in the hearth; a precursor of Christmas decorations and candles. It was believed to be bad luck if the yule log was allowed to burn out before the twelve days of Christmas had finished. For many centuries, it was also believed to be bad luck to decorate a home before Christmas Eve, and in Britain, it was said that leaving decorations up after the end of Twelfth Night was also a bad omen, although in many Catholic countries, Christmas decorations are habitually left in place until Candlemas on 2 February.

The British Christmas suffered a sharp setback during the time of the Interregnum (1649-60) when the celebrating of Christmas was seen as "giving liberty to carnal and sensual delights". The festivities were banned, traders were ordered to keep working on 25 December and people were expected to fast on Christmas Day. People who wanted to hold religious services, celebratory dinners or family parties at Christmas had to do so in secret or risk having legal penalties imposed on them. In 1660, the short-lived English republic came to an end and King Charles II – son of the executed King Charles I – was crowned. During his reign, the celebration of Christmas became important again. Not everyone was happy about this new style of celebrating Christmas, however, and many clergymen and lawmakers complained it was a time of increased drunkenness and crime. The celebrating of Christmas continued to grow in popularity over the coming centuries, although it changed as British society changed and each ageing generation complained that Christmas was not as it had been in their childhood. By the beginning of the nineteenth century, there was a feeling that too many Christmas traditions had fallen out of fashion and that a Christmas renaissance was needed.

In Georgian England, when Dickens was a child, holly, ivy, pine needles and other greenery were used to decorate homes for Christmas, just as they had been used in pagan times. The Christian church had appropriated many earlier traditions and declared the plants to have religious significance, such as holly being symbolic of Christ's crown of thorns. If a family could afford it, large swags of greenery would be used to decorate rooms, staircases and windows and to frame paintings and mirrors. Many households also displayed a wreath, but these were usually made of simple greenery; it was not yet the fashion to have the more elaborate decorations which would become popular in Victorian Britain. Mistletoe had long been a popular part of Christmas decorations and Regency cartoons depict couples underneath a 'kissing bunch' of mistletoe – although in very religious households, mistletoe was considered scandalous and banned. In *Christmas Festivities*, the first Christmas story written by Dickens, in 1835, the grandfather tells his grandchildren that he kissed their grandmother under mistletoe when he was still a boy. He also included a mistletoe scene in *The Pickwick Papers* (1837):

> 'They all three repaired to the large kitchen, in which the family were by this time assembled, according to annual custom on Christmas Eve... From the centre of the ceiling of this kitchen, old Wardle had just suspended, with his own hands, a huge branch of mistletoe, and this same branch of mistletoe instantaneously gave rise to a scene of general and most delightful struggling and confusion; in the midst of which, Mr. Pickwick, with a gallantry that would have done honour to a descendant of Lady Tollimglower herself, took the old lady by the hand, led her beneath the mystic branch, and saluted her in all courtesy and decorum.'

Another Christmas tradition which the young Dickens children would have enjoyed, was seeing a baker's window displaying an elaborate Twelfth Cake. If they had been visiting London, they might have been taken to see the windows at Gunter's on Berkeley Square. Gunter's was known for its Italian-born confectioner William Jarrin, who became famed for his Twelfth Cakes (as well as for his ice cream).

In 1820, Queen Charlotte was presented with a 'very large and exceedingly rich' twelfth cake, created to look like a crown, by a Mr G. Button of Fleet Street. In *The Times*, Mr Button described his gift as:

'most beautifully and tastefully ornamented, with Justice standing on a rock, trampling venomous reptiles under her feet, in allusion to her Majesty's late sufferings and trial. On each side of the rock were horns of plenty, richly overflowing with great abundance of delicious fruits.'

Throughout the nineteenth century, the fashion for producing highly decorated cakes to celebrate Twelfth Night became increasingly popular and crowds would gather outside bakers' windows to see the latest creations, all designed to show off a confectioner's skill. Cakes would be laden with ropes and swags of sugar, almonds and marzipan decorations. The most elaborate of cakes would be layered – similarly to a wedding cake – with each layer being covered with symbols, animals or figures. Descriptions survive of cakes being decorated with troupes of dancers in beautiful costumes, wild animals such as tigers, bears or lions, domestic scenes or with figures from storybooks and the theatre, including characters from fairytales and Shakespeare, or the always popular Harlequin and Columbine.

'The celebration of Twelfth-Day with the costly and elegant Twelfth-cake has much declined within the last half-century. Formerly, in London, the confectioners' shops on this day were entirely filled with Twelfth-cakes, ranging in price from several guineas to a few shillings; the shops were tastefully illuminated, and decorated with artistic models, transparencies, &c. We remember to have seen a huge Twelfth-cake in the form of a fortress, with sentinels and flags; the cake being so large as to fill two ovens in baking.

'One of the most celebrated and attractive displays was that of Birch, the confectioner, No. 15, Cornhill, probably the oldest shop of its class in the metropolis. The business was established in the reign of King George I.'

from Chambers, Robert, *The Book of Days, a Miscellany of Popular Antiquities*, 1862

DICKENS AND CHRISTMAS

In the 1820s and 1830s, the author William Hone published a weekly pamphlet entitled, *The Every-day Book, or a Guide to the Year*. These pamphlets were designed to be bound together at the end of the year to form an almanac. His illustrator was George Cruikshank, who would later become one of Dickens's illustrators and friends. In his *Every-day Book* for 1838, William Hone left a description of how London confectioners were presenting their twelfth cakes in the first years of the Victorian era:

> '... countless cakes of all prices and dimensions ... stand in rows and piles on the counters and sideboards and in the windows ... one, enormously superior to the rest in size, is the chief object of all curiosity; and all are decorated with all imaginable images of things animate and inanimate. Stars, castles, kings, cottages, dragons, trees, fish, palaces, cats, dogs, churches, lions, milkmaids, knights, serpents, and innumerable other forms in snow-white confectionary, painted with variegated colours.'

This heralded a time when ostentatious decoration, rather than the taste of the cake itself, had started to become the most important element of a fashionable Twelfth Night party. In 1853, Dickens published a critical article about this fashion in his magazine *Household Words*. The article, entitled 'Slang', was written by George Augustus Sala, a prolific journalist, and artist, who had known Dickens since childhood; his mother had been an actress who starred in two of Dickens's plays. It was his work for Dickens's *Household Words* that helped Sala make his name as a journalist, and he went on to work for the *Daily Telegraph* and the *Illustrated London* News. He became renowned as a foreign correspondent, including writing about the American Civil War. In his 1853 article for Dickens, Sala complained about the fad for enormous cakes and the hyperbolic language that surrounded the confectioners' advertisements:

> '... touching the use of the terms, 'monster,' 'mammoth,' 'leviathan,' how very trying have those misplaced words become! ... every re-union of four-and-twenty fiddlers in a row was dubbed a monster concert; a loaf made with a double allowance of dough was a monster loaf; every confectioner's new year's raffle was a monster twelfth cake.'

A Recipe for Twelfth Cake

Take seven pounds of flour, make a cavity in the centre, set a sponge with a gill and a half of yeast and a little warm milk; then put round it one pound of fresh butter broke into small lumps, one pound and a quarter of sifted sugar, four pounds and a half of currants washed and picked, half an ounce of sifted cinnamon, a quarter of an ounce of pounded cloves, mace, and nutmeg mixed, sliced candied orange or lemon peel and citron.

When the sponge is risen, mix all the ingredients together with a little warm milk; let the hoops be well papered and buttered, then fill them with the mixture and bake them, and when nearly cold ice them over with sugar prepared for that purpose as per receipt; or they may be plain.

John Mollard, *The Art of Cookery,* 1803

Hone's guide for 1826 included help on hosting a decorous Twelfth Night party, notably without any elements of the 'misrule' for which the festival was renowned. In the Twelfth Night cards sold by bakers, popular characters included such names as Toby Tipple, Mrs Prittle-Prattle, Miss Frolic and Lord Flirtaway. Hone was not a fan of shop-bought character cards, complaining, 'Twelfth-night characters sold by the pastrycooks, are either commonplace or gross – when genteel they are inane; when humorous, they are vulgar.' His instructions for a home-made Twelfth Night party were:

'First, buy your cake. Then, before your visitors arrive, buy your characters, each of which should have a pleasant verse beneath. Next look at your invitation list, and count the number of ladies you expect; and afterwards the number of gentlemen. Then, take as many female characters as you have invited ladies; fold them up, exactly of the same size, and number each on the back; taking care to make the King No. 1, and the Queen No. 2. The prepare and number the gentleman's characters.

"Cause tea and coffee to be handed to your visitors as they drop in. When all are assembled and tea over, put as many ladies' characters in a reticule as there are ladies present; next put the gentlemen's characters in a hat. Then call on a gentleman to carry the reticule to the ladies as they sit, from which each lady is to draw one ticket, and to preserve it unopened. Select a lady to bear the hat to the gentlemen for the same purpose. There will be one ticket left in the reticule, and another in the hat, which the lady and gentleman who carried each is to interchange, as having fallen to each other.

'Next, arrange your visitors according to their numbers; the King No. 1, the Queen No. 2, and so on. The king is then to recite the verse on his ticket; then the queen the verse on hers; and so the characters are to proceed in numerical order. This done, let the cake and refreshments go round, and hey! for merriment!'

In his *Book of Days*, published in 1862, author Robert Chambers looked back on the Twelfth Night celebrations of his youth:

'Twelfth Night cards represented ministers, maids of honour, and other attendants of a court, and the characters were to be supported throughout the night.... They were sold in small packets to pastrycooks, and led the way to a custom which annually grew to an extensive trade.'

Throughout the nineteenth century, the celebrating of Twelfth Night changed and by the end of the century the holiday had dwindled in importance. It was always very popular in the Dickens household, however, and Charles Dickens insisted on it being celebrated in style. In 1892, his daughter Mamie was quoted in the *Ladies Home Journal*:

'My father was ... in his element at the Twelfth Night parties ... He would have something droll to say to every one, and under his attentions the shyest child would brighten and become merry. No one was overlooked or forgotten by him; like the young Cratchits, he was 'ubiquitous.' Supper was followed by songs and recitations from the various members of the company, my father acting always as master of ceremonies, and calling upon first one child, then another for his or her contribution to the festivity. I can see now the anxious faces turned toward the beaming, laughing eyes of their host. How attentively he would listen, with his head thrown slightly back, and a little to one side, a happy smile on his lips. O, those merry, happy times, never to be forgotten by any of his own children, or by any of their guests. Those merry, happy times!'

By the end of Dickens's life, Twelfth Night had become a shadow of its former self, while Christmas had become increasingly elaborate. By the end of the century, the style of celebrating Christmas had evolved into something very different from that which would have been recognised by Dickens's ancestors – and yet many of these changes were due to Charles Dickens himself.

First, all the wild heads of the parish, conventing together, chuse them a grand captain (of mischief), whom they ennoble with the title of my Lord of Misrule, and him they crown with great solemnity, and adopt for their king. This king annointed chuseth for him twenty, forty, three score, or a hundred lusty guts, like to himself, to wait upon his lordly majesty, and to guard his noble person. Then, every one of these his men he investeth with his liveries of green, yellow, or some other wanton colour. And as though that were not gaudy enough, they bedeck themselves with scarfs, ribbons and laces, hanged all over with gold rings, precious stones, and other jewels; this done, they ties about either leg twenty or forty bells, with rich handkerchiefs in their hands, and sometimes laid across over their shoulders and necks, borrowed for the most part of their party of pretty Mopsies and loving Bessies for bussing them in the dark.

From 'Bringing in Christmas', the *Illustrated London News*, 20 December 1845

CHAPTER THREE

'He's Behind You!' – The Theatre at Christmas

'The floor was swept and watered, the lamps were trimmed, fuel was heaped upon the fire; and the warehouse was as snug, and warm, and dry, and bright a ball-room, as you would desire to see upon a winter's night.

'In came a fiddler with a music-book, and went up to the lofty desk, and made an orchestra of it, and tuned like fifty stomach-aches. In came Mrs Fezziwig, one vast substantial smile. In came the three Miss Fezziwigs, beaming and lovable. In came the six young followers whose hearts they broke.... There were more dances, and there were forfeits, and more dances, and there was cake, and there was negus, and there was a great piece of Cold Roast, and there was a great piece of Cold Boiled, and there were mince-pies, and plenty of beer. But the great effect of the evening came after the Roast and Boiled, when the fiddler (an artful dog, mind. The sort of man who knew his business better than you or I could have told it him.) struck up 'Sir Roger de Coverley.' Then old Fezziwig stood out to dance with Mrs Fezziwig. Top couple, too; with a good stiff piece of work cut out for them; three or four and twenty pair of partners; people who were not to be trifled with; people who would dance, and had no notion of walking.

'But if they had been twice as many – ah, four times – old Fezziwig would have been a match for them, and so would Mrs Fezziwig. As to her, she was worthy to be his partner in every sense of the term. If that's not high praise, tell me higher, and I'll use it. A positive light appeared to issue from Fezziwig's calves. They shone in every part of the dance like moons. You couldn't have predicted, at any given time, what would have become of them next. And when old Fezziwig and Mrs Fezziwig had gone all through the dance; advance and retire, both hands to your partner, bow and curtsey, corkscrew, thread-the-needle, and back again to your place; Fezziwig cut — cut so deftly, that he appeared to wink with his legs, and came upon his feet again without a stagger.

'When the clock struck eleven, this domestic ball broke up. Mr and Mrs Fezziwig took their stations, one on either side of the door, and shaking hands with every person individually as he or she went out, wished him or her a Merry Christmas.'

Charles Dickens, A Christmas Carol, 1843

Dickens left very few reminiscences of his own childhood Christmases, although he made a great effort to ensure his own children's Christmases were memorable. Much of what we know about his early life comes from a biography written by his friend John Forster. The two men met in 1836, at a party given by the novelist William Harrison Ainsworth, and became friends instantly. Forster had intended to become a lawyer, but gave up his studies in order to be "a man of letters". He wrote articles and poetry and made a living as a literary critic, but today, he is best remembered as Dickens's first biographer. When Forster published *The Life of Charles Dickens*, in 1872-1874, he did so with the aid of his friend's papers and unfinished autobiography, which Forster had been bequeathed. It is notable that Christmas is barely mentioned in the first chapters of the biography of the man whose name was to become synonymous with the season. One memory of an early Christmas appeared in *Household Words*, in December 1850. In the article 'A Christmas Tree', however, his overwhelming memory is a sense of fear, as he recalls toys he found sinister and confusing:

'I look into my youngest Christmas recollections! All toys at first, I find. Up yonder, among the green holly and red berries, is the Tumbler with his hands in his pockets, who wouldn't lie down, but whenever he was put upon the floor, persisted in rolling his fat body about, until he rolled himself still, and brought those lobster eyes of his to bear upon me—when I affected to laugh very much, but in my heart of hearts was extremely doubtful of him. Close beside him is that infernal snuff-box, out of which there sprang a demoniacal Counsellor in a black gown, with an obnoxious head of hair, and a red cloth mouth, wide open, who was not to be endured on any terms, but could not be put away either.... The cardboard lady in a blue-silk skirt, who was stood up against the candlestick to dance, and whom I see on the same branch, was milder, and was beautiful; but I can't say as much for the larger cardboard man, who used to be hung against the wall and pulled by a string; there was a sinister expression in that nose of his; and when he got his legs round his neck (which he very often did), he was ghastly, and not a creature to be alone with.

'When did that dreadful Mask first look at me? Who put it on, and why was I so frightened that the sight of it is an era in my life?... Nothing reconciled me to it.... Nor was it any satisfaction to be shown the Mask, and see that it was made of paper, or to have it locked up and be assured that no one wore it. The mere recollection of that fixed face, the mere knowledge of its existence anywhere, was sufficient to awake me in the night all perspiration and horror, with, "O I know it's coming! O the mask!".'

Another of Dickens's childhood memories was published in *Household Words* on I January 1859, of being young enough to need to be carried downstairs to look in upon what he remembered as a rather cheerless New Year party.

'I have a vivid remembrance of the sensation of being carried downstairs in a woman's arms, and holding tight to her ... a New Year's Party revealed itself to me, as a very long row of ladies and gentlemen sitting against a wall, all drinking at once out of little glass cups with handles, like custard-cups. What can this Party have been! I am afraid it must have been a dull one, but I know it came off ... There was no speech-making, no quick movement and change of action, no demonstration of any kind. They were all sitting in a long row against the wall – very like my first idea of the good people in Heaven, as I derived it from a wretched picture in a Prayer-book – and they had all their heads a little thrown back, and were all drinking at once.'

In the same article, he recalled another new year at which he and his little sister (presumably Letitia) had somehow been made to keep a strange secret:

'On what other early New Year's Day can I possibly have been an innocent accomplice in the secreting – in the coal cellar too – of a man with a wooden leg! ... I clearly remember that we stealthily conducted the man with the wooden leg – whom we knew intimately – into the coal cellar, and that, in getting him over the coals to hide him behind some partition there was beyond, his wooden leg bored itself in among the small coals, and his hat flew off, and he fell backward and lay prone: a spectacle of helplessness ... I have not the least idea who 'we' were, except that I had a little sister for another innocent accomplice, and that there must have been a servant girl for principal: neither do I know whether the man with the wooden leg robbed the house, before or afterwards, or otherwise nefariously distinguished himself.... But I know that some awful reason compelled us to hush it all up, and that we 'never told'. For many years, I had this association with a New Year's Day entirely to myself, until at last, the anniversary being come round again, I said to the little sister, as she and I sat by chance among our children, 'Do you remember the New Year's Day of the man with the wooden leg?' Whereupon, a thick black curtain which had overhung him from her infancy went up, and she saw just this much of the man, and not a jot more.'

As a child, Charles Dickens's burning ambition was to become an actor. He had fond memories of being taken to the theatre as a child, and as soon as he started his first adult job (at the age of fifteen), he used any spare money to buy cheap theatre tickets. He wanted to write plays and star in them and he had dreams of travelling around the country as an actor-manager, following in the footsteps of one of his heroes, William Shakespeare. This was partly inspired by childhood Christmases, as the Georgian Christmas season was not complete without a visit to the pantomime. In the year of Dickens' birth, The *London Courier and Gazette* named the two top pantomimes for that season as *Harlequin and the Red Dwarf, or the Adamant Rock* at the Covent Garden Theatre; and *Harlequin and Humpo* by Mr T. Dibdin, at the Drury Lane Theatre. *Harlequin and the Red Dwarf, or the Adamant Rock* was based on the tales from *Arabian Nights*, one of his favourite books.

References to themes or stories from *The Arabian Nights* can be found throughout Dickens's writing. As such, he may well have been enthralled by *Harlequin and the Red Dwarf, or the Adamant Rock*, had he been old enough to attend, although this particular performance, from 1812, received an unfavourable review from one indignant critic, angry because the live stag-hunting scene, was, in his view, disappointing:

'His [the stag's] performance of the forest scene totally failed, and he disappointed the spectators fully as much as his great forerunner, the elephant, last season. The dogs (said to belong to a certain Baronet and a new County Member) were entirely at fault, and walked about the stage with the most perfect unconcern. We hope that the Managers will take warning from the repeated marks of disapprobation which this exhibition received on Saturday night, and abandon the hideous absurdity of introducing brutes on the stage for whom nature has done nothing even to render them diverting in such a situation.'

The theatre appears frequently in Charles Dickens's novels. Those childhood trips to the pantomime probably inspired him to write in *Nicholas Nickleby* (1839):

'Miss Snevellicci's papa, who had been in the profession ever since he had first played the ten-year-old imps in the Christmas pantomimes; who could sing a little, dance a little, fence a little, act a little, and do everything a little, but not much; who had been sometimes in the ballet, and sometimes in the chorus, at every theatre in London; who was always selected in virtue of his figure to play the military visitors and the speechless noblemen; who always wore a smart dress, and came on arm-in-arm with a smart lady in short petticoats, – and always did it too with such an air that people in the pit had been several times known to cry out "Bravo!" under the impression that he was somebody.'

In the winter of 1837 to 1838, Dickens was commissioned to edit the memoirs of one of his heroes, the famous clown Joseph Grimaldi (1778-1837). Although Dickens ended up writing much of the book, he was initially commissioned to work as the editor, not the author, of the notes made on the memoirs by the previous author Mr Egerton Wilks. By this date. Dickens had already begun to make his name with *Sketches by Boz* (1836) and *The Pickwick Papers* (1837), but this was not good enough for a fan of Grimaldi's, who disliked the biography and claimed that the author was too young ever to have been able to see Grimaldi perform. Dickens counteracted these comments by writing a letter to be published in the magazine he was editing, *Bentley's Miscellany* (the magazine in which *Oliver Twist* was serialised). The letter, which was never published, reveals a rare memory of Dickens's childhood Christmases:

> 'I understand that a gentleman unknown is going about this town privately informing all ladies and gentlemen of discontented natures that, on a comparison of dates ... he has made the profound discovery that I can never have seen Grimaldi whose life I have edited, and that the book must therefore of necessity be bad. Now, sir, although I was brought up from remote country parts in the dark ages of 1819 and 1820 to behold the splendor [sic] of Christmas pantomimes and the humour of Joe [Grimaldi], in whose honor [sic] I am informed I clapped my hands with great precocity, and although I even saw him act in the remote times of 1823, yet as I had not then aspired to the dignity of a tail-coat, though forced by a relentless parent into my first pair of boots.'

In 1819, while the Dickens children were watching Grimaldi's pantomime at the Covent Garden Theatre, the nearby Drury Lane Theatre produced its historic production of *Jack and the Beanstalk*. Although the story had been a play for many years, it was this 1819 performance that is considered the very first true 'pantomime' in the modern sense. Although the word had been in use for many years, it was this particular production that introduced many of the traditions that now define the genre, including being the first pantomime to feature a 'principal boy'; the male hero being played by a female actress in alluring 'male' attire has now become a tradition in every pantomime. The *Theatrical Journal* published a glowing review:

> Pantomime has now superseded Tragedy, Comedy, Opera, and Farce; and for this time Grimaldi is a hero ... Covent Garden has, as usual, produced a superb pantomime; and Drury Lane has laboured hard to outstrip its renowned competitor.' (27 December 1819)

The Grimaldi performance that the Dickens children would have seen in 1820, was the pantomime *Harlequin and Friar Bacon* by Bonnor and O'Keefe. Several newspapers published the same review:

> 'The delight of children of all ages, and the triumph of wands, motley jackets, light feet, and party-coloured faces, Pantomime, commenced

on Tuesday night. Covent-garden has had an old celebrity in this work of genius ... We let the prospectus speak for itself.'

An illustration of Grimaldi in his clown make-up and costume was painted by George Cruikshank in 1820. It depicts him with wild but smiling eyes, an unruly wig and eyebrows and his face spread thickly with red and white greasepaint.

The following year, the pantomime was *Harlequin and Mother Bunch, or The Yellow Dwarf*, in which, as the *Evening Mail* commented, 'Grimaldi kept the house in a roar by his drollery and humour.' Just two years later, Grimaldi made headline news again, when the *Hampshire Advertiser* informed their readers in a simple sentence which became the notice of Grimaldi's retirement from the stage:

'Grimaldi is so seriously unwell as to be unable to appear in the Christmas pantomime at Covent Garden, which will, we understand, be produced this season without a clown. This deficiency the management intend to supply by a celebrated pulchinello from Paris.' (29 December 1823).

In the ghosted *Memoirs of Joseph Grimaldi*, Dickens wrote

'The delights – the ten thousand million delights of a pantomime – come streaming upon us now – even of the pantomime which came lumbering down in Richardson's wagons at fairtime to the dull lumbering little town in which we had the honour to be brought up.... We feel again all the pride of standing in a body on the platform, the observed of all observers in the crowd below ... we catch a glimpse (too brief, alas!) of the lady with a green parasol in her hand, on the outside stage of the next show but one, who supports herself on one foot, on the back of a majestic horse ... and our hearts throb with emotion, as we deliver our cardboard check into the very hands of the Harlequin himself, who, all glittering with spangles, and dazzling with many colours, deigns to give us a word of encouragement and commendation as we pass into the booth! ... What mattered it that the stage was three yards wide, and four deep? *We* never saw it. We had no eyes, ears or corporeal senses, but for the pantomime.' Charles Dickens was inspired by these visits to the theatre, and, when he was nine years old, he wrote a play: *Miznar, Sultan of India*. The author left little indication of what it was about, except that it was inspired by the tale of "The Enchantress" from James Kenneth Ridley's book *Tales of the Genii* (1764), which was, in turn, based on *The Arabian Nights*.

By the time of the family's visits to see Grimaldi perform, they been living in Kent for several years. In 1852, Dickens published *The Child's Story*, an article in which he reminisced about a carefree existence of roaming around the countryside, playing games at the seaside and lazing along the banks of the River Medway:

> 'they were not always learning; they had the merriest games that ever were played. They rowed upon the river in summer, and skated upon the ice in Winter. – They had holidays, too, and Twelfth cakes, and parties, where they danced till midnight.'

These carefree days came to an end at around the same time that Grimaldi was being supplanted by a 'pulchinello from Paris'. In 1822, John Dickens's place of work was relocated from the Navy offices at Chatham Dockyard to the Navy offices at Somerset House, in central London. By this date, the family consisted of Fanny (aged twelve), Charles (aged ten), Letitia (aged six), Fred (aged two) and baby Alfred, who was born in March 1822. Two other siblings – a boy named Alfred Allen and a girl named Harriet – had died as babies. John Dickens found the costs of supporting a growing family, as well as to the medical costs and funerals of two infants, crippling. He was in debt when he left Kent and the costs of moving to such an expensive city as London made the problem even worse. Soon his debts began spiralling out of control.

When his family moved to London, Charles remained in Chatham, boarding at the home of his schoolmaster, William Giles. In the 1880s, the schoolmaster's sister was interviewed and she described the young Charles Dickens as 'quite at home at all sorts of parties, junkettings, and birth-day celebrations, and ... he took great delight in Fifth of November festivities around the bon-fire.' In just a few months, however, Charles's happy career at William Giles's school, on the idyllic sounding Clover Lane, was at an end. John Dickens could no longer afford his son's school fees, so Charles left Kent in a stage coach, sitting inside it alongside a heap of "damp straw in which he was packed and forwarded like game, carriage-paid". He wrote of the journey many years later, 'There was no other inside passenger, and I consumed my sandwiches in solitude and dreariness, and it rained hard all the way, and I thought life sloppier than I expected to find it.'

His new life in a strange city was made doubly painful by the loss of his older sister, Fanny, who had been accepted as a boarder at the Royal Academy of Music, in Tenterden Street, Mayfair, a very fashionable part of town. The rest of the family was living in straitened circumstances at 16, Bayham Street, in Camden Town, North London. Dickens saw Camden Town through the eyes of unhappiness and poverty and in his mind, it was the meanest place he could think of. In *A Christmas Carol*, he places the poverty stricken home of the Cratchit family in Camden Town, it being the cruellest place he could imagine. John Forster evoked the misery of Dickens's recollections of that time in his biography:

'Bayham Street was about the poorest part of the London suburbs then, and the house was a mean small tenement, with a wretched little back-garden abutting on a squalid court. Here was no place for new acquaintances to him: not a boy was near with whom he might hope to become in any way familiar. A washerwoman lived next door, and a Bow Street officer lived over the way. Many, many times has he spoken to me of this, and how he seemed at once to fall into a solitary condition apart from all other boys of his own age, and to sink into a neglected state at home which had always been quite unaccountable to him. "As I thought," he said on one occasion very bitterly, "in the little back garret in Bayham Street, of all I had lost in losing Chatham, what would I have given, if I had had anything to give, to have been sent back to any other school, to have been taught something anywhere!."'

Charles Dickens spent much 1823 running errands for his parents and visiting his disabled uncle, Thomas Barrow (Elizabeth Dickens's brother), whose leg had to be amputated after a bad break. Dickens had vivid memories of spending time being his uncle's 'little companion and nurse' at his lodgings in Gerrard Street, Soho (now the centre of London's Chinatown).

All through this time, a looming fear hung over the Dickens children, who knew that things were very bad at home. A couple of months before Christmas, the family made a surprising move from Bayham Street to 4, North Gower Street, just off the Euston Road. This was a more salubrious address, and the reason for renting the house was so that Elizabeth Dickens could set up a school. Charles remembered the day on which a large brass plate was attached to the front door engraved with the words 'Mrs Dickens's Establishment'. He recalled how he and his younger siblings took flyers announcing the new school to houses all around the area, but no pupils ever applied to the school and the family's finances grew even worse. By the end of 1823, the family were living in increasingly desperate circumstances. In his unfinished autobiography, Dickens commented, 'I know that we got on very badly with the butcher and baker; that very often we had not too much for dinner.' At the Christmas of 1823, while John Dickens struggled to afford the rent, there would have been little in the way of heating and comfort, let alone festive food or presents. John and Elizabeth Dickens were convinced Fanny's musical talent would enable her to earn a good living and be able to save the family's finances in the future, but eleven-year-old Charles needed to start work and bring in money immediately. He was found a job at Warren's Blacking Factory, but his meagre wages were not enough to pays his father's creditors. John Dickens was arrested for debt and, as he was being led away by the arresting officers, he spoke to his eldest son. Charles Dickens never forgot the words his father said to him, and many years later wrote, 'I really believed at the time, that they had broken my heart.' John was taken to the Marshalsea Debtors' Prison in Southwark, South London.

Warren's Blacking Factory, where Dickens worked six days a week, was on the Strand, on the north bank of the River Thames. Before the building of London's Embankment and the sewers, the Thames was a stinking filthy river, into which much of the city's sewage and rubbish was emptied. While Fanny was becoming one of the Academy's star pupils, winning prizes for her singing and piano playing, her brother was working ten-hour days at the factory. He was also living alone in a lodging house he hated in the misery of Camden Town. Not long after her husband's imprisonment, Elizabeth had accepted the inevitable and she and the younger Dickens children had moved into the Marshalsea to share John's cell. Realising how unhappy Charles was, his parents managed to use their contacts to find him new lodgings in Lant Street, Southwark, just a short walk from the prison. Throughout these months, Charles walked alone in the dark to and from work, the prison and his lodgings, learning to survive in some of the most dangerous streets in London. These experiences helped to form some of his most famous fictional characters, and particularly inspired the unloved and uncared for children in *A Christmas Carol*.

By the time Christmas of 1824 arrived, the Dickens family had been through a whirlwind year of change, descending into prison, poverty, child labour and the depths of despair, before being lifted out of prison and the factory, back into their own home and a return to their previous lives. It was the death of John Dickens's mother which enabled the family to be freed from prison. She left both her sons a small legacy and John's enabled him to pay off his debts and go back to his former job. By the end of the year, in a miraculous turnaround, Charles was once more a respectable schoolboy, living with his family, enrolled at Wellington House Academy in Hampstead, North London, trying – in vain – to forget about the blacking factory and his lodging house.

That Christmas was a marked contrast to the year before. For once, the family was living without fear of the bailiff and the rent collector. Their feelings might have echoed those expressed in *The Sunday Times* that Boxing Day:

'Whatever may be said of the dissipation of Christmas, we think its recurrence is attended with many excellent effects. In a commercial country like England, where the merchant during the entire year is glued to his desk, and wholly intent on his selfish schemes, his feelings are apt to be frozen over by the palsying power of interest. In counting over his gains, he forgets that others, connected with him, and his equals in rank, and character, may claim a right to share his coffers or his society; and hence the impulse of avarice too often disserves the links in the chain of the family bond, and which go far to injure the strength and durability of the greater chain of society. But when all the members of the family once assemble under the same roof – to commemorate the Nativity of Him who came to destroy all fictitious distinctions, and to partake anew of that festive mirth which delighted their early years, there is a mingling of affection, and a re-union of sympathy, the effect of which is to render men better when they emerge anew into the troubled waters of busy life.'

CHAPTER FOUR

Love at Christmas

'In reading [*A Christmas Carol*], one becomes Scrooge himself: feels with him the terrible power his ghostly visitants have over him, the softening influence of the various scenes through which he passes, the very pangs that are caused by the ghosts' rebukes. One feels too, how very natural and delightful it is when he is ultimately reclaimed.'

R.L.Stewart in *The Dickensian* (1907)

Over the next few years, the Dickens family continued to struggle with John's inability to handle his finances. In 1827, when Charles was fifteen and Fanny was seventeen, John Dickens was arrested again, although this time he was not imprisoned as he managed to borrow enough money to pay off his debts. Both Charles and Fanny left school and started work. Fanny became a teacher at the Royal Academy of Music and Charles was found a job as a clerk with a firm of solicitors named Ellis and Blackmore. In the same year, Elizabeth Dickens gave birth to her final child, Augustus – known in the family as Boz. Some years later, when Charles Dickens was in need of a pen name, he would choose his baby brother's nickname.

Charles Dickens spent eighteen months working as a legal clerk, but he was determined to move into a different world. He visited the theatre as frequently as possible and still dreamt of becoming an actor; he also took the practical step of learning shorthand before leaving his job to become a freelance journalist. He became renowned for his accuracy in reporting speeches and found regular working writing for radical newspapers, including the *True Sun* and the *Mirror of Parliament*. In 1830, he fell in love with Maria Beadnell, the daughter of a banker and his wife. Maria was two years older than Dickens and her parents thought a struggling writer with ambitions of going on the stage an unprepossessing suitor.

One of Dickens's friends at this time, was a bank clerk, Henry Kolle, who was engaged to Maria's sister, Anne Beadnell and colluded with Charles by taking secret messages between him and Maria. On 20 December 1832, Dickens wrote to Kolle, 'How are you engaged on Christmas Day? – If you do not join any family party of your own, will you dine with us – It will I need hardly say give us all the greatest pleasure to see you.' A couple of weeks later, on 5 January 1833, Dickens wrote to him again, postponing a proposed party to which Kolle and his brother had been invited. The letter gives us a glimpse into the Dickens family's domestic life at this date, as they prepared to move house. One of Charles Dickens's chief preoccupations is with his sister Fanny's piano and the impossibility of having a party without it:

> 'Will you excuse my postponing the pleasure of seeing yourself and Brother until Sunday week? – My reason is this:- we are having coals in at the new place, cleaning &c we cannot very well remove until Tuesday or Wednesday next. The piano will most likely go to Bentinck St. to-day & I have already said we cannot accompany it – so that the Piano will be in one place and we in another. In addition to this, we shall all be in a bustle, and I fear should impress your Brother with a very uncomfortable idea of our domestic arrangements …'

Dickens's hopes of marrying Maria Beadnell were firmly quashed in February 1833, when he told her he loved her and she rejected him. Shortly afterwards, her parents sent her abroad, in an attempt to get over what they saw as an unsuitable romance. Perhaps the heartbreak made Dickens more determined to succeed, and by the end of the year he had some very exciting Christmas news to share with Henry Kolle, who was now Maria's brother-in-law. Dickens wrote to Henry suggesting he buy a copy of the *Monthly Magazine*, because it had published his very first work of fiction. On 3 December 1833, Dickens wrote to Kolle, 'look for the Article. It is the same that you saw lying on my table but the name is transmogrified from "A Sunday out of town" to "A dinner at Poplar Walk" … I am so dreadfully nervous, that my hand shakes to such an extent as to prevent my writing a word legibly.'

He was not paid anything for the story and he wrote again to Kolle a week later, to say his story had been plagiarised and reprinted by a magazine with the appropriate title of *The Thief*. The *Monthly Magazine* asked him to write more stories, although, as he noted wryly, 'they are "rather backward in coming forward" with the needful'. Dickens was longing for this news of his success to make its way to the ears of Maria Beadnell. He lost contact with her until 1855, by which time he was a world-famous author, married with ten children, and she was the rather lonely wife of Mr Henry Winter, the manager of a saw-mill in North London, with children of her own. It was only when they met again, over two decades after she had rejected him, that he realised at last that he was no longer in love with her.

Dickens wrote nine stories that were published in the *Monthly Magazine*, although he was not paid for any of them. Their success made him determined to make money as a writer, having failed in his mission to become an actor. In 1832, he had applied for an audition at the Covent Garden Theatre company. The manager, George Bartley, arranged an audition for April 1832, but on the day he was supposed to attend, Dickens was ill with 'a terrible bad cold and an inflammation of the face' and missed his chance. Although thwarted in his theatrical dreams, he was doing well in his journalistic career and, just before the Christmas of 1834, he moved out of the family home and into his first bachelor lodgings. This was an apartment at 13, Furnival's Inn, a newly reconstructed lodgings on the site of a medieval Inn of Court. He took his younger brother Fred with him, to ease some of the financial burden on his parents, and to try and encourage Fred not to follow their father's example of living in debt.

Through his work on the *Morning Chronicle*, Charles Dickens began a lifelong friendship with Thomas Beard, a fellow journalist. Many of his letters to Beard survive, including one dated 16 December 1834, from Furnival's Inn. Dickens writes about a proposed party (which he describes as a 'flare') and the chaos he is in since moving house:

> 'As I have *no* dishes, no curtains, and no french polish, I think we had better, for all our comforts, defer the projected flare until Saturday … Pray tell your father, that I place implicit reliance upon him; and be kind enough to remember on your own account that I have got some really *extraordinary* french brandy.'

A few days later, Dickens was still suffering from the vagaries of his new home, complaining to his friend Henry Austin that he has been unable to find anyone to clean for him on a Sunday:

> 'Dear Henry,
> I am obliged to give you the very ridiculous notice that if you come and see me tomorrow we must *go out and get our dinner*. I think the

best way will be to walk somewhere; the fact is that I have had an explosion with nineteen out of the twenty Laundresses [the general term for female servant] in the Inn already, and can't get "done for" Some Methodistical ruffian has been among 'em, and they have all got the can about "profaning the Sabbath" – and wiolating that commandment which embraces within its scope not only the stranger within the gates, but cattle of every description, including Laundresses.

'Tomorrow is my Mother's birth day, so I have promised on behalf of yourself and Beard that we will go from here, and the spend the Evening there. If you will be down her as early as you can tomorrow morning – shall we say to breakfast; for I don't take that meal until half past ten? – we can walk to Norwood, or some pretty place where we can get a chop, and return here to our grog.'

It is possible that, by the Christmas of 1834, Charles Dickens had already met the woman who was to become his wife. She was Catherine Hogarth, the eldest daughter of George Hogarth, editor of the *Evening Chronicle*, the man who first paid him to write some of the short stories which later became known as *Sketches by Boz*. The date of their first meeting is not recorded, but in February 1835, Dickens felt he knew Catherine well enough to invite her to his twenty-third birthday party. After the party, she wrote to a cousin, 'Mr Dickens improves greatly on acquaintance'. By the following December they were preparing for their wedding. It was at that Christmas of 1835 that Charles Dickens wrote his very first Christmas story. It was entitled *Christmas Festivities* and was published in the weekly newspaper *Bell's Life in London*, on 27 December. A few weeks later it was published as part of *Sketches by Boz*, under the new title of *A Christmas Dinner*. The story begins with the words, 'Christmas time! That man must be a misanthrope indeed, in whose breast something like a jovial feeling is not roused – in whose mind some pleasant associations are not awakened – by the recurrence of Christmas.' In the story, Dickens describes a family party, at which prejudices and resentments are all healed by the spirit of Christmas. It ends with the words:

'And thus the evening passes, in a strain of rational good-will and cheerfulness, doing more to awaken the sympathies of every member of the party in behalf of his neighbour, and to perpetuate their good feeling during the ensuing year, than half the homilies that have ever been written, by half the Divines that have ever lived.'

LOVE AT CHRISTMAS

'The Christmas family-party ... is an annual gathering of all the accessible members of the family, young or old, rich or poor; and all the children look forward to it, for two months beforehand, in a fever of anticipation. Formerly, it was held at grandpapa's; but grandpapa getting old, and grandmamma getting old too, and rather infirm, they have given up house-keeping, and domesticated themselves with uncle George; so, the party always takes place at uncle George's house, but grandmamma sends in most of the good things, and grandpapa always WILL toddle down, all the way to Newgate-market, to buy the turkey, which he engages a porter to bring home behind him in triumph, always insisting on the man's being rewarded with a glass of spirits, over and above his hire, to drink "a merry Christmas and a happy new year" to aunt George. As to grandmamma, she is very secret and mysterious for two or three days beforehand, but not sufficiently so, to prevent rumours getting afloat that she has purchased a beautiful new cap with pink ribbons for each of the servants, together with sundry books, and pen-knives, and pencil-cases, for the younger branches; to say nothing of divers secret additions to the order originally given by aunt George at the pastry-cook's, such as another dozen of mince- pies for the dinner, and a large plum-cake for the children.'

Charles Dickens, *Christmas Festivities* (1835)

That year, Dickens worked throughout the twelve days of Christmas, trying to earn as much money as possible before getting married. He ended the year and began the new one by writing another sketch entitled *The New Year*, which was also published in *Bell's Life in London*. It was written on New Year's Eve itself, as he explained in a note to his friend Thomas Mitton, 'Dear Tom, I am at home to-night and alone. I am writing as I was when I last saw you, but Fred is disengaged for a rubber at Cribbage, and I shall be very happy to see you.'

'The New Year' begins with the words:

'Next to Christmas-day, the most pleasant annual epoch in existence is the advent of the New Year. There are a lachrymose set of people who usher in the New Year with watching and fasting, as if they were bound to attend as chief mourners at the obsequies of the old one. Now, we cannot but think it a great deal more complimentary, both to the old year that has rolled away, and to the New Year that is just beginning to dawn upon us, to see the old fellow out, and the new one in, with gaiety and glee.'

The next twelve months in Charles Dickens's life were to prove extraordinarily successful: he would become known as the author of *Sketches by Boz* and *The Pickwick Papers* and would write a 'comic burletta', *The Strange Gentleman* and the words for an opera, *The Village Coquettes*.

In preparation for his marriage, Charles moved into 15, Furnival's Inn, a larger apartment, where there was room for him and Catherine, as well as for Fred Dickens and Catherine's younger sister, Mary Hogarth. The wedding took place on 2 April 1836 at the Hogarth family's parish church, St Luke's, in Chelsea. It was, according to the best man, Thomas Beard, 'altogether a very quiet piece of business'. Henry Burnett, who would later marry Fanny Dickens, wrote of the wedding, '… all things passed off very pleasantly, and all seemed happy, not the least so Dickens and his young girlish wife. She was a bright, pleasant bride, dressed in the simplest and neatest manner.'

Their first child was conceived on the honeymoon and, by Christmas, Catherine was due to give birth. While she prepared for the baby, her husband must have reflected on the past year; he had married, was about to become a father, had become recognised as an author and had entered the world of the theatre, when *The Strange Gentleman* and *The Village Coquettes* were performed at the St James's Theatre. That December, as he worked towards his deadlines with an awareness of impending fatherhood, he declined an invitation with the words, 'I am so engaged with my respectable friend Pickwick (on whom I have only just commenced) that I cannot get out this week, even to the Theatre.'

At the end of December 1836, Dickens wrote to Thomas Beard:

'We propose giving the Turkey until 4 tomorrow, in order that he may be well done. Be punctual .... I arrived home at one oClock this morning dead drunk, & was put to bed by my loving missis. We are just going to Chapman's sisters' quadrille party, for which you may imagine I feel remarkably disposed.'

Charles Culliford Boz Dickens was born on 6 January 1837, and both of his grandmothers rushed to Furnival's Inn to help the new mother. Mary Hogarth wrote to a cousin that her brother-in-law was 'kindness itself to [Catherine], and is constantly studying her comfort'. For Catherine, this was a very difficult time as she suffered – and would continue to do so following the births of their future children – from what would be recognised today as post-natal depression. Charley (as the baby quickly became known) was to be the eldest of ten children. Between 1837 and 1852, Catherine would give birth to seven sons and three daughters (as well as suffering at least two miscarriages).

That Charley was born on Twelfth Night, made the holiday even more special in the Dickens family. Although in most households the celebrating of Twelfth Night diminished steadily throughout Queen Victoria's reign, the Dickens family held a party every year for the double celebration of Twelfth Night and Charley's birthday. Mamie Dickens, Charley's younger sister, recalled these children's parties in her memoirs:

'Miss Coutts, now the Baroness Burdett Coutts, was in the habit of sending my brother, on this his birthday anniversary, the most gorgeous of Twelfth-cakes, with an accompanying box of bonbons and Twelfth Night characters. The cake was cut, and the favors and bonbons distributed at the birthday supper, and it was then that my father's kindly, genial nature overflowed in merriment.'

In 1849, the *Illustrated London News* gave a lavish description of the royal household's Twelfth Night celebrations, beginning with a visit to the theatre, followed by eating an enormous Twelfth Cake:

'... designed and carried out by her Majesty's confectioner, Mr. Mawditt. The Cake was of regal dimensions, being about 30 inches in diameter, and tall in proportion: round the side the decorations consisted of strips of gilded paper, bowing outwards near the top, issuing from an elegant gold bordering. The figures, of which there were sixteen, on the top of the Cake, represented a party of beaux and belles of the last century enjoying a repast al fresco, under some trees; whilst others, and some children, were dancing to minstrel strains.'

Yet despite enjoying such celebrations, it was alleged that Queen Victoria felt the celebrating of Twelfth Night encouraged drunkenness and debauchery and wanted the emphasis on public celebration to be shifted from Twelfth Night to Christmas Day. By the end of her reign, the Christmas season had been reduced from twelve days down to three; Christmas Eve, Christmas Day and Boxing Day (26 December). Although, as *The Times* reported in 1877, the change was not effective in ending antisocial behaviour:

'Christmas is threatened by the multitude that choose to honour and observe it in their own way ... Christmas for a large part of the people recalls the pagan Saturnalia without even the picturesque forms and social graces of paganism. The devotees reel about the streets, make nights hideous, turn their houses upside down, and crowd the police court ...'

Perhaps it is fortunate that Dickens was no longer alive by the time that the government attempted to crush the celebrating of Twelfth Night. In 1871, a year after his death, the Bank Holidays Act was passed, which gave official recognition to four bank holidays, on which everyone was permitted the day off work. The four holidays were: Easter Monday; the Monday in Whitsun week (May); the first Monday in August; and Boxing Day, unless 26 December fell at a weekend, if so, the holiday would be the first weekday after that day. This Act made it mandatory for employers to give their workers paid holidays for four days of the year, and was seen as a step forward in workers' rights, especially for those who had bad employers attempting not to permit their workers any time off. Although this new Act did not prohibit celebrating Twelfth Night celebrations, it did not include the holiday in the official British Calendar, and this contributed to the decline of Twelfth Night celebrations. On 5 November 1873, the *London Evening Standard* mourned this and other changes:

"A curious history might be written of our old English holidays, of their origin, of the period of their full glory, and of their final disappearance ...There was once, for instance, a time when every red-letter day in the Calendar was a holiday; and even now Michaelmas-day still has its recognised place in our business books, although as a festival it has long since disappeared. May-day would be entirely forgotten were it not for the fact that in some of our larger towns and cities the chimney-sweepers make it the occasion of an annual appeal to their customers for a gratuity. Twelfth-night would have long since faded from our list of Christmas gatherings did not the memory of its ancient glories still survive in the custom of Twelfth-cakes for the children. Indeed, almost all our old holidays have been, to all intents and purposes, superseded by the modern institution of Bank Holidays.'

In many parts of the British Isles, Boxing Day was the day on which the servants were given time off, after working very hard on Christmas Day. The name 'Boxing Day' comes from the tradition of servants and other workers, such as rubbish collectors and chimney sweeps, being given 'Christmas boxes'; sometimes these were presents, but more usually they were parcels of money. Boxing Day was also the day on which the charity boxes (or 'alms boxes'), placed in churches, were opened and the money was given out to the poor of the parish. For working-class people who were not domestic servants, Christmas Eve and Boxing Day were normal working days and, as Dickens would emphasise in *A Christmas Carol*, many working people were also expected to work on Christmas Day. Ebenezer Scrooge berates Bob Cratchit for wanting Christmas Day as a holiday and claims the practice of giving workers a paid day was a form of 'picking a man's pocket every 25th of December'.

In nineteenth century Scotland, however, the big seasonal celebration was not Christmas Day or Boxing Day, which were seen as very English celebrations. In Scotland, Hogmanay, on 31 December was most important date of the season. It was usual to celebrate New Year's Eve and New Year's Day throughout the British Isles, but in Scotland, this was the main celebration. Until the sixteenth century, Christmas had been celebrated widely in Scotland, but with the Reformation of the church, the celebration of Christmas was considered Catholic and the celebrating of it was frowned upon as 'Popish'. In 1640, an Act passed by the Scottish Parliament made it illegal to celebrate 'Yule'. Although the Act was repealed in the 1680s, the Presbyterian church made it clear that it considered Christmas a remnant of a Pagan festival, not Christian in origin and not connected with the New Testament. Throughout the nineteenth century and into the twentieth, as people in the rest of the British Isles were becoming obsessed with celebrating Christmas, the fashion for a Dickensian Christmas remained largely uncelebrated in Scotland. A law that made 25 December a public holiday in Scotland was finally passed in 1958.

Throughout the rest of Britain, it was not until the mid-nineteenth century that Christmas Day was accepted as the most important feast day of the winter calendar, and that change was partly due to the Industrial Revolution. When Britain was still largely an agricultural society, each region of the country celebrated in its own way and 25 December wasn't necessarily the day on which all communities celebrated. Different areas celebrated different aspects of the season, and for many, the celebration was dictated depending on the local workers. For example, in regions where apples were the main crop, wassailing was the principal celebration, and usually happened on or around Twelfth Night. Many agricultural communities celebrated on the first Monday after Twelfth Night, which was known as 'Plough Monday'. It marked the first day back at work after the twelve days of Christmas, even though most labourers worked throughout the twelve days. Plough Monday was a day on which people danced, sang, collected alms from the wealthy and ate a special 'Plough Pudding'. As the Industrial Revolution took hold, and increasing numbers of people moved away from working on the land to working in the cities, many of the old country traditions started to die out. This helped the focus shift from the twelve days of Christmas to celebrating only on 25 December.

The Factory Act of 1833 named Christmas Day and Good Friday as the two days in the year (other than Sundays) on which factory workers were permitted the day off work, but not all employees were made aware of their rights – and not all employers chose to adhere to the new law. It was also common for workers to choose to work on 25 December, because they preferred to take 1 January as a holiday instead. Although it became an accepted tradition in the Victorian age to give presents at Christmas, for centuries it had been more common to give and receive gifts at New Year. In *The Chimes*, his second Christmas book, Dickens makes reference to this:

'The streets were full of motion, and the shops were decked out gaily. The New Year, like an Infant Heir to the whole world, was waited for, with welcomes, presents, and rejoicings. There were books and toys for the New Year, glittering trinkets for the New Year, dresses for the New Year, schemes of fortune for the New Year; new inventions to beguile it.'

'Lavish profusion is in the shops: particularly in the articles of currants, raisins, spices, candied peel, and moist sugar. An unusual air of gallantry and dissipation is abroad; evinced in an immense bunch of mistletoe hanging in the greengrocer's shop doorway, and a poor little Twelfth Cake, culminating in the figure of a Harlequin – such a very poor little Twelfth Cake, that one would rather called it a Twenty-fourth Cake or a Forty-eighth Cake – to be raffled for at the pastrycook's, terms one shilling per member.'

Charles Dickens, *The Mystery of Edwin Drood* (1870)

CHAPTER FIVE

Traditions – Old and New

'Christmas was close at hand, in all his bluff and hearty honesty; it was the season of hospitality, merriment, and open-heartedness; the old year was preparing, like an ancient philosopher, to call his friends around him, and amidst the sound of feasting and revelry to pass gently and calmly away. Gay and merry was the time; and right gay and merry were at least four of the numerous hearts that were gladdened by its coming. And numerous indeed are the hearts to which Christmas brings a brief season of happiness and enjoyment. How many families, whose members have been dispersed and scattered far and wide, in the restless struggles of life, are then reunited, and meet once again in that happy state of companionship and mutual goodwill, which is a source of such pure and unalloyed delight; and one so incompatible with the cares and sorrows of the world, that the religious belief of the most civilised nations, and the rude traditions of the roughest savages, alike number it among the first joys of a future condition of existence, provided for the blessed and happy! How many old recollections, and how many dormant sympathies, does Christmas time awaken!'

Charles Dickens The Pickwick Papers (1837)

The most famous of Dickens's early Christmas stories appears in *The Pickwick Papers*, which was serialised between March 1836 and October 1837. All of Dickens's novels were published in serial form, as either weekly or monthly instalments in magazines. They were only published as complete novels once the final instalment had been published. Dickens did not write them as complete novels and then serialise them; he wrote to a deadline every week or month. The exception to this was his Christmas Books, all of which were short novellas, not novels, and they were published as books. In *The Pickwick Papers*, on Christmas Eve, Mr Wardle sits with his friends by the fireside at Dingley Dell and relates 'The Story of the Goblins who stole a Sexton'. The sexton of the title is a grumpy individual named Gabriel Grub, who needs reforming, just as Ebenezer Scrooge does in *A Christmas Carol*. Mr Wardle's story begins with a description of Gabriel as a mean-spirited old man who despises Christmas:

'A little before twilight, one Christmas Eve, Gabriel shouldered his spade, lighted his lantern, and betook himself towards the old churchyard; for he had got a grave to finish by next morning, and, feeling very low, he thought it might raise his spirits, perhaps, if he went on with his work at once. As he went his way, up the ancient street, he saw the cheerful light of the blazing fires gleam through the old casements, and heard the loud laugh and the cheerful shouts of those who were assembled around them; he marked the bustling preparations for next day's cheer, and smelled the numerous savoury odours consequent thereupon, as they steamed up from the kitchen windows in clouds. All this was gall and wormwood to the heart of Gabriel Grub; and when groups of children bounded out of the houses, tripped across the road, and were met, before they could knock at the opposite door, by half a dozen curly-headed little rascals who crowded round them as they flocked upstairs to spend the evening in their Christmas games, Gabriel smiled grimly, and clutched the handle of his spade with a firmer grasp, as he thought of measles, scarlet fever, thrush, whooping-cough, and a good many other sources of consolation besides.

'In this happy frame of mind, Gabriel strode along, returning a short, sullen growl to the good-humoured greetings of such of his neighbours as now and then passed him, until he turned into the dark lane which led to the churchyard.'

By the end of the story he is 'an altered man'. Embarrassed about the way he has lived his life until now, he leaves the village to make a new start amongst people who know nothing about the grumpy man he was before.

In *The Pickwick Papers*, Dickens also gives an evocative description of a late Regency Christmas party, the types of parties John and Elizabeth Dickens and their young children would have attended. When Dickens writes about Mr Pickwick playing Blind Man's Buff, he might be recalling a scene he remembered from childhood:

> 'Mr Pickwick, blinded ... with a silk handkerchief, falling up against the wall, and scrambling into corners, and going through all the mysteries of blindman's buff, with the utmost relish for the game, until at last he caught one of the poor relations, and then had to evade the blind-man himself, which he did with a nimbleness and agility that elicited the admiration and applause of all beholders.'

He would later write a similarly joyous scene in *A Christmas Carol* to describe Mr Fezziwig's party.

As a child, Charles Dickens had loved the work of the American writer, Washington Irving, who had famously written about Christmas. Washington Irving had lived in England in the 1810s and early 1820s. His sister, Sarah, had married an American who took British nationality and they set up home in Birmingham in England. While staying with them, Irving became fascinated by a nearby Jacobean mansion, Aston Hall, which was then being leased to James Watt, the son of the famous Scottish inventor. Under the pseudonym of Geoffrey Crayon, Irving published a series of short stories *The Sketch Book of Geoffrey Crayon, Gent*, which included *Rip van Winkle* (1819 and *The Legend of Sleepy Hollow* (1820), both stories known to the young Charles Dickens.

Irving then wrote a series of stories inspired by Aston Hall (but named Bracebridge Hall and relocated to Yorkshire). In *The Keeping of Christmas at Bracebridge Hall* (1822), Irving mourned how the Christmas season, in Britain and America, was becoming less important in the eyes of the general populace, and that the old customs were falling out of fashion. Irving's story was intended to celebrate the 'old English' ways of marking Christmas, and to record some of the traditions for future generations.

The Keeping of Christmas at Bracebridge Hall begins with the words:

> 'Nothing in England exercises a more delightful spell over my imagination, than the lingerings of the holiday customs and rural games of former times ... I regret to say that they are daily growing more and more faint, being gradually worn away by time – but still more obliterated by modern fashion.'

Irving was nostalgic for an old-fashioned English Christmas that had once 'brought the peasant and the peer together, and blended all ranks in one warm generous flow of joy and kindness', and he railed against the 'modern refinement' which had wrought havoc 'among the hearty old holiday customs … Many of the games and ceremonials of Christmas have entirely disappeared'.

'Of all the old festivals, however, that of Christmas awakens the strongest and most heartfelt associations. There is a tone of solemn and sacred feeling that blends with our conviviality, and lifts the spirit to a state of hallowed and elevated enjoyment. The services of the church about this season are extremely tender and inspiring. They dwell on the beautiful story of the origin of our faith, and the pastoral scenes that accompanied its announcement. They gradually increase in fervour and pathos during the season of Advent, until they break forth in full jubilee on the morning that brought peace and good will to men. I do not know a grander effect of music on the moral feelings, than to hear the full choir and the pealing organ performing a Christmas anthem in a cathedral, and filling every part of the vast pile with triumphant harmony.

'It is a beautiful arrangement, also, derived from days of yore, that this festival, which commemorates the announcement of the religion of peace and love, has been made the season for gathering together of family connections, and drawing closer again those bands of kindred hearts, which the cares and pleasures and sorrows of the world are continually operating to cast loose: of calling back the children of a family, who have launched forth in life, and wandered widely asunder, once more to assemble about the paternal hearth, that rallying-place of the affections, there to grow young and loving again among the endearing mementos of childhood.

DICKENS AND CHRISTMAS

'There is something in the very season of the year that gives a charm to the festivity of Christmas ... in the depth of winter, when nature lies despoiled of every charm, and wrapped in her shroud of sheeted snow, we turn for our gratifications to moral sources. The dreariness and desolation of the landscape, the short gloomy days and darksome nights, while they circumscribe our wanderings, shut in our feelings also from rambling abroad, and make us more keenly disposed for the pleasure of the social circle. Our thoughts are more concentrated: our friendly sympathies more aroused. We feel more sensibly the charm of each by dependence on each other for enjoyment. Heart calleth unto heart; and we draw our pleasures from the deep wells of loving-kindness, which lie in the quiet recesses of our bosoms; and which, when resorted to, furnish forth the pure element of domestic felicity.

'The pitchy gloom without makes the heart dilate on entering the room filled with the glow and warmth of the evening fire. The ruddy blaze diffuses an artificial summer and sunshine through the room, and lights up each countenance in a kindlier welcome. Where does the honest face of hospitality expand into a broader and more cordial smile where is the shy glance of love more sweetly eloquent than by the winter fireside? and as the hollow blast of wintry wind rushes through the hall, claps the distant door, whistles about the casement, and rumbles down the chimney, what can be more grateful than that feeling of sober and sheltered security, with which we look round upon the comfortable chamber and the scene of domestic hilarity?'

Washington Irving, *The Keeping of Christmas at Bracebridge Hall* (1822)

The Keeping of Christmas at Bracebridge Hall, which was published when Charles Dickens was ten, was very popular and achieved the author's aim of making his readers nostalgic for an old-fashioned Christmas. It was this spirit of aiming to bring back the old Christmas traditions, and railing against the cynical modernity of the current era that would also make both the Christmas story in *The Pickwick Papers* and *A Christmas Carol* so popular.

TRADITIONS – OLD AND NEW

Irving's narrator takes a stagecoach to Yorkshire, where he has planned to spend Christmas at a country inn. Amongst his fellow companions are three schoolboys, released from boarding school for the holidays and whose excited conversation the narrator enjoys listening to, while watching the countryside go past the window:

> 'Perhaps the impending holiday might have given a more than usual animation to the country, for it seemed to me as if everybody was in good looks and good spirits. Game, poultry, and other luxuries of the table, were in brisk circulation in the villages; the grocers, butchers, and fruiterers shops were thronged with customers. The housewives were stirring briskly about, putting their dwellings in order; and the glossy branches of holly, with their bright red berries, began to appear at the windows.'

On Christmas Eve, as the coach arrives at the inn, which is brightened by festive decorations and lit by a roaring fire, the narrator bumps into an old friend, Frank Bracebridge, with whom he 'had once travelled on the Continent'.

Frank Bracebridge invites him to stay at his father's country house:

> 'As we approached the house, we heard the sound of music, and now and then a burst of laughter, from one end of the building. This, Bracebridge said, must proceed from the servants' hall, where a great deal of revelry was permitted, and even encouraged, by the squire, throughout the twelve days of Christmas, provided everything was done conformably to ancient usage. Here were kept up the old games of hoodman blind, shoe the wild mare, hot cockles, steal the white loaf, bob apple, and snap dragon: the Yule log and Christmas candle were regularly burnt, and the mistletoe, with its white berries, hung up, to the imminent peril of all the pretty housemaids. So intent were the servants upon their sports, that we had to ring repeatedly before we could make our selves heard ... The mistletoe is still hung up in farmhouses and kitchens at Christmas, and the young men have the privilege of kissing the girls under it, plucking each time a berry from the bush. When the berries are all plucked, the privilege ceases.'

Throughout the narrator's stay, Frank's father, 'the squire', is at great pains to tell his guest about the customs they enjoy and which he encourages all his tenants to celebrate. The squire bemoans the fact that so many of the traditions are being ignored and, he believes, this is making their time a more selfish and unkind age:

> 'The squire went on to lament the deplorable decay of the games and amusements which were once prevalent at this season among the lower orders ... "Our old games and local customs," said he, "had a great effect in making the peasant fond of his home, and the promotion of them by the gentry made him fond of his lord. They made the times merrier, and kinder, and better ... The nation" continued he, "is altered; we have almost lost our simple true-hearted peasantry."'

One of the squire's greatest delights was in the wassail bowl and its customs:

> 'The Wassail Bowl was sometimes composed of ale instead of wine; with nutmeg, sugar, toast, ginger, and roasted crabs [crab apples]; in this way the nut-brown beverage is still prepared in some old families, and round this mighty bowl. Having raised it to his lips, with a hearty wish of a merry Christmas to all present, he sent it brimming round the board, for every one to follow his example, according to the primitive style; pronouncing it "the ancient fountain of good-feeling, where all hearts met together." There was much laughing and rallying as the honest emblem of Christmas joviality circulated, and was kissed rather coyly by the ladies ...'

CHAPTER SIX

'Ring in the New'

'Hackney-coaches and carriages keep rattling up the street and down the street in rapid succession, conveying, doubtless, smartly-dressed coachfuls to crowded parties; loud and repeated double knocks at the house with green blinds, opposite, announce to the whole neighbourhood that there's one large party in the street at all events; and we saw through the window, and through the fog too, till it grew so thick that we rung for candles, and drew our curtains, pastry-cooks' men with green boxes on their heads, and rout-furniture-warehouse-carts, with cane seats and French lamps, hurrying to the numerous houses where an annual festival is held in honour of the occasion … Take the house with the green blinds for instance. We know it is a quadrille party, because we saw some men taking up the front drawing-room carpet while we sat at breakfast this morning, and if further evidence be required, and we must tell the truth, we just now saw one of the young ladies "doing" another of the young ladies' hair, near one of the bedroom windows, in an unusual style of splendour, which nothing else but a quadrille party could possibly justify … More double knocks! what an extensive party! what an incessant hum of conversation and general sipping of coffee! … The toast is drunk with acclamation ... and the whole party rejoin the ladies in the drawing-room. Young men who were too bashful to dance before supper, find tongues and partners; the musicians exhibit unequivocal symptoms of having drunk the new year in, while the company were out; and dancing is kept up, until far in the first morning of the new year.'

Charles Dickens, 'The New Year' (1836)

As the new year of 1837 dawned, Dickens needed to concentrate on practical matters. With Charley's birth, they had outgrown their apartments at Furnival's Inn, so he took on the lease of a new home and, on 25 March 1837, the family, including Fred Dickens and Mary Hogarth, moved into 48, Doughty Street (now the Charles Dickens museum). This was the grandest house that he had ever lived in, and the fact that he had managed to afford to do so through his writing and hard work, was a source of great pride. He described it as 'a frightfully first-class Family Mansion, involving awful responsibilities' and he must have felt that he was, at last, leaving behind the spectre of the Marshalsea prison and his time as a 'little labouring hind', pasting labels onto blacking bottles. Whilst living at Doughty, Street Dickens completed *The Pickwick Papers* and *Oliver Twist* (the first instalment of which had been published in February 1837, a month before the family left Furnival's Inn) and wrote *Nicholas Nickleby*. He moved into 48, Doughty Street as a rising star, and when he moved out less than three years later, he had become a dazzling household name.

The first year in their new home, however, was not a good one and the first family Christmas at Doughty Street was suffused with sadness. The year had begun very well, with Catherine and the baby thriving and Charles's writing becoming increasingly successful, but on the night of Saturday 6 May 1837, everything changed. Charles, Catherine and Mary Hogarth had spent the evening at St James's Theatre, watching a farce written by Charles, *Is She His Wife?, or, Something Singular!*. Shortly after they returned home, seventeen-year-old Mary collapsed. By the following afternoon, she was dead. The family had been in their new home only a few weeks and Mary died just days before Catherine's twenty-second birthday. Catherine, who was pregnant again, suffered a miscarriage, caused by the shock of her sister's death.

In September 1837, the family celebrated the marriage of Fanny Dickens to her fellow musician Henry Burnett, but Christmas was still subdued and sad without Mary Hogarth. The new year was ushered in by a party at Doughty Street, for a select gathering of friends and family, and Henry Burnett remembered:

'It was near the hour of twelve, when we went up to the windows, and each person became mute, excepting an excusable whisper every now and then from two or three ladies. The constrained silence was at an end as soon as the first stroke of a distant clock came upon the ear. Then a muffled counting was heard from one or two, and then the clear voice of our Host called out, "Best Wishes and a kiss for each lady, and a Happy New Year to us all!.""

On 1 January 1838, Dickens wrote in his diary:

'A sad new Year's Day in one respect, for at the opening of last year poor Mary was with us. Very many things to be grateful for, since then, however. Increased reputation and means – good health and prospects. We never know the full value of blessings, 'till we lose them …'

Between New Year and Twelfth Night, letters and diaries record that Dickens spent time going to parties and gatherings, working on his biography of Joseph Grimaldi and planning a book about the history of London with his friend William Harrison Ainsworth – it was never written. On 2 January, Dickens noted, 'With Ainsworth all day ... Afterwards to the ruins of the fire in the Borough, thence to the top of Saint Saviour's Church; back to his Club to dinner, and afterwards to Covent Garden where we met Browning.' The fire had broken out on 31 December, at a warehouse in Tooley Street, near London Bridge. The church that he mentions was renamed Southwark Cathedral in 1905; it would have held a special charm for Dickens because of its connections with Shakespeare. In early January, Fanny Burnett 'sang beautifully' at a party that her brother attended, and which he described in his diary as 'full of City people – and rather dull'. Another guest recorded, 'Met Boz – looks quite a boy.'

Twelfth Night was spent with friends and Dickens recorded in his diary:

'Our boy's birth day – one year old. A few people at night – only Forster, the Degex's, John Ross, Mitton and the Beards besides our families – to Twelfth Cake and forfeits.'

By Charley's birthday Catherine was in her seventh month of a new pregnancy, with the baby due in the spring, and by their second Christmas at Doughty Street the family home was made up of Charles, Catherine, 'Uncle Fred', toddler Charley and baby Mamie (christened Mary, after her deceased aunt).

On Christmas Eve 1838, Charles went to a rehearsal of the pantomime, *Harlequin and Fair Rosamund,* with John Forster and the poet Robert Browning. It was being performed at the Covent Garden Theatre, by their friend, the actor-manager William Charles Macready. Dickens had promised to write a review. On Christmas Day, Catherine, who was a talented cook, helped her servants create a Christmas feast at 48, Doughty Street. In her memoirs, Mamie Dickens wrote about how her father would study a dinner party menu with delight and 'then he would discuss every item in his humorous, fanciful way with his guests ... and he would apparently be so taken up with the merits or demerits of a menu that one might imagine he lived for nothing but the coming dinner'. Mamie loved setting the table for Christmas, recalling:

'A prettily decorated table was [father's] special pleasure, and from my earliest girlhood the care of this devolved upon me. When I had everything in readiness, he would come with me to inspect the result of my labors, before dressing for dinner, and no word except of praise ever came to my ears.'

Charley Dickens recalled a memory of that Christmas of 1838, when he was almost two years old:

'I am not at all sure that the first recollection of my father is not more derived from tradition than actual memory ... But I seem to remember very well on Christmas Day dinner at Doughty Street when, owing to the non-appearance of one of the guests the party consisted of thirteen and I was brought down from the nursery to fill the gap and afterwards set on a footstool on the table close to my father at dessert time. It was one of his few superstitions, by the by, this thirteen at the table.'

Christmas was a time when everyone tried to look their best. In *A Christmas Carol*, the impoverished Cratchit family attempt to make their shabby clothes look as smart as possible and Mrs Cratchit is described as being 'dressed out but poorly in a twice-turned gown, but brave in ribbons, which are cheap and make a goodly show for sixpence'. In the 1850s, Dickens wrote in a letter, 'My mother has a strong objection to being considered in the least old, and usually appears here on Christmas Day in a juvenile cap, which takes an immense time in the putting on.' As Christmas grew in popularity, so the tailors and shops began to sell special clothes for the Christmas season and church pews during services on Christmas Day were filled with people wearing the latest fashions.

In between Christmas of 1838 and New Year, Charles Dickens attended three dinners given by male friends: the pioneering doctor John Elliotson; the novelist William Harrison Ainsworth; and the politician Thomas Noon Talfourd, to whom Dickens had dedicated *The Pickwick Papers*. On New Year's Eve, he and Catherine hosted a dinner party at Doughty Street. In addition to all this socialising, he worked steadily on the serialisation of *Nicholas Nickleby* and he was also thinking about an idea for another novel, which would eventually be published as *Barnaby Rudge*. On 3 January 1839, Dickens wrote to John Forster, 'The beginning is made and – which is more – I can go on, so I hope the book is in training at last.' He kept on thinking about this idea for a novel, but other ideas kept coming to him and so it was put off until it was serialised between February and November 1841. Twelfth Night in 1839 was an even bigger celebration than usual in the Dickens household, because Mamie was christened on 5 January. The party to celebrate both the christening and Charley's second birthday could not, however, be held on 6 January, as it was a Sunday. This meant that all Twelfth Night celebrations had to be delayed by a day until 7 January.

It was to be their final Christmas at 48, Doughty Street. In October 1839, Catherine gave birth to a second daughter, Catherine Elizabeth Macready Dickens, known as Katey. This sent Dickens into another frenzy of practicality as he sought to move his expanding family into a bigger home. With the success of *Nicholas Nickleby*, he was able to afford to do so in style and, in December 1839, just days before the seasonal festivities began, the family moved into 1, Devonshire Terrace. This was a beautiful house at the end of a fashionable row of large homes, opposite the York Gate of the Regent's Park. Charles Dickens signed an eleven-year lease at the cost of £800, a sum of money that would have made his father's eyes water. The rent was an additional £160 per year. One of the essential changes the author asked to be made to the house at Devonshire Terrace was to have the study soundproofed. It was in this study that he would write, amongst other books, his novella *A Christmas Carol*.

The Christmas season of 1839 to 1840, with two toddlers and a baby in the house, was one of great celebration. In addition to the toddlers and the baby was a somewhat unusual pet; Grip, a talkative and mischievous raven. The earliest surviving reference to Grip in one of Dickens's letters dates from 13 February 1840, when he wrote a jokey letter to Daniel Maclise stating, 'I love nobody here but the Raven.' Grip was a domineering personality, whom Dickens adored. He strutted around the house and garden commanding attention – and inspiring the author as he continued to make notes for what would become his fifth novel, *Barnaby Rudge*. The initial title for this was *Gabriel Varden*, but by the time it was published (after *The Old Curiosity Shop*) its title had changed. This novel was a long time coming; although he published four novels before it, it was in fact the first idea for a full length book which he had come up with.

His diary entry for 1 January 1840 records, 'Dinner party at home – Tom Hill, Blanchard, Stone, Thompson, Collinson, Hullah and wife, Maclise, Forster, Kate, and I.' On 2 January 1840, Charles Dickens wrote a jovial letter to the publishers, Bradbury and Evans:

'My Dear Sirs,
I determined not to thank you for the Turkey until it was quite gone, in order that you might have a becoming idea of its astonishing capabilities.

The last remnant of that blessed bird made its appearance at breakfast yesterday – I repeat it, yesterday – the other portions having furnished forth seven grills, one boil and a cold lunch or two.

Accept my warm thanks (in which Mrs Dickens begs to join) for your annual recollection of us, which we value very highly as one of the pleasant circumstances of a pleasant season – and couple with them my hearty wishes for many happy years to both of you and both of yours – and of good health and good work and good feeling to all of us.'

The following day he wrote to John Forster cancelling their engagement to visit the theatre, explaining that as he had kept the servants 'up very late indeed for a great many nights' and because he had so much writing to do he had 'determined to resist the Pantomime and to come straight home like a good boy – for which resolution blame Christmas and the New Year; not me.'

CHAPTER SEVEN

'Pure as the New Fallen Snow'

'Christmas was always a time which in our home was looked forward to with eagerness and delight, and to my father it was a time dearer than any other part of the year, I think. He loved Christmas for its deep significance as well as for its joys, and this he demonstrates in every allusion in his writings to the great festival, a day which he considered should be fragrant with the love that we should bear one to another, and with the love and reverence of his Saviour and Master. Even in his most merry conceits of Christmas, there are always subtle and tender touches which will bring tears to the eyes, and make even the thoughtless have some special veneration for this most blessed anniversary.'

Mamie Dickens, *Charles Dickens by his Eldest Daughter* (1894)

Ever since the mid-1840s, the name Charles Dickens has become synonymous with Christmas, but this was not how his early contemporaries would have thought of him.

After *Sketches by Boz* (1836) and *The Pickwick Papers* (1837), Dickens's first novels make scant mention of Christmas. When Christmas is mentioned, in *Oliver Twist* (1838), *Nicholas Nickleby* (1839), *The Old Curiosity Shop* (1841) *Barnaby Rudge* (1841) and *Martin Chuzzlewit* (1844), it is only in passing, or to mark the passage of time.

Charles Dickens spent much of the Christmas season of 1840 to 1841 agonising over the plot of *The Old Curiosity Shop*. As he struggled to cope with the death of Little Nell, Dickens wrote to his friends that it brought back sad memories about the death of Mary Hogarth. Fans from all over the world, who were waiting eagerly for every new chapter to be published, wrote to Dickens begging him not to allow Little Nell to die, but he refused to change his mind, because he felt that the world was too unkind to sustain an impoverished child such as Little Nell. Just before Christmas 1840, he wrote instructions to his illustrator, George Cattermole, accompanied by the words, 'I am breaking my heart over this story, and cannot bear to finish it.' His brother-in-law Henry Burnett said, 'Little Nell was an object of his life ... he mourned her loss for a month after her death, and felt as if one of his own dear ones had left a vacant chair.'

On Christmas Eve, Charles and Catherine invited friends to Devonshire Terrace to play charades; they were also planning a New Year's Eve party. On 18 December, Charles Dickens sent invitations to friends. To the actor and printer John Pritt Harley he wrote:

'Come and dine here on the last day of this good old year, at 6 sharp ... We have no serious party ... and want to see the year out with some charades and other frolics. I won't tell you simply that you could come in dirty boots, but that stockings alone would be considered court dress.'

To William Harrison Ainsworth he wrote:

'...I want to make you promise to dine here on the last day of the old year at 6 exactly – quite at home and unceremoniously to see it out with forfeits and such like exercises.'

Charley's birthday and Twelfth Night party was a small one that year, with only Daniel Maclise and John Forster invited. Catherine was, once again, heavily pregnant, and due to give birth in a month. Walter Landor Dickens was born on 8th February 1841, a day after his father's twenty-ninth birthday. His new son was described by Dickens as being 'very fat ... like a plump turkey'.

A few weeks after his son's birth, the author was mourning the death of his pet raven. Grip was the victim of his own greed, having managed to prise off the lids of cans of lead paint and drink the contents. He took several days to die, and Dickens lovingly recorded his last words and movements. In a letter to Daniel Maclise, Dickens reported:

'On the clock striking twelve he appeared slightly agitated, but soon recovered, walking twice or thrice along the coach-house, stopped to bark, staggered, exclaimed "Halloa old girl" (his favourite expression) and died. He behaved throughout with a decent fortitude, equanimity, and self-possession, which cannot be too much admired ... The children seem rather glad of it. He bit their ankles. But that was play.'

It was a feverish atmosphere in Devonshire Terrace in the winter of 1841. Grip had been replaced by a second raven, also named Grip, as well as by a pet eagle. In addition to the usual preparations for Christmas and New Year, Charles and Catherine were making preparations to leave the country – and, in doing so, to leave behind their four children, including the new baby, whose christening had to be arranged. Walter was christened on 4 December 1841 and a celebratory party was held afterwards.

Charles Dickens was excited about his approaching tour of America and Canada, but Catherine, terrified of leaving her children, was frightened and apprehensive. Her husband's enthusiasm and excitement bursts through in his correspondence of the time. Their friend, Charles Smithson, a lawyer who lived at Malton in Yorkshire, had sent the Dickens family a large festive pie; it was also he who had given the second Grip to Dickens as a present when his first raven died. On 20 December Dickens wrote to him,

'My Dear Smithson,
The Pie was no sooner brought into my room yesterday evening, than I fainted away.

Topping put his shoulder out, in carrying it from the waggon to the hall-door, and John is in the hospital with a damaged spine – having rashly attempted to lift it!

There never <u>was</u> such a Pie! We are mad to know what it's made of, but haven't the courage to cut it. Indeed we haven't a knife large enough for the purpose. We think of hiring Fletcher to eat it. We sit and stare at it in dull astonishment and grow dizzy in the contemplation of its enormous magnitude.

It prevents my writing at any length, as my faculties are absorbed in crust. I have a shadowy recollection that I owe Mrs Smithson a large sum of money, and that it preys upon my mind. Fred was to have told me the amount but he forgot it on his way home. I seem to remember too, that you paid for THE Raven – Good God! – if you could only hear him talk, and see him break the windows!

You will be glad to hear – I can only hint at his perfections – that he disturbs the church service, and that his life is threatened by the Beadle. Maclise says he <u>knows</u> he can read and write. I quite believe it; and I go so far as to place implicit reliance on his powers of cyphering.... Since writing the above, I have looked at the Pie and I am very weak [his signature given as a feeble cross].'

The festive season was a whirl of social engagements before leaving the country, leading Dickens to apologise to Angela Burdett-Coutts, "Every day this week I am engaged". On Christmas Eve, Dickens and John Forster went to the Drury Lane Theatre to see a rehearsal of Macready's latest production, *The Merchant of Venice*. On 27 December, Dickens went back again, to watch his friend in the role of Shylock on opening night. He reserved the rest of the week after Christmas to spend with his children, refusing invitations from friends.

On 1 January 1842, Catherine and Charles had a farewell dinner given by John Forster. On the following day, they left London for Liverpool, where they would board their ship to America. They sailed on 4 January 1842, on board the SS *Britannia* – their departure date was two days before their eldest child's fifth birthday and a month before their baby's first birthday. Catherine, Charles and their maid Anne Brown spent Twelfth Night feeling seasick in terrible weather, or as Dickens recorded in *American Notes*:

'It was not exactly comfortable below. It was decidedly close; and it was impossible to be unconscious of the presence of that extraordinary compound of strange smells, which is to be found nowhere but on board ship, and which is such a subtle perfume that it seems to enter at every pore of the skin, and whisper of the hold. Two passengers' wives (one of them my own) lay already in silent agonies on the sofa; and one lady's maid (my lady's) was a mere bundle on the floor, execrating her destiny, and pounding her curl-papers among the stray boxes. Everything sloped the wrong way: which in itself was an aggravation scarcely to be borne. I had left the door open, a moment before, in the bosom of a gentle declivity, and, when I turned to shut it, it was on the summit of a lofty eminence. Now every plank and timber creaked, as if the ship were made of wicker-work; and now crackled, like an enormous fire of the driest possible twigs. There was nothing for it but bed; so I went to bed.

'It was pretty much the same for the next two days, with a tolerably fair wind and dry weather. I read in bed (but to this hour I don't know what) a good deal; and reeled on deck a little; drank cold brandy-and-water with an unspeakable disgust, and ate hard biscuit perseveringly: not ill, but going to be.'

In New York, Charles Dickens was thrilled to meet Washington Irving, who hosted a dinner in honour of the English author. At the dinner, Dickens made a speech saying, 'I do not go to bed two nights out of seven without taking Washington Irving under my arm upstairs to bed with me'. The two men got on very well and an ongoing friendship seemed to be ensured – until Irving read Dickens's resulting travelogue *American Notes* (1842). Although he described Irving in the book as 'my dear friend' and 'this charming writer', Irving disliked the book and felt his country had been offended.

Charles and Catherine returned to London at the end of June 1842, determined never to go away again without their children. Charley, Mamie, Katey and Walter had spent the six months being cared for by the servants, Uncle Fred and Catherine's younger sister, fifteen-year-old Georgina Hogarth. By the time their parents returned, the children had grown so attached to Georgina, whom they called 'Aunty Georgy', that Charles and Catherine asked if she would like to move into their home permanently. It was common in nineteenth century Britain, where girls and women were expected to be carefully chaperoned at all times, for an unmarried sister to move in with a married sister's family; although this was usually expected to be a temporary arrangement, until she married.

A few weeks before Christmas, Dickens went travelling to Cornwall, with John Forster and the artists Daniel Maclise and Clarkson Stanfield. Dickens and Forster wrote and made notes about everything they saw, and Maclise and Stanfield drew and painted. One of the people they met on their journey was a Dr Miles Marley, and Dickens stored away the name. The doctor was reputedly proud of his unusual name; he could have had no idea how many people would be talking about a man named Marley by the end of the following year.

As was usual on his travels, Dickens tried to see as much as he could of social and working conditions. In Cornwall, he was humbled by his visit to a tin mine, and remembered the landscapes and living conditions of those miners when he came to write the scene in *A Christmas Carol* when Scrooge is taken by the Ghost of Christmas Present to witness the conditions in which poor, working people live:

'And now, without a word of warning from the Ghost, they stood upon a bleak and desert moor, where monstrous masses of rude stone were cast about, as though it were the burial-place of giants; and water spread itself wheresoever it listed, or would have done so, but for the frost that held it prisoner; and nothing grew but moss and furze, and coarse rank grass. Down in the west the setting sun had left a streak of fiery red, which glared upon the desolation for an instant, like a sullen eye, and frowning lower, lower, lower yet, was lost in the thick gloom of darkest night.

"What place is this?" asked Scrooge.

"A place where Miners live, who labour in the bowels of the earth," returned the Spirit. "But they know me. See."

'A light shone from the window of a hut, and swiftly they advanced towards it. Passing through the wall of mud and stone, they found a cheerful company assembled round a glowing fire. An old, old man and woman, with their children and their children's children, and another generation beyond that, all decked out gaily in their holiday attire. The old man, in a voice that seldom rose above the howling of the wind upon the barren waste, was singing them a Christmas song – it had been a very old song when he was a boy – and from time to time they all joined in the chorus. So surely as they raised their voices, the old man got quite blithe and loud; and so surely as they stopped, his vigour sank again.

'The Spirit did not tarry here, but bade Scrooge hold his robe, and passing on above the moor, sped – whither. Not to sea. To sea. To Scrooge's horror, looking back, he saw the last of the land, a frightful range of rocks, behind them; and his ears were deafened by the thundering of water, as it rolled and roared, and raged among the dreadful caverns it had worn, and fiercely tried to undermine the earth.

'Built upon a dismal reef of sunken rocks, some league or so from shore, on which the waters chafed and dashed, the wild year through, there stood a solitary lighthouse. Great heaps of sea-weed clung to its base, and storm-birds – born of the wind one might suppose, as sea-weed of the water – rose and fell about it, like the waves they skimmed.

'But even here, two men who watched the light had made a fire, that through the loophole in the thick stone wall shed out a ray of brightness on the awful sea. Joining their horny hands over the rough table at which they sat, they wished each other Merry Christmas in their can of grog; and one of them: the elder, too, with his face all damaged and scarred with hard weather, as the figure-head of an old ship might be: struck up a sturdy song that was like a Gale in itself.'

With all these images stored away in his imagination, Dickens was back in London at the start of November, in time to start preparing for a family Christmas. It was particularly jubilant this year, as Charles and Catherine tried to make up for the six months away from their children. In her memoirs, Mamie Dickens left the following description of Christmas preparations in the Dickens family:

'In our childish days my father used to take us every 24th day of December to a toy shop in Holborn where we were allowed to select our Christmas present and also any we wished to give to our little companions. Although I believe we were often an hour of more in the shop before our several tastes were satisfied, he never showed the least impatience, was always interested and desirous as we were that we should choose exactly what we liked best.'

On Christmas Eve of 1842, Dickens also paid a visit to the theatre, to see Macready's latest pantomime, *Harlequin and William Tell, or, The Genius of the Ribstone Pippin*. It seems likely it was Dickens who wrote a very favourable review of Macready's pantomime for the *Examiner* of 31 Dec, stating that it was 'the best we have had for years'. New Year's Eve was spent at John Forster's home, celebrating in what Dickens described as 'a small style', but they made up for this with a party planned for Twelfth Night. Charles Dickens wrote to several friends to make it clear the party was not just for children. To the illustrator Frank Stone, he wrote:

'All manner of childish amusements are coming off here on Twelfth Night, in honor of my eldest son attaining the tremendous age of six years. It has occurred to me that a few older boys and girls (all of whom you know) might protract the festivities on their own account, and make a merry evening of it.'

To Leigh Hunt, he wrote:

'Next Friday – Twelfth Night – is the Anniversary of my Son and Heir's birthday ... I have asked some children of a larger growth (all of whom you know) to come and make merry on their own account.'

DICKENS AND CHRISTMAS

On the last day of 1842, Dickens wrote to Cornelius Felton, a Harvard professor he had met in Boston, to wish him a happy new year and to describe the party he had planned for Charley's birthday:

> 'The actuary of the National Debt couldn't calculate the number of children who are coming here on Twelfth Night ... But the best of it, is, that Forster and I have purchased between us the entire stock in trade of a conjuror, the practice and display whereof is entrusted to me. And oh my dear eyes, Felton, if you could see me conjuring the company's watches into impossible tea caddies, and causing pieces of money to fly, and burning pocket handkerchiefs without hurting 'em, – and practising in my own room, without anybody to admire – you would never forget it as long as you live. In those tricks which require a confederate I am assisted (by reason of his impertubable good humour) by Stanfield, who always does his part exactly the wrong way: to the unspeakable delight of all beholders.'

At the party, a special present was unwrapped. The Dickens children would remember for years to come their shining excitement at beholding their very own Magic Lantern, to a Victorian child this was the height of technological sophistication – a device that could project images onto a screen or wall and make it look as though it were glowing with light. It was the Victorian equivalent of a cinema screen. For the Dickens family, and for Charles Dickens in particular, this was to be their last Christmas without the extraordinary level of elevated celebrity that would be caused by the publication of *A Christmas Carol*.

CHAPTER EIGHT

'Bah! Humbug!'

> "'There are many things from which I might have derived good, by which I have not profited, I dare say," returned the nephew. "Christmas among the rest. But I am sure I have always thought of Christmas time, when it has come round – apart from the veneration due to its sacred name and origin, if anything belonging to it can be apart from that – as a good time; a kind, forgiving, charitable, pleasant time: the only time I know of, in the long calendar of the year, when men and women seem by one consent to open their shut-up hearts freely, and to think of people below them as if they really were fellow-passengers to the grave, and not another race of creatures bound on other journeys. And therefore, uncle, though it has never put a scrap of gold or silver in my pocket, I believe that it has done me good, and will do me good; and I say, God bless it!'"
>
> Charles Dickens, *A Christmas Carol* (1843)

Although Charles Dickens began the new year in a mood of great optimism, he had a difficult year ahead. For the first time his sales decreased, and his publishers, Chapman and Hall, began to lose confidence in him. Many of Dickens's American readers had been angered by what they considered his rudeness about their country in *American Notes*, complaining that he had abused their hospitality. Although Dickens had written many favourable things in his travelogue, his wry jokes and outright criticisms – in particular of slavery, which was still legal in the USA at that date – made many of his former fans turn against him.

DICKENS AND CHRISTMAS

In January 1843, the first episode of *Martin Chuzzlewit*, was published. It continued, in monthly instalments, until July 1844. The novel includes characters who travel to America, and once again Dickens berated the country for believing itself to be 'civilised' when it still permitted the atrocity of slavery. In *Martin Chuzzlewit* he wrote such lines as:

'An American gentleman ... stuck his hands deep into his pockets, and walked the deck with his nostrils dilated, as already inhaling the air of Freedom which carries death to all tyrants, and can never (under any circumstances worth mentioning) be breathed by slaves.'

He also wrote scathingly about the fictional town of Eden, an ironic name for a place that could not be less like the biblical version of paradise. Eden was based on a town named Cairo, in Illinois. People in Illinois, and all over America, were incensed and Dickens's once-golden reputation in America was rapidly becoming tarnished.

An even bigger problem was that *Martin Chuzzlewit* also did not capture the interest of the usual number of Dickens's readers at home. As there was no international copyright law, he received no money for books sold in America so home sales were important, he campaigned for an international copyright law for decades. Although there were those who loved it as much as his other novels, there were also a large number who just stopped reading it partway through. Dickens felt this keenly and when he and Catherine realised there would be a fifth baby in the household by the following January, he began to be frightened about money. No matter how famous he became, Dickens could never rid himself of the twin spectres of the Marshalsea and the blacking factory; he was terrified of his earning potential disappearing.

During the blacking factory months, Dickens had become a wary street child. He had to learn whom to avoid and whom he could trust, which areas to skirt around the edge of, which streets never to walk along, and how to recognise danger. As an adult, Dickens often suffered from insomnia; when that happened, he would walk around London at night, often with his dogs as company. On these walks, he took inspiration for his stories, worked out plotlines, observed characters and came to a genuine understanding about the lives of London's poorest communities. Throughout 1843, he grew increasingly concerned about the plight of impoverished children and the many sickening dangers that lay in wait for them. Children were forced to work in some of the nastiest jobs in the country, for which they were paid a fraction of what adults earned – if they were paid at all. They did jobs that were injurious to health, and which could often prove fatal, and they had scant laws protecting them. Of those laws that were in place, very few of the children even knew of their existence. Many children were forced into prostitution, as England's archaic sexual consent laws, which had not been changed since the thirteenth century, permitted sex with a child at the age of twelve, which remained in place until a new law in 1875 raised the age to thirteen. This had helped to make England, and London in particular, a centre of paedophile prostitution.

On his walks around the city, Dickens saw the misery in which increasing numbers of children were living. The Industrial Revolution had seen a massive increase in people migrating from the countryside to the cities but even while this urban sprawl was continuing to grow, technology was changing all the time and these changes meant a more mechanised workplace. This, in turn, meant the need for fewer human workers. Many of the families who had moved to London and were unable to find work were living in terrifying slums and eking out an existence through begging or stealing. Dickens had brought the plight of these children to his public in *Oliver Twist* yet nothing seemed to be changing in the lives of the country's poorest children.

During his months in America, Dickens had altered his religion, from being a member of the Church of England, to becoming a Unitarian. He had done so because he felt that the Unitarian church would be more proactive in helping the poor and desperate. A year on from his return from the United States, he was feeling despondent about whether such great changes would – or indeed *could* – ever happen. While he was writing *Martin Chuzzlewit*, and continuing to work on articles for magazines and newspapers, Dickens was thinking about the plight of the country's children and what he could do to help. He had read the 1843 parliamentary report on child labourers in Britain's factories, written by the pioneering doctor Thomas Southwood Smith. He had been 'perfectly stricken down' by reading it and wrote to Southwood Smith that he intended to write a pamphlet titled *An Appeal to the People of England, on Behalf of the Poor Man's Child*, 'with my name attached, of course'. He spent weeks thinking about how best to make the general public aware enough to bring about change.

All through 1843, Dickens paid even more attention than usual to the injustice of British society, and felt sickened by the enormous gulf between the wealthy and the desperate. In May, he went to a fundraising dinner for the Charterhouse Square infirmary, a charity which took care of elderly, poverty-stricken men. Ironically, the majority of those who attended the dinner were very wealthy men, mostly bankers who made their fortunes in the City of London. Dickens wrote a contemptuous letter to his friend Douglas Jerrold describing his fellow diners as 'sleek, slobbering, bow-paunched, overfed, apoplectic, snorting cattle'.

He spent hours talking to the philanthropist and heiress Angela Burdett-Coutts, discussing what they could do to bring about societal change. Both were convinced that one vital way forward was education, and Dickens began to visit ragged schools; he also visited prisons, to see what effect a lack of education had on criminality. On 24 September, he wrote to Burdett-Coutts about the pupils at a ragged school:

> 'There are fewer girls than boys; but the girls are more numerous than you would suppose, and much better behaved – although they are the wretchedest of the wretched. But there is much more Good in Women than in Men, however Ragged they are. People are apt to think otherwise, because of the outward degredation of a woman strikes them more forcibly than any amount of hideousness in a man. They have no better reasons.'

On the same day, he wrote to Lord Brougham, a pioneering lawyer and politician who had fought against slavery. By the time he knew Dickens, he was concerning himself with educational reform. The author wrote the letter from Broadstairs, in Kent, where he had taken his family for the summer:

> 'Since I had the pleasure of seeing you, I have gone very much about the Jails and byeplaces of London, and although they are old sights to me, am more than ever amazed at the Ignorance and Misery that prevail ... I would that I were a Police Magistrate ... I think I should be a pretty good one, with my knowledge of the kind of people that come most commonly within their Jurisdiction; and I would never rest from practically shewing all classes how important it has become to educate, on bold and comprehensive principles, the Dangerous Members of Society. I have often had this desire on my mind, but never so strongly as now.'

This feeling that he should be making genuine physical changes to the society in which he lived had been growing all year. He was desperate to write something that would actually make a difference to the lives of the poor children he encountered every day, and the more he thought about his pamphlet report for the government, the less he felt it would have any effect at all – it would be read by a tiny minority and possibly ignored. Instead, he needed to write something that would make people pay attention, that would strike 'a sledgehammer blow' on behalf of 'the poor man's child'. He needed to produce something that would have 'twenty thousand times the force' of a government pamphlet.

In October 1843, Dickens travelled to Manchester, where he had been invited to give a speech in support of the Athenaeum, a charity which provided educational opportunities for working men and women. He was also able to spend time with Fanny, who lived in Manchester. She and Henry Burnett now had two children. At the time of their uncle's visit, Harry Burnett was nearly four and Charles Burnett was two and a half. Dickens was deeply moved by witnessing the difficulties Harry suffered due to his disability. Harry had been born with unspecified disabilities, and the family feared that he was not destined to live into adulthood. Seeing his little nephew struggle with his health made Dickens think about the realities of what life was like for impoverished disabled children, whose lives were even harder than those of their able-bodied siblings.

In Manchester, Dickens walked around the city, just as he liked to do in London. Before this visit, he thought he had witnessed all the degradations of poverty in his home town, but he was horrified by the sight of families living in abject misery and poverty. He saw families living on the streets, all in danger of starving, and he was chilled at the breadth of poverty in post-Industrial Revolution Manchester. This was the time of the 'Hungry Forties', when Britain was experiencing an economic depression, when unemployment was growing exponentially, when two consecutive harvests failed and when the price of everyday foods was beyond the reach of many families. Within a couple of years, the situation would have grown even worse, with the Potato Famine, which began in 1845 and killed an estimated one million people in Ireland.

Charles Dickens's speech at the Athenaeum on 5 October was passionate in its call for reform. Fired by the social injustices he had witnessed, his words burned with the author's fury and his feelings of powerlessness. He railed at the way in which the upper class of wealthy privileged men seemed determined never to share their riches with those who needed the most help:

'... How often have we heard from a large class of men wise in their generation, who would really seem to be born and bred for no other purpose than to pass into currency counterfeit and mischievous scraps of wisdom, as it is the sole pursuit of some other criminals to utter base coin – how often have we heard from them, as an all-convincing argument, that "a little learning is a dangerous thing?" Why, a little hanging was considered a very dangerous thing, according to the same authorities, with this difference, that, because a little hanging was dangerous, we had a great deal of it; and, because a little learning was dangerous, we were to have none at all. Why, when I hear such cruel absurdities gravely reiterated, I do sometimes begin to doubt whether the parrots of society are not more pernicious to its interests than its birds of prey. I should be glad to hear such people's estimate of the comparative danger of "a little learning" and a vast amount of ignorance; I should be glad to know which they consider the most prolific parent of misery and crime. Descending a little lower in the social scale, I should be glad to assist them in their calculations, by carrying them into certain gaols and nightly refuges I know of, where my own heart dies within me, when I see thousands of immortal creatures condemned, without alternative or choice, to tread, not what our great poet calls the "primrose path" to the everlasting bonfire, but one of jaded flints and stones, laid down by brutal ignorance, and held together, like the solid rocks, by years of this most wicked axiom …'

His speech was reported in newspapers all over the British Isles.

By the time Dickens travelled back to London from Manchester, he was burning with the desire to write something monumentally important, something that would campaign against the 'ignorance and want' that seemed to him to be so pervasive. The first known mention of *A Christmas Carol* can be found in a letter to the Scottish academic and magazine editor, Professor MacVey Napier. On 24 October 1843, Dickens wrote to him, 'I plunged headlong into a little scheme I had held in abeyance during the interval which had elapsed between my first letter and your answer; set an artist at work upon it...' The artist was Dickens's great friend John Leech, who would become famous as one of the leading cartoonists for the satirical magazine *Punch*. For weeks, Dickens worked furiously on his 'little scheme', while continuing to write *Martin Chuzzlewit*. Chapman and Hall were less than enthusiastic about his idea for a Christmas novella. They agreed to publish it only if Dickens bore a large amount of the costs, not least for the very expensive hand-coloured illustrations on which he was insisting.

All the while he was writing the story, Dickens's financial woes were nagging at the back of his mind, as was the knowledge that the expense of another baby – and the attendant medical bills for Catherine – was imminent. He wrote to a friend:

'Mrs. Dickens sends her love and best regards. We think of keeping the New Year, by having another child. I am constantly reversing the Kings in the Fairy Tales, and importuning the Gods not to trouble themselves: being quite satisfied with what I have. But they are so generous when they do take a fancy to one!'

To add to his concerns, his parents had, once again, fallen into debt and, once again, expected him to pay their bills. At the end of September, Dickens had received from his father what he described to his friend Thomas Mitton as 'a threatening letter'. Dickens wrote in pain to his friend, 'I am amazed and confounded by the audacity of his ingratitude. He, and all of them, look upon me as something to be plucked and torn to pieces for their advantage ... My soul sickens at the thought ...'

One of the people to whom Dickens confided his financial woes was his lawyer friend Charles Smithson in Yorkshire. The letter suggests Smithson had previously pointed out that Chapman and Hall's contracts were not at all favourable to Dickens. The author responded, 'The Oliver agreement was of my own making, and so was the Pickwick. It was a consequence of the astonishing rapidity of my success and the steady rise of my fame that the enormous profits of these books should flow into hands other than mine. It has always been so ...' Dickens also mentioned that another publishing company, Bradbury and Evans, was courting him, but that he was not interested in changing firms. He was soon to change his mind.

All the time he was writing *A Christmas Carol,* Dickens's letters show his constant preoccupation with the story. He wrote to George Cruikshank, 'I am finishing a little Book for Christmas, and contemplate a Bolt, to do so in peace. As soon as I have done, I will let you know, and then I hope we shall take a glass of Grog together.' And to Marion Ely, 'I have been working from morning until night upon my little Christmas Book; and have really had no time to think of anything but that.'

A Christmas Carol was finished on 2 December 1843. It had taken its author just six weeks to write. Despite being triumphant about finishing it, he was panicking about his finances, knowing his bank account was overdrawn, which was worryingly reminiscent of his father's ineptitude with money. Dickens was also furious that Chapman and Hall were making so little effort to publicise the book. Bradbury and Evans were happy to point out his current publisher's misdemeanours. Two days after finishing *A Christmas Carol*, he wrote a furious letter to his friend Thomas Mitton:

'I have been obliged to write [Chapman and Hall] a most tremendous letter, and have told them not to answer it, or come near me, but simply to do what I have ordered them. Can you believe that with the exception of Blackwood's, the Carol is not advertised in One of the Magazines! Bradbury would not believe it when I told him on Saturday last. And he says that nothing but a tremendous push can possibly atone for such fatal negligence … I have shewn the book to two or three Judges of very different views and constitutions. I have never seen men, personally and mentally opposed to each other, so unanimous in their predictions, or so hot in their approval.'

Dickens sent Mitton a copy of his manuscript, and Mitton responded very warmly. Dickens's reply shows how strong his own feelings were about the story:

'I am extremely glad you feel the Carol. For I knew I meant a good thing. And when I see the effect of such a little whole as that, on those for whom I care, I have a strong sense of the immense effect I could produce with an entire book. I am quite certain of that … I am sure if will do me a great deal of good; and I hope it will sell, well.'

In writing *A Christmas Carol*, Charles Dickens was encapsulating the zeitgeist. For some years, people had been feeling nostalgic for the ways in which Christmas used to be celebrated and the British Isles was ripe for a renaissance in the ways in which they viewed the Christmas season. As the Enlightenment of the eighteenth century had made way for the technological wizardry of the nineteenth, there was a renewed interest in the past – but as an historic fascination, rather than a desire to live within it. With every decade that passed, greater numbers of British people were becoming literate and educated, and the desire to know more about their country's history was increasing. Stories of how the ancient Britons used to celebrate their pagan winter festival captured the imagination, and the fashion of dressing one's home for Christmas with ever more elaborate decorations and greenery began to become even more popular.

The year 1843, was to mark a turning point in how the British – and much of the wider world – celebrated Christmas. Not only was it the year in which *A Christmas Carol* was published; it was also the year in which the very first Christmas card was produced commercially. The name Henry Cole is little remembered today, but he was a true pioneer of the Victorian age. He was involved in the reformation of the postal service, was a pioneer of the railways and was one of the main instigators and creators – together with Prince Albert – of the Great Exhibition – full title 'The Great Exhibition of the Works of Industry of All Nations' – in 1851. Through that, he also helped with the creation of the South Kensington Museums and the Royal Albert Hall. He began his career as a civil servant at the Public Records Office, and went on to become the very first director of the South Kensington Museum, now known as the Victoria and Albert Museum, or the V&A.

For the perennially busy Henry Cole, the Christmas tradition of sending long, handwritten letters was proving impossible alongside his already very crowded working schedule. He simply did not have the time to sit and write letters to everyone he wanted to keep in touch with. Thanks to Henry Cole's efficiency in helping the reformer and campaigner Rowland Hill create the new and improved 'Penny Post' in 1840, increasing numbers of letters were arriving daily, all of which needed an answer. Overwhelmed by the demands of the season, Henry Cole came up with the idea of creating a card he could send instead of writing letters. He asked an artist friend, John Callcott Horsley, to draw a picture of the Cole family celebrating Christmas together.

John Callcott Horsley, was a well-respected artist, who had trained at the Royal Academy and gained initial fame for his portraiture. He also became known for the frescoes he painted at the new Houses of Parliament (which had been rebuilt following a fire in 1834). His sister, Elizabeth, had married the great railway engineer, Isambard Kingdom Brunel. Today, he is remembered as the designer of his first Christmas card, but in his own time, he was best known – and satirised – not for the Christmas card, but for the zeal with which he campaigned against nudity. He was infuriated when the Royal Academy started permitting students to draw from naked female models. All of the Royal Academy's students, at this time, were male and Horsley led a campaign to insist that, although male models could be sketched nude, all female models should be clothed. The campaign earned him the nickname of 'Clothes Horsley' and made him the subject of many cartoons.

On 17 December 1843, two days before *A Christmas Carol* was published, Henry Cole recorded in his diary, 'In the Evg Horsley came & brought his design for Christmas cards'. The design was based on a triptych, but it was not a religious scene. In the central section, is a sketch of three generations of Henry Cole's family raising their glasses in a toast to Christmas. On the two side panels are images of almsgiving of food and warm clothing being given to the poor, one of the central tenets of an old-fashioned Christmas. The Cole family is depicted sitting on a trellised balcony, from which is draped a banner that reads 'A Merry Christmas And A Happy New Year To You'. At the bottom of the card is printed 'Published at Summerly's Home Treasury Office, 12 Old Bond Street, London'. To Henry Cole's friends, this would have been significant, as, in addition to his work as a civil servant in the Public Record Office, Cole wrote books under the pseudonym Felix Summerly.

The cards were printed as lithographs by Joseph Cundell, and then hand tinted by the professional colourer William Mason. That Christmas, while much of the world was responding with an extraordinary fervour to the publication of *A Christmas Carol*, Henry Cole sent out his very first cards. He had commissioned the printer to produce one thousand copies, so, after he had taken all the cards he needed, he put up the remaining stock for sale, at the price of one shilling each. An advertisement from the *Athenaeum* magazine described 'Felix Summerly's' card as 'Just published. A Christmas Congratulation Card: or picture emblematical of Old English Festivity to Perpetuate kind recollections between Dear Friends.'

The first Christmas card proved controversial. Henry Cole was the father of eight children, and the depiction of some of his children on the Christmas card caused a furore. In the foreground a woman carefully helps a child sip from a glass of red wine, while in the background another child's face is obscured by the bottom of a wine glass and a little boy stands eagerly, apparently waiting for his drink. The Temperance Society was outraged, concerned that the card would cause an increase in drunkenness at Christmas time and lead to the moral corruption of children. The Temperance Society was also angered by the Cratchit family's Christmas lunch in *A Christmas Carol*, as Bob Cratchit is described as having made:

'some hot mixture in a jug with gin and lemons, and stirred it round and round and put it on the hob to simmer ... Then all the Cratchit family drew round the hearth, in what Bob Cratchit called a circle, meaning half a one; and at Bob Cratchit's elbow stood the family display of glass. Two tumblers, and a custard-cup without a handle.

74

These held the hot stuff from the jug, however, as well as golden goblets would have done; and Bob served it out with beaming looks, while the chestnuts on the fire sputtered and cracked noisily.'

In 1845, the *Gloucester Journal* included an account of a Temperance Society Christmas tea party at which the chairman's speech was recorded:

'He wanted to see people support temperance for virtue's sake, not for fashion. If Prince Albert was a teetotaller, all the nobility would follow his example ... The object of this society was to abolish drunkenness. With what sort of conscience could parents teach their children to drink! ... He thought that if the 600 members of the House of Commons were to give up their wine, they would do more good than by all their laws.'

Initially, Henry Cole's idea was a commercial failure, because few people grasped the concept of a Christmas card, and a shilling was a very expensive price for a single card. Within a couple of years, however, the idea had grown in popularity, helped largely by the renewed fervour for Christmas, prompted by the popularity of *A Christmas Carol*. By the end of the decade, Henry Cole's idea was well on its way to becoming as important a part of celebrating Christmas as Charles Dickens's Christmas novella had become. By the 1860s, Christmas cards were being mass produced, with artists and printers from all over the country cashing in on Henry Cole's idea, although very few early commercial Christmas cards featured religious pictures, most of the designs were of food, parties or saccharine illustrations of young children, usually depicted either naked in the role of a fairy or dressed in 'Sunday best' clothes. In 1883, *The Times* wrote that the new fashion for buying Christmas cards had:

'created a new trade, and has opened up a new field of labour for artists, lithographers, engravers, printers, ink and pasteboard makers ... All the year round brains are at work devising new designs and inventing novelties. The very cheap Christmas cards come from Germany where they can be produced at a much cheaper rate, but all the more artistic and more highly finished cards are the result of English workmanship.'

The astonishing and immediate success of *A Christmas Carol* surprised even its author. One of its most fervent supporters was the novelist William Thackeray. In his heartfelt review in *Fraser's Magazine*, Thackeray commented, 'Who can listen to objections regarding such a book as this? It seems to me a national benefit, and to every man or woman who reads it a personal kindness.' Dickens had foreseen that *A Christmas Carol* would be popular, but even he was not prepared for just how rapidly the book would sell. The first print run of 6,000 copies was published on 19 December 1843, and on Christmas Eve Dickens received a letter from Chapman and Hall to say the book was about to sell out 'and that as the orders were coming in fast from town and country, it would soon be necessary to reprint'. The national fervour that grew out of the book's publication was unprecedented – and this was despite its publishers having made so little effort to publicise the new title. As a consequence, Charles Dickens ended his contract with Chapman and Hall in 1844 and began working with Bradbury and Evans.

The plot of *A Christmas Carol* brought back into the public consciousness the need for Christmas to be centred on charity. Three days after the publication of Dickens's sensational new publication, the *Chelmsford Chronicle* published a stirring article:

'Well, Christmas is with us again, or close upon the door-step. His approach, like that of some great or royal personage, is prefaced by the bustle in our streets and households … Christmas in the march of time has, perhaps, lost a part of his portly form … It is not, perhaps, in the gay halls and gilded dining-rooms of wealth that the charm of Christmas is so strongly felt. There the feast of plenty comes to often to give that zest to the holiday table, which is felt in the home where … the little luxury can count a year between. But there is a class lower still than this – aye, so low that they cannot reach even the semblance of a Christmas meal, until the welcome tap of heaven-born benevolence be heard at their cottage door. The charitable alms of the rich fall at this season upon the poor like the refreshing dew upon the parched grass of summer, and a mere trifle may carry to many a lonely home of poverty that "merry Christmas".'

'"Do you know whether they've sold the prize Turkey that was hanging up there – Not the little prize Turkey: the big one."

"What, the one as big as me." returned the boy.... "It's hanging there now"....

"Is it.' said Scrooge... 'Go and buy it, and tell them to bring it here, that I may give them the direction where to take it. Come back with the man, and I'll give you a shilling. Come back with him in less than five minutes and I'll give you half-a-crown."

'The boy was off like a shot. ... "I'll send it to Bon Cratchit's," whispered Scrooge, rubbing his hands, and splitting with a laugh. "He shan't know who sends it. It's twice the size of Tiny Tim.".

'It was a Turkey. He never could have stood upon his legs, that bird. He would have snapped them short off in a minute, like sticks of sealing-wax.

'"Why, it's impossible to carry that to Camden Town," said Scrooge. "You must have a cab."

'The chuckle with which he said this, and the chuckle with which he paid for the Turkey, and the chuckle with which he paid for the cab, and the chuckle with which he recompensed the boy, were only to be exceeded by the chuckle with which he sat down breathless in his chair again, and chuckled till he cried.

'Shaving was not an easy task, for his hand continued to shake very much; and shaving requires attention, even when you don't dance while you are at it. But if he had cut the end of his nose off, he would have put a piece of sticking-plaster over it, and been quite satisfied.

'He dressed himself all in his best, and at last got out into the streets. The people were by this time pouring forth, as he had seen them with the Ghost of Christmas Present; and walking with his hands behind him, Scrooge regarded every one with a delighted smile. He looked so irresistibly pleasant, in a word, that three or four good-humoured fellows said, "Good morning, sir. A merry Christmas to you." And Scrooge said often afterwards, that of all the blithe sounds he had ever heard, those were the blithest in his ears.... He went to church, and walked about the streets, and watched the people hurrying to and fro, and patted children on the head, and questioned beggars, and looked down into the kitchens of houses, and up to the windows, and found that everything could yield him pleasure. He had never dreamed that any walk – that anything – could give him so much happiness....

'"A merry Christmas, Bob," said Scrooge, with an earnestness that could not be mistaken, as he clapped him on the back. "A merrier Christmas, Bob, my good fellow, than I have given you for many a year. I'll raise your salary, and endeavour to assist your struggling family, and we will discuss your affairs this very afternoon, over a Christmas bowl of smoking bishop, Bob. Make up the fires, and buy another coal-scuttle before you dot another i, Bob Cratchit."

'Scrooge was better than his word. He did it all, and infinitely more; and to Tiny Tim, who did not die, he was a second father. He became as good a friend, as good a master, and as good a man, as the good old city knew, or any other good old city, town, or borough, in the good old world. Some people laughed to see the alteration in him, but he let them laugh, and little heeded them; for he was wise enough to know that nothing ever happened on this globe, for good, at which some people did not have their fill of laughter in the outset; and knowing that such as these would be blind anyway, he thought it quite as well that they should wrinkle up their eyes in grins, as have the malady in less attractive forms. His own heart laughed: and that was quite enough for him.

'He had no further intercourse with Spirits, but lived upon the Total Abstinence Principle, ever afterwards; and it was always said of him, that he knew how to keep Christmas well, if any man alive possessed the knowledge. May that be truly said of us, and all of us! And so, as Tiny Tim observed, God bless Us, Every One!'

Charles Dickens, *A Christmas Carol* (1843)

'BAH! HUMBUG!'

It was pure coincidence that *A Christmas Carol* was published in the same year in which Henry Cole created his Christmas card, but it demonstrates that Dickens was capturing the nostalgic mood of the time. Dickens wrote *A Christmas Carol* in a very specific style, deliberately calling each section a 'stave' not a 'chapter', this echoed the musical theme of the novella's title, as well as giving it religious overtones. The main character is the miserly moneylender Ebenezer Scrooge, whose most famous expression is a contemptuous 'Bah, humbug!' with which he expresses his irritation at everything cheerful and, in particular, the celebrating of Christmas.

The story begins on Christmas Eve, the seventh anniversary of the death of Scrooge's business partner and fellow miser, Jacob Marley. That night, Scrooge is visited by Marley's ghost, who tells him he has to change his life or be condemned to the same terrible afterlife that Marley is suffering. He tells Scrooge that he will be visited by three more ghosts; the spirits of Christmas Past, Christmas Present, and Christmas Yet to Come.

By the end of the story, Scrooge has been reminded of his childhood, his lost love and the way in which money began to assume more importance to him than people; he has witnessed the miseries of poverty that he has not only done nothing to alleviate, but which he has wittingly made worse; and he has seen into his future, as a man for whom no one cares. The four ghosts achieve their goal of making Ebenezer Scrooge a kind, good, charitable man of whom, by the end of the story, 'it was always said ... that he knew how to keep Christmas well'.

The tale of this conversion of an old skinflint and miser into a man determined to help those who need it, struck at the heart of Victorian sentiment. Dickens wrote many more Christmas stories, but none ever achieved the greatness of *A Christmas Carol*, because it was written with such passion and fire. Dickens wrote it not solely as a story, but as a means to bring about social change, he wrote it because he was determined to make a difference to the lives of poverty-stricken children and this was the most effective way he could envisage doing so. All his subsequent Christmas books were written because his readers demanded one and because it made good business sense. None of them have the power of *A Christmas Carol*.

In the first stave of *A Christmas Carol*, Scrooge utters the unforgettable comment that poor people who are unable to work and don't want to be forced into prison or the workhouse should die and 'decrease the surplus population'. In writing those words Dickens was voicing what he believed many of his readers felt about the poor, the way he felt people had once viewed him as the labouring child of a prisoner. They are words that haunt

79

Scrooge throughout the story, and he grows to be deeply ashamed for having thought of human life as worthless.

In the third stave of the book, the Ghost of Christmas Present visits Scrooge. Dickens makes it explicit that he is writing about his readers' present time, when the ghost comments that he has 'more than eighteen hundred brothers' (each 'brother' indicating a year). When Scrooge finds the ghost, he is surrounded by the type of conspicuous consumption that typified a middle- or upper-class Christmas in a Victorian home:

'It was his own room. There was no doubt about that. But it had undergone a surprising transformation. The walls and ceiling were so hung with living green, that it looked a perfect grove; from every part of which, bright gleaming berries glistened. The crisp leaves of holly, mistletoe, and ivy reflected back the light, as if so many little mirrors had been scattered there; and such a mighty blaze went roaring up the chimney, as that dull petrification of a hearth had never known in Scrooge's time, or Marley's, or for many and many a winter season gone. Heaped up on the floor, to form a kind of throne, were turkeys, geese, game, poultry, brawn, great joints of meat, sucking-pigs, long wreaths of sausages, mince-pies, plum-puddings, barrels of oysters, red-hot chestnuts, cherry-cheeked apples, juicy oranges, luscious pears, immense twelfth-cakes, and seething bowls of punch, that made the chamber dim with their delicious steam.'

Dickens worked very closely with John Leech on the illustrations, and the picture Leech painted of Dickens's 'jolly Giant' of a ghost is closely allied both to the traditional image of the mummers' Father Christmas and to the ancient pagan Green Man. Traditionally, and all through the nineteenth century in Britain, Father Christmas wore green and white; some illustrations depict him in blue and white, which was a throwback to the Norse god of Jul. Although he was often depicted wearing red in North America, the dominance of the modern-day image of Father Christmas dressed in red and white began in earnest in Britain after the Coca-Cola company started using his image in their advertising campaigns and changed his robes to suit their brand colours. Dickens describes the Ghost of Christmas Present as being:

'clothed in one simple green robe, or mantle, bordered with white fur. This garment hung so loosely on the figure, that its capacious breast was bare, as if disdaining to be warded or concealed by any artifice.

Its feet, observable beneath the ample folds of the garment, were also bare; and on its head it wore no other covering than a holly wreath, set here and there with shining icicles. Its dark brown curls were long and free; free as its genial face, its sparkling eye, its open hand, its cheery voice, its unconstrained demeanour, and its joyful air. Girded round its middle was an antique scabbard; but no sword was in it, and the ancient sheath was eaten up with rust.'

John Leech's ghost is duly dressed in a flowing green robe trimmed with white fur and wears a wreath of green holly leaves around his head. He is intended to look fatherly and benign, and to provide a rich contrast to the cringeing, stooped Scrooge in his white nightshirt. The Ghost of Christmas Present is synonymous with the spirit of Christmas:

'The Spirit stood beside sick beds, and they were cheerful; on foreign lands, and they were close at home; by struggling men, and they were patient in their greater hope; by poverty, and it was rich. In almshouse, hospital, and jail, in misery's every refuge, where vain man in his little brief authority had not made fast the door and barred the Spirit out, he left his blessing, and taught Scrooge his precepts.'

In creating the character of Scrooge and in writing about his conversion, Dickens wanted his readers to recognise that there was a bit of Scrooge in each of them too. He wanted to prick the consciences of those readers who might call themselves good Christians and go to church every Sunday, but then gave no thought to the starving people they passed on their walk, or carriage ride, home and who paid no heed to the child labourers working in their factories or who produced the clothes they wore, or who were being abused by their employers in all manner of terrifying and often fatally dangerous jobs that made the readers' lives easier – such as chimney sweeps' assistants, factory machine cleaners, seamstresses, miners and brickmakers.

In this third stave, Dickens also uses Scrooge as his own mouthpiece. At one point, it is Ebenezer Scrooge who criticises a lack of compassion, when he questions the spirit as to why bakers' shops are closed on Sundays. For those without an oven in their own home – the vast majority of the labouring class – the one chance of eating a hot meal was if the local baker let them use their oven, after the bread had been baked. Shops had to be closed on Sundays, the Christian Sabbath – but Sunday was the only day that poor people had off work. This meant that there was not a single day in the week when they could eat a hot meal. When Scrooge asks the ghost why he had decreed this, the ghost responds angrily that even though people might pretend it is being done in his name, it is not:

> "'You would deprive them of their means of dining every seventh day, often the only day on which they can be said to dine at all," said Scrooge. "Wouldn't you."
>
> "I," cried the Spirit.
>
> "You seek to close these places on the Seventh Day." said Scrooge. "And it comes to the same thing."
>
> "I seek." exclaimed the Spirit.
>
> "Forgive me if I am wrong. It has been done in your name, or at least in that of your family," said Scrooge.
>
> "There are some upon this earth of yours," returned the Spirit, "who lay claim to know us, and who do their deeds of passion, pride, ill-will, hatred, envy, bigotry, and selfishness in our name, who are as strange to us and all our kith and kin, as if they had never lived. Remember that, and charge their doings on themselves, not us.'"

For the author, the essence of *A Christmas Carol* is a section that is often left out of adaptations of the story. Dickens had had the idea for the book when thinking about the government's report into child health, and he had wanted to make his story a way of raising awareness of the plight of labouring children. He wanted it to make his readers feel guilty enough to do something to alleviate child poverty. When the Ghost of Christmas Present is starting to age and fade away, Scrooge notices something underneath the spirit's robe. Initially he thinks it is an animal's claw, but then he realises it is a human hand so skinny there is almost no flesh on it:

> 'From the foldings of its robe, it brought two children; wretched, abject, frightful, hideous, miserable. They knelt down at its feet, and clung upon the outside of its garment … They were a boy and a girl. Yellow, meagre, ragged, scowling, wolfish; but prostrate, too, in their humility. Where graceful youth should have filled their features out, and touched them with its freshest tints, a stale and shrivelled hand, like that of age, had pinched, and twisted them, and pulled them into shreds. Where angels might have sat enthroned, devils lurked, and glared out menacing. No change, no degradation, no perversion of humanity, in any grade, through all the mysteries of wonderful creation, has monsters half so horrible and dread.

'Scrooge started back, appalled. Having them shown to him in this way, he tried to say they were fine children, but the words choked themselves, rather than be parties to a lie of such enormous magnitude.

"Spirit. are they yours." Scrooge could say no more.

"They are Man's," said the Spirit, looking down upon them. "And they cling to me, appealing from their fathers. This boy is Ignorance. This girl is Want. Beware them both, and all of their degree, but most of all beware this boy, for on his brow I see that written which is Doom, unless the writing be erased …"'

This scene was the crux of Dickens's message and his main reason for writing *A Christmas Carol.* He wanted his readers to realise that, if they continued to deny poor children the necessities of life – such as food, shelter, warm clothing, good health and an education – they would grow up to become dangerous, violent adults. The child born in a workhouse who was not as fortunate as Oliver Twist and didn't die young like Little Nell would grow up to become another Bill Sikes, Fagin, Nancy or Daniel Quilp.

'Bob, turning up his cuffs – as if, poor fellow, they were capable of being made more shabby – compounded some hot mixture in a jug with gin and lemons, and stirred it round and round and put it on the hob to simmer; Master Peter, and the two ubiquitous young Cratchits went to fetch the goose, with which they soon returned in high procession.

'Such a bustle ensued that you might have thought a goose the rarest of all birds; a feathered phenomenon, to which a black swan was a matter of course – and in truth it was something very like it in that house. Mrs Cratchit made the gravy (ready beforehand in a little saucepan) hissing hot; Master Peter mashed the potatoes with incredible vigour; Miss Belinda sweetened up the apple-sauce; Martha dusted the hot plates; Bob took Tiny Tim beside him in a tiny corner at the table; the two young Cratchits set chairs for everybody, not forgetting themselves, and mounting guard upon their posts, crammed spoons into their mouths, lest they should shriek for goose before their turn came to be helped. At last the dishes were set on, and grace was said. It was succeeded by a breathless pause, as Mrs Cratchit, looking slowly all along the carving-knife, prepared to plunge it in the breast; but when she did, and when the long expected gush of stuffing issued forth, one murmur of delight arose all round the board, and even Tiny Tim, excited by the two young Cratchits, beat on the table with the handle of his knife, and feebly cried Hurrah.

'There never was such a goose. Bob said he didn't believe there ever was such a goose cooked. Its tenderness and flavour, size and cheapness, were the themes of universal admiration. Eked out by apple-sauce and mashed potatoes, it was a sufficient dinner for the whole family; indeed, as Mrs Cratchit said with great delight (surveying one small atom of a bone upon the dish), they hadn't ate it all at last. Yet every one had had enough, and the youngest Cratchits in particular, were steeped in sage and onion to the eyebrows. But now, the plates being changed by Miss Belinda, Mrs Cratchit left the room alone – too nervous to bear witnesses – to take the pudding up and bring it in.

'Suppose it should not be done enough. Suppose it should break in turning out. Suppose somebody should have got over the wall of the back-yard, and stolen it, while they were merry with the goose – a supposition at which the two young Cratchits became livid. All sorts of horrors were supposed.

'Hallo. A great deal of steam. The pudding was out of the copper. A smell like a washing-day. That was the cloth. A smell like an eating-house and a pastrycook's next door to each other, with a laundress's next door to that. That was the pudding. In half a minute Mrs Cratchit entered – flushed, but smiling proudly – with the pudding, like a speckled cannon-ball, so hard and firm, blazing in half of half-a-quartern of ignited brandy, and bedight with Christmas holly stuck into the top.

'Oh, a wonderful pudding. Bob Cratchit said, and calmly too, that he regarded it as the greatest success achieved by Mrs Cratchit since their marriage. Mrs Cratchit said that now the weight was off her mind, she would confess she had had her doubts about the quantity of flour. Everybody had something to say about it, but nobody said or thought it was at all a small pudding for a large family. It would have been flat heresy to do so. Any Cratchit would have blushed to hint at such a thing.'

Charles Dickens *A Christmas Carol* (1843)

On 17 December, Dickens sent advance copies of *A Christmas Carol* to several friends, and they rushed to write their appreciation to him. In response to a letter from Charles Mackay, Dickens wrote:

'Believe me that your pleasure in the Carol, so earnestly and spontaneously expressed, gives me real gratification of heart. It has delighted me very much ... I was very affected by the little Book myself; in various ways, as I wrote it ... I shall not forget your note, easily.'

To other friends he apologised for being unable to send a copy of the book on the day it came out, as copies were selling so fast he had been unable to find any. Three days after publication day he penned a letter to Reverend William Harkness, 'I have run short of copies of the Carol, owing to the demand, or I would have sent you this before.' At New Year he wrote to the poet Thomas Hood, 'A thousand thanks for your kind and charming notice of the Carol.'

Dickens's excitement at his book's success, comes across in an exuberant letter sent to Daniel Maclise on Christmas Day, reminding the artist he was invited to dinner:

'Recreant of the Castle. The banquet hour on this eventful day, is when the turret chimes denote Half Past Five. If, in accordance with a Sacred Custom, you dine with the Bozonian Knight be punctual. If with Royalty, be hungry and be jovial ...'

A Christmas Carol changed Charles Dickens's life forever. From that year onwards, Christmas became the busiest – and, by the end of his life, the most stressful – time of his year.

DICKENS AND CHRISTMAS

On Boxing Day 1843, while Dickens was still on a high, he and Catherine took their family to a party to celebrate the birthday of thirteen-year-old Nina Macready. Charles Dickens and John Forster performed a spectacular magic show, at which the adult guests were as impressed as the children. Among those guests was Jane Carlyle (wife of the historian and writer Thomas Carlyle), who wrote to a friend that it was:

'… the <u>very</u> most agreeable party that ever I was at in London … Dickens and Forster above all exerted themselves till the perspiration was pouring down and they seemed <u>drunk</u> with their efforts! Only think of that excellent Dickens playing the <u>conjuror</u> for one whole hour – the <u>best</u> conjuror I ever saw – (and I have paid money to see several) – and Forster acting as his servant. This part of the entertainment concluded with a plum pudding made out of raw flour, raw eggs – all the usual raw ingredients – boiled in a gentleman's hat – and tumbled out reeking – all in one minute before the eyes of the astonished children and astonished grown people! That trick – and his other of changing ladies' pocket handkerchiefs into comfits – and a box of bran into a box full of – a live guinea pig! would enable him to make a handsome subsistence, let the bookseller trade go as it please-!

Catherine Dickens was just weeks away from giving birth to her fifth child, but her children were able to join in the boisterous dancing. Amongst their dancing partners was William Thackeray, the father of Mamie and Katey Dickens's good friends, Anny and Minny. At this date, William Thackeray was a very rare thing in Victorian Britain – a single father bringing up his two daughters admirably (with the help of servants).

One person who missed the party was Nina's father, William Charles Macready, who was touring America with his theatrical company. On 3 January Dickens wrote to him,

'Oh that you had been in Clarence Terrace on Nina's birthday! Good God how we missed you, talked of you, drank your health, and wondered what you were doing! ... Forster and I conjured bravely – that a hot plum pudding was produced from an empty saucepan, held over a blazing fire, kindled in Stanfield's hat, without damage to the lining – that a box of bran was changed into a live Guinea Pig, which ran between my God child's [Henry Macready] feet, and was then the cause of such a shrill uproar and clapping of hands that you might have heard it (and I daresay did) in America – that three half crowns being taken from Major Burns and put into a tumbler-glass before his eyes did then and there give jingling answers unto questions asked of them by me, and knew where you were, and what you were doing; to the unspeakable admiration of the whole assembly. ... we are going to do it again, next Saturday, with the addition of Demoniacal dresses from a Masquerade Shop ... I have sent you ... a little book I published on the 17th of December, and which has been a most prodigious success – the greatest, I think, I have ever achieved. It pleases me to think that it will bring you Home for an hour or two. And I long to hear that you have read it, on some quiet morning.'

On the day after the party Dickens wrote to Angela Burdett-Coutts (who was Charley's godmother):

'If every Christmas that comes to you, only makes you, or finds you, one half as happy and merry as I wish you to be, you will be the happiest and merriest person in all the world ... Charley is in great force, and with his sisters, desire his hearty love. They all went, with us, last night to a juvenile party at Mrs Macready's, and came out very strong – especially Charley who called divers [sic] small boys by their Christian names (after the manner of a Young Nobleman on the Stage) and indulged in numerous phases of genteel dissipation. I have made a tremendous hit with a conjuring apparatus, which includes some of Doëbler's best tricks, and was more popular last evening after cooking a plum pudding in a hat, and producing a pocket handkerchief from a Wine Bottle, than ever I have been in my life....

[*postscript*] You will be glad to hear, I know, that my Carol is a prodigious success.'

On the same day, the *Belfast Commercial Chronicle* included a lavish article about *A Christmas Carol* which is described as 'A tale to make the reader laugh and cry – open his hands, and open his heart to charity even towards the uncharitable, – wrought up with a thousand minute and tender touches of the true 'Boz' workmanship ... Smellfungus himself would be puzzled how to cut up this jovial, genial piece of Christmas fare otherwise than lovingly.' Smellfungus was a hyper-criticial character from Laurence Sterne's novel *A Sentimental Journey Through France and Italy* (1768) and readers of the time would have been familiar with the reference.

87

DICKENS AND CHRISTMAS

On 2 January 1844, Dickens wrote to Cornelius Felton at Harvard:

'Now, if instantly on receipt of this, you will send a free and independent citizen down to the Cunard Wharf at Boston, you will find that Captain Hewitt of the Britannia Steam Ship (my ship [the one he and Catherine had travelled to America in]) has a small parcel for Professor Felton of Cambridge; and in that parcel you will find a Christmas Carol in Prose. Being a Ghost Story of Christmas by Charles Dickens. Over which Christmas Carol, Charles Dickens wept, and laughed, and wept again, and excited himself in a most extraordinary manner, in the composition; and thinking whereof, he walked about the black streets of London, fifteen and twenty miles, many a night when all the sober folks had gone to bed … Its success is most prodigious. And by every post, all manner of strangers write all manner of letters to him about their homes and hearths, and how this very same Carol is read aloud there, and kept on a very little shelf by itself. Indeed it is the greatest success as I am told that this Ruffian and Rascal has ever achieved … Such dinings, such dancings, such conjurings, such blindmans-buffings, such theatre-goings, such kissings-out of old years and kissings-in of new ones, never took place in these parts before. To keep the Chuzzlewit going, and do this little book, the Carol, in the odd times between two parts of it, was, as you may suppose, pretty tight work. But when it was done, I broke out like a Madman. And if you could have seen me at a children's party at Macreadys the other night, going down a Country dance something longer than the Library at Cambridge with Mrs. M. you would have thought I was a country Gentleman of independent property, residing on a tip-top farm, with the wind blowing straight in my face every day.'

That year the family's Twelfth Night party was even more exciting than normal, as Dickens and Forster had so enjoyed being conjurers that they decided to do the show again, but with even more theatricality. Dickens sent his younger brother, Fred, on an errand, noting on 4 January:

'I want to hire for Twelfth Night, a Magician's Dress – that is to say a black cloak with hieroglyphics on it – some kind of doublet to wear underneath – a grave black beard – and a high black sugar-loaf hat – and a wand with a snake on it, or some such thing. Forster wants a similar set of garments in fiery red.'

'BAH! HUMBUG!'

Within a short time of *A Christmas Carol* being published, Dickens discovered that it was being plagiarised. At a printing office on Drury Lane, the author bought an illegal copy of his own work – for which he was receiving no royalties – printed by Richard Egan Lee and John Haddock. Dickens brought a legal injunction against them and, within a few days, on 18 January, wrote to Forster with jubilation, 'The pirates are beaten flat. They are bruised, bloody, battered, smashed, squelched, and utterly undone.' This was only the beginning of the plagiarism and pirating of his most famous work. No matter how much he, his publishers, and his friends in the legal profession, such as Thomas Noon Talfourd, attempted to prevent his work being printed illegally, it was a losing battle. In February 1844, at least three theatrical productions of *A Christmas Carol* were recorded as being performed in London alone. The story had captured the heart of the nation. The little novella, in which Chapman and Hall had placed so little faith, was famous all over the country. To Dickens, this was the beginning of what would become an industry of Christmas. By the end of his career, he would come to dread the festive season for its overwhelming workload, but at the start of 1844, he was simply overwhelmed with excitement.

'On Christmas Day we all had our glasses filled, and then my father, raising his, would say: "Here's to us all. God bless us!" a toast which was rapidly and willingly drunk. His conversation, as may be imagined, was often extremely humorous, and I have seen the servants, who were waiting at table, convulsed often with laughter at his droll remarks and stories. Now, as I recall these gatherings, my sight grows blurred with the tears that rise to my eyes. But I love to remember them, and to see, if only in memory, my father at his own table, surrounded by his own family and friends—a beautiful Christmas spirit.'

Mamie Dickens, *My Father As I Recall Him*

CHAPTER NINE

'A New Heart for a New Year, Always'

' ... the bells of the churches ring incessantly; not in peals, or any known form of sound, but in a horrible, irregular, jerking, dingle, dingle, dingle: with a sudden stop at every fifteenth dingle or so, which is maddening. This performance is usually achieved by a boy up in the steeple, who takes hold of the clapper, or a little rope attached to it, and tries to dingle louder than every other boy similarly employed. The noise is supposed to be particularly obnoxious to Evil Spirits; but looking up into the steeples, and seeing (and hearing) these young Christians thus engaged, one might very naturally mistake them for the Enemy.'

Charles Dickens, *Pictures from Italy* (1846)

Dickens began 1844 on a high, but within a few weeks he was exhausted and depressed. On 15 January, Catherine gave birth to their fifth child, a son named Francis Jeffrey Dickens, known as Frank. The medical expenses for her and the new baby came at a time when Dickens was already in debt and this was compounded by his parents' continual overspending and expecting their son to pay their bills. At the same time, Dickens was fighting a tide of plagiarism of his earlier books and trying to finish writing *Martin Chuzzlewit*, whose sales figures were still causing him stress. Soon he and Catherine were both suffering from depression.

Dickens was always happier in summer than winter, so he made the decision to move his family to a warmer climate. He chose Italy, partly because he was a fan of the Romantic poet, Lord Byron, and he longed to be inspired by the same place that had inspired him, and because the cost of living in Italy was much lower than living in London.

'A NEW HEART FOR A NEW YEAR, ALWAYS'

In July 1844, with the family home at Devonshire Terrace rented out, the Dickens family were packed into a large carriage, which Dickens had commissioned specially for the journey. There were eleven people in the carriage; Charles, Catherine and their five children, Georgina Hogarth, Catherine's maid Anne Brown, the family's cook and Timber, a Havana Spaniel. Timber was a very well-travelled dog, having been given to Catherine and Charles in America. Also travelling with them was their invaluable courier Louis Roche (a courier took the role of a modern-day tour guide). He could speak the languages they needed to help them travel through France and Switzerland into Italy, he sorted out all the paperwork, bought any necessary tickets and ensured that every border crossing was easy and every travel problem was smoothed over.

It must have been a tremendous sight to witness the family party setting off from London for their two-week journey through France and Switzerland to Italy. They left London on 2 July and arrived in Albaro, just outside Genoa on 16 July. Today, Albaro is a part of Genoa, but when the Dickens family lived there, it was a separate village outside the city. Their first home was a pretty pale-terracotta-coloured villa which Dickens had been told was called Villa di Bella Vista, but which the locals all called Villa di Bagnerello, after its owner, Signor Bagnerello, a 'drunken butcher'. Although it was a very pretty house with a stunning view of the Mediterranean and ample space for the family, Dickens was disappointed. It was not as grand as he had hoped and he nicknamed it 'the Pink Jail'. He began searching for a new family home. He planned to live in Italy for a least a year, and he wanted to do so in style.

By Christmas, the family was happily installed in a home that satisfied every one of Charles Dickens's Italian dreams. He described their new home, the Palazzo Peschiere, in his second travelogue *Pictures from Italy* (1846):

'There is not in Italy, they say (and I believe them), a lovelier residence than the Palazzo Peschiere, or Palace of the Fishponds, whither we removed as soon as our three months' tenancy of the Pink Jail at Albaro had ceased and determined.

'It stands on a height within the walls of Genoa, but aloof from the town: surrounded by beautiful gardens of its own, adorned with statues, vases, fountains, marble basins, terraces, walks of orange-trees and lemon-trees, groves of roses and camellias. All its apartments are beautiful in their proportions and decorations; but the great hall, some fifty feet in height, with three large windows at the end, overlooking the whole town of Genoa, the harbour, and the neighbouring sea, affords one of the most fascinating and delightful prospects in the world. Any house more cheerful and habitable than the great rooms are, within, it would be difficult to conceive; and certainly nothing more delicious than the scene without, in sunshine or in moonlight, could be imagined. It is more like an enchanted place in an Eastern story than a grave and sober lodging.

'How you may wander on, from room to room, and never tire of the wild fancies on the walls and ceilings, as bright in their fresh colouring as if they had been painted yesterday; or how one floor, or even the great hall which opens on eight other rooms, is a spacious promenade; or how there are corridors and bed-chambers above, which we never use and rarely visit, and scarcely know the way through; or how there is a view of a perfectly different character on each of the four sides of the building; matters little. But that prospect from the hall is like a vision to me. I go back to it, in fancy, as I have done in calm reality a hundred times a day; and stand there, looking out, with the sweet scents from the garden rising up about me, in a perfect dream of happiness.'

At last, Dickens felt happy. He said that it was the first time in his life he had ever truly understood what it was to relax. He continued the Italian lessons he had been taking in London (although he was put to shame by his cook, who learnt Italian quickly and easily) and he felt his mood elevate. He played in the gardens with the children, loving to see how much freedom they felt in racing around among the citrus trees, playing with the water in the fountains and gazing into the fishponds. Poor Timber suffered terribly from fleas; then he suffered the indignity of having his hair shaved off in an attempt to get rid of them. Dickens wrote to friends that the tenacity of the Italian flea was far superior to that of an English one.

The continued success of *A Christmas Carol* and the satisfactory conclusion of *Martin Chuzzlewit* in July 1844, left the author eager to start working on another Christmas story. He was inspired by the constant sound of the church bells all around Albaro and Genoa and called his second Christmas book *The Chimes*. In October, Dickens wrote to Forster:

'I am in regular, ferocious excitement with the Chimes; get up at seven; have a cold bath before breakfast; and blaze away, wrathful and red-hot, until three o'clock or so: when I usually knock off (unless it rains) for the day ... I am fierce to finish."'

The Chimes was written in 'Quarters', mimicking the chiming of each quarter of the hour. On 18 October 1844, Dickens sent the first quarter to Forster, for his opinion. He told him that he planned to send him one a week, every Monday, for the next three weeks. Within a couple of days of his letter, Dickens was brought down into a gloom, once again by the weather, although his writing was continuing to go well. He wrote again to Forster:

'I am still in stout heart with the tale. I think it well-timed and a good thought ... Weather worse than any November English weather I have ever beheld, or any weather I have had experience of anywhere. So horrible to-day that all power has been rained and gloomed out of me. Yesterday, in pure determination to get the better of it, I walked twelve miles in mountain rain. You never saw it rain. Scotland and America are nothing to it.'

Just as he had done with *A Christmas Carol*, Dickens worked on *The Chimes* in a fever of energy, allowing the story to absorb and exhaust him. *The Chimes* is another supernatural Christmas story, but this one is not of ghosts, but of goblins; an echo of the Christmas story in *The Pickwick Papers*. The book's full title is *The Chimes: A Goblin Story of Some Bells That Rang An Old Year Out and a New Year In*. The main character, Toby Veck, better known by his nickname of Trotty Veck, is a poorly paid 'ticket porter', or deliverer of messages, who waits for employment at the foot of a bell tower. He is a widower with one child, Margaret, known as Meg.

Trotty Veck has been depressed by his experience of life and by the way he has been conditioned by society to believe that working-class people – including himself – are worth less than the wealthy and well-connected. On a cold and blustery New Year's Eve, Meg, who has been waiting a long time to marry her fiancé, Richard, comes to find her father at his waiting post, bringing with her a welcome hot meal. She tells him she and Richard have decided to marry the following morning, explaining:

'"Richard says ... another year is nearly gone, and where is the use of waiting on from year to year, when it is so unlikely we shall ever be better off than we are now? He says we are poor now, father, and we shall be poor then, but we are young now, and years will make us old before we know it. He says that if we wait: people in our condition: until we see our way quite clearly, the way will be a narrow one indeed – the common way – the Grave, father … So Richard says, father; as his work was yesterday made certain for some time to come, and as I love him, and have loved him full three years – ah! longer than that, if he knew it! – will I marry him on New Year's Day; the best and happiest day, he says, in the whole year, and one that is almost sure to bring good fortune with it."'

This news should make Trotty Veck happy, but he has become so conditioned to think of people like himself as being unwise to marry, or have children, or to do anything except live a miserable existence, that he finds himself believing it. Like Scrooge, Trotty Veck needs to stop seeing the worst in everything.

Throughout *The Chimes*, Dickens introduces pompous characters, including Alderman Cute and the politician Sir Joseph Bowley, who are convinced of the superiority of their own class. There are marked similarities between the way in which these characters behave and talk and the way in which Ebenezer Scrooge dismisses the poor as those who should die 'and decrease the surplus population'. *The Chimes* was an overt message to the middle and upper classes that they need to change the way they treat those poorer than themselves.

Charles Dickens also uses the book to express his fury at what he sees as the media sensationalising, and making its money from, human misery. The reasons behind Trotty Veck's perceived misanthropy are stories he reads in newspapers and the attitudes of the wealthy people he delivers messages for. Both the newspapers and the moneyed classes engender in Trotty Veck a belief that his people, the working class, are inherently bad, that they are born bad and are unable to be changed. Trotty has been made world weary and disillusioned by newspaper stories, such as that of a woman who killed her baby because she could not afford to feed it. He no longer wants Meg to marry and give birth to a new generation, as he believes that next generation is doomed to keep making the same mistakes as their parents and grandparents. The news stories that fill Trotty Veck with disgust for his fellow humans, were based on stories that had shocked and angered Dickens himself.

Late that night, on New Year's Eve, Trotty Veck feels himself being called by the bells of the church whose belltower he stands beside every day. He climbs to the very top, where he encounters the spirits of the bells, attended by goblins. The goblin leader scolds him for losing his faith in humanity and leads Trotty to believe that he has died in a fall from the belltower and that he is now a spirit. The goblins show him a vision of Meg, Richard and their friends, a difficult and heartbreaking life that Trotty Veck, now he is dead, is unable to change. His cynicism and misanthropy have been passed onto his daughter. Meg's personality has changed and, with it, her happy future. As Trotty watches the people he cares for living miserable lives of alcoholism, prostitution, destitution and despair, Trotty begs the goblins, and the Chimes themselves, to allow him to save his daughter.

The story ends with Trotty waking up in his own home. It is New Year's Day and Meg and Richard are excited about their wedding. As with *A Christmas Carol*, the ending is one of redemption and happiness – and the readers are left to consider their own lives and actions, and whether they bear any comparison to Alderman Cute, Sir Joseph Bowley, Mr Filer or the misanthropic version of Trotty Veck.

On 3 November, Dickens wrote triumphantly to Forster:

'Half-past two, afternoon. Thank God! I have finished the Chimes. This moment. I take up my pen again to-day, to say only that much; and to add that I have had what women call "a real good cry!"'

To Thomas Mitton, he confided:

'I have worn myself to Death, in the Month I have been at work. None of my usual reliefs have been at hand; I have not been able to divest myself of the story – have suffered very much in my sleep, in consequence – and am so shaken by such work in this trying climate that I am as nervous as a man who is dying of Drink: and as haggard as a Murderer. I believe I have written a tremendous Book; and knocked the Carol out of the field.'

Baby Frank, who was just a few months old when his father finished *The Chimes*, was given the nickname of 'the Chickenstalker', after the character of Mrs Chickenstalker in the new story.

For his family, the completion of *The Chimes* was a happy event, as Dickens was back in a happy mood and his exhilaration was always catching. Filled with a renewed energy, he planned a business trip back to London, to talk to his publishers and promote *The Chimes*. He travelled back England at the end of November 1844, guided by Louis Roche. He wrote to Catherine en route:

> 'I arrived here at halfpast five tonight, after 50 hours of it, in a French coach. I was so beastly dirty when I got to this house, that I had quite lost all sense of my identity, and if anybody had said "Are you Charles Dickens?" I should unblushingly have answered "No, I never heard of him". A good wash, and a good dress, and a good dinner have revived me, however.'

In London, he lodged at the Piazza Coffee House in Covent Garden, from where he wrote constant letters and enlisted several artist friends to illustrate the new book; these included John Leech, who had illustrated *A Christmas Carol* (and whose illustration of Trotty Veck seemingly in the act of the trotting motion that led to his nickname became emblematic of the book), Daniel Maclise, Clarkson Stanfield and Richard Doyle. *The Chimes* was a joint venture between Dickens's old and new publishers: Bradbury and Evans printed the book and Chapman and Hall published it. The publication date was set for 16 December. John Forster arranged select parties so Dickens could read *The Chimes* aloud. On 2 December, Dickens wrote triumphantly to Catherine:

> 'The little book is now, so far as I am concerned, all ready … Anybody who has heard it, has been moved in the most extraordinary manner. Forster read it (for dramatic purposes) to A Beckett – not a man of very quiet feeling. He cried so much, and so painfully, that Forster didn't quite know whether to go on or stop; and he called next day to say that any expression of his feeling was beyond his power.... As the reading comes off tomorrow night, I had better not despatch my letter to you until Wednesday's post …
>
> 'P.S. If you had seen Macready last night – undisguisedly sobbing, and crying on the sofa, as I read – you would have felt (as I did) what a thing it is to have Power.'

On 3 December, there was another reading for which Forster held a 'tea party'; as he explained in his invitations, 'D. objecting to anything more jovial'. Dickens did not want his friends' listening skills to be impaired by alcohol, he wanted to ensure all attention was on him and *The Chimes*. The reading took place at John Forster's home in Lincoln's Inn Fields. Amongst those present were the historian Thomas Carlyle, the playwright Douglas Jerrold, the artists Daniel Maclise and Clarkson Stanfield, the novelist and journalist Samuel Laman Blanchard, the Unitarian minister and social campaigner Rev. William Johnson Fox, and the Scottish writer Alexander Dyce. The party was immortalised in a pencil sketch by Daniel Maclise, who sent it to Catherine Dickens with a letter, '… there was not a dry eye in the house ... We should borrow the high language of the minor theatre and even then not do justice – shrieks of laughter – there were indeed –and floods of tears as a relief to them – I do not think that there ever was such a triumphant hour for Charles...' Dickens wrote to his sister Fanny that he had been told even the printers 'laughed and cried' as they read the story while printing it.

Forewarned by what had happened with *A Christmas Carol*, Dickens also made use of his time in London, to sort out an agreement with his friends Gilbert A Beckett and Mark Lemon – a close friend and the first editor of *Punch* – that they could have the rights to dramatize *The Chimes* – officially – for the Adelphi Theatre. He also spent his time in London trying to get help for the widow and children of a man who had died some months earlier. John Overs, a cabinet maker and aspiring writer, had sent several manuscripts to Dickens, who had attempted to help him get the works published. When that had failed, Dickens started sending Overs money to try and help him out in his illness. Being ill in Victorian Britain could cause financial devastation; not only did it mean that the ill person was no longer earning a wage, but they were also incurring medical expenses. It needed only one fairly minor illness to push a working family into the abyss of poverty. Dickens spent much of his week in London trying to find solutions for the family – in which he was successful, managing to secure a pension for Mrs Overs and work for her daughters.

The Chimes was published while Dickens was travelling back to Italy. Most of the reviews were praiseworthy, although some were brave enough to suggest *The Chimes* was not as good as its predecessor. Dickens must have been amused by the review in a right-wing magazine *John Bull* which accused Dickens of fanning the flames of 'low Radical doctrines of the day'. *The Chimes* was frequently compared unfavourably with *A Christmas Carol*. In Ireland, the *Cork Examiner* complained:

'The "Carol" was a generous book ... it showed its handywork by brightening the page of its story as it went on, and finally achieved its great purpose, by leaving all parties, actors, and readers, better and happier than they sat down. This is high praise; but Mr Dickens in his "Carol", deserves it ... The success which attended this little incipient 'annual was very great – much greater we opine, proportionately, that that which has attended any other of this popular author's productions; and it was not unreasonable to suppose that he would endeavour to follow up ... this festive season ... Accordingly his second 'carol', for so we may call the 'Chimes', has been produced, and is already before us and some thousands of readers.

'How do those thousands of readers like its tone? For ourselves we confess it pleases us not. It is not a fair "second" to the melody of the first ... Mr Dickens, having become popular, has fallen into the popular error of substituting exaggeration and extravagance for the truth and force to which he owes his popularity ... As a story, nothing can be more unartistic or more commonplace than this production.'

As had happened with *Pickwick Papers* and *A Christmas Carol*, plagiarism of *The Chimes* was rife. By the end of December 1844, less than a fortnight after the book itself had been published, theatres were advertising performances of 'Dickens's *Christmas Chimes*' – although Dickens himself didn't receive any royalties or copyright payments. Hastily created plays based on his Christmas books now rivalled pantomimes for Christmas audiences.

By 20 December, Dickens was back in Albaro with his family. He had travelled via Paris and was pleased at having been recognised, on the ship from Marseilles to Genoa, by an American tourist. Just two days after his return, the family was thrilled to receive from Angela Burdett-Coutts a 'Twelfth Cake weighing ninety pounds, magnificently decorated' for her godson, Charley. In a letter to Forster, Dickens wrote how perturbed the 'Jesuitical surveillance' of the customs officers had been by seeing a cake decorated with Twelfth Night characters. The family celebrated Christmas in style in their wing of the Palazzo Peschiere and they celebrated New Year's Eve at a party with the palazzo's other residents, which included a Spanish duke and his family, about whom Dickens loved to tell his friends scandalous stories.

The public loved Dickens's second Christmas book, and the first print run of 20,000 copies sold rapidly. On 8 January 1845, the *Inverness Courier* began its 'Miscellaneous' column with the sentence, 'Above 30,000 copies of Mr Dickens's Christmas story, the *Chimes*, have been sold within a fortnight.' *A Christmas Carol* was still the people's favourite, though and, despite the fact that *The Chimes* had been inspired by Genoa, when Dickens was invited to perform a reading at the house of the British Consul before leaving Italy, it was *A Christmas Carol* that the Consul was eager to hear. The reading took place, very unseasonally, in June 1845, just before the author and his family returned to London.

Stealing a Christmas Dinner

Early on the morning of Christmas-day, some daring thief contrived to obtain entrance to the house of Mr M. Bishop, in Old-street-road, and watching his opportunity succeeded in abstracting from the kitchen a fine large turkey, which was intended for the Christmas dinner, as also a quantity of raisins and currants and other et ceteras.

Morning Chronicle, 27 December 1845

CHAPTER TEN

'The Luckiest Thing in All the World'

'It may have entertained the Cricket too, for anything I know; but, certainly, it now began to chirp again, vehemently.

"Heyday!" said John, in his slow way. "It's merrier than ever, to-night, I think."

"And it's sure to bring us good fortune, John! It always has done so. To have a Cricket on the Hearth, is the luckiest thing in all the world!"

'John looked at her as if he had very nearly got the thought into his head, that she was his Cricket in chief, and he quite agreed with her ... "The first time I heard its cheerful little note, John, was on that night when you brought me home – when you brought me to my new home here; its little mistress. Nearly a year ago ... Its chirp was such a welcome to me! It seemed so full of promise and encouragement. It seemed to say, you would be kind and gentle with me ... all the Cricket tribe are potent Spirits, even though the people who hold converse with them do not know it (which is frequently the case); and there are not in the unseen world, voices more gentle and more true, that may be so implicitly relied on, or that are so certain to give none but tenderest counsel, as the Voices in which the Spirits of the Fireside and the Hearth address themselves to human kind."'

Charles Dickens, *The Cricket on the Hearth* (1845)

The Dickens family returned to London in the summer of 1845. On 21 August, Dickens wrote gloomily to his friend Arthur Cunynghame, 'London is as flat as can be. There is nothing to talk about but Railroad shares. And as I am not a Capitalist, I don't find anything very interesting in that.' It may have been August, but Dickens's mind was already looking ahead to Christmas and he continued the letter, 'The Gin Punch shall be yours in the snowy time (I hope) of Christmas; and it shall be preceded by a glass of rather better wine than one can get in the City of Palaces.'

That Autumn, as Catherine was preparing to give birth to their sixth child, a son with the splendid name of Alfred D'Orsay Tennyson Dickens, her husband was working on his third Christmas book, *The Cricket on the Hearth*. The story, which is divided into three sections known as 'Chirps', is the story of the Peerybingle family and their friends the Plummers. John and Dot Peerybingle have a baby son and a humorously inept young nanny. The presence of a cricket singing from its home on their hearth conjures up an image of a cosy room warmed by a glowing fire.

The Peerybingles' friend, Caleb Plummer, is living in impoverished circumstances, caring for his blind daughter, Bertha, and trying to reconcile himself to the fact that his long-lost son, Edward, is believed dead. When he left England, Edward was engaged to his sweetheart, May Fielding. Believing Edward has died, May has rsigned herself to making a loveless, but sensible marriage. Edward returns in secret, having heard May is to be married and not wanting to ruin her happiness. He disguises himself, so family and friends won't know he has returned. Pretending to be an elderly stranger, Edward becomes a lodger in the Peerybingles' household – although Dot soon realises his true identity. She knows that her friend May, only agreed to marry because she was worn down by her overbearing mother. May's fiancé is Caleb Plummer's miserly employer, Mr Tackleton:

'Tackleton the Toy-merchant, pretty generally known as Gruff and Tackleton – for that was the firm, though Gruff had been bought out long ago; only leaving his name, and as some said his nature, according to its Dictionary meaning, in the business – Tackleton theToy-merchant, was a man whose vocation had been quite misunderstood by his Parents and Guardians ... cramped and chafing in the peaceable pursuit of toy-making, he was a domestic Ogre, who had been living on children all his life, and was their implacable enemy. He despised all toys ... In appalling masks; hideous, hairy, red-eyed Jacks in Boxes; Vampire Kites; demoniacal Tumblers who wouldn't lie down, and were perpetually flying forward, to stare infants out of countenance; his soul perfectly revelled. They were his only relief, and safety-valve. He was great in such inventions ... safe to destroy the peace of mind of any young gentleman between the ages of six and eleven, for the whole Christmas or Midsummer Vacation … Still, Tackleton, the toy-merchant, was going to be married. In spite of all this, he was going to be married. And to a young wife too, a beautiful young wife.'

Although living in pinching poverty, in 'a little cracked nutshell of a wooden house, which was, in truth, no better than a pimple on the prominent red-brick nose of Gruff and Tackleton', Caleb pretends to his daughter they are living in a beautiful, comfortable home and, because she can't see how shabby their possessions have become, she is happy to believe him. As Dickens commented:

'I should have said that Caleb lived here, and his poor Blind Daughter somewhere else – in an enchanted home of Caleb's furnishing, where scarcity and shabbiness were not, and trouble never entered. Caleb was no sorcerer, but ... [the] Blind Girl never knew that ceilings were discoloured, walls blotched and bare of plaster here and there, high crevices unstopped and widening every day, beams mouldering and tending downward. The Blind Girl never knew that iron was rusting, wood rotting, paper peeling off; the size, and shape, and true proportion of the dwelling, withering away. The Blind Girl never knew that ... sorrow and faintheartedness were in the house; that Caleb's scanty hairs were turning greyer and more grey, before her sightless face.'

Caleb is a toymaker and Bertha makes dolls and their dresses, themes to which Dickens returned in *Our Mutual Friend*. Caleb also pretends to his daughter that Tackleton is a kind man whose abusive comments are meant in jest; unfortunately this has led Bertha to be secretly, and unrequitedly, in love with the good man she believes Tackleton to be. As a loving parent, Caleb builds a protective world of happiness around his daughter, hoping she will never discover it is fabricated.

Contrary to the loving opinion that Bertha has formed of him, Tackleton tries to kill happiness where he sees it, and this includes his desire to stamp upon the Peerybingles' cheerful cricket:

'… "why don't you kill that Cricket? I would! I always do. I hate their noise."

102

"You kill your Crickets, eh?" said John.
"Scrunch 'em, sir," returned the other, setting his heel heavily on the floor.'

John, wisely, does not kill his cricket, and in the final Chirp of the book, the cricket, 'in fairy shape', saves him from making a fatal mistake. *The Cricket on the Hearth* is not a redemption story in the same sense as *A Christmas Carol* or *The Chimes*, nor does it centre around Christmas. It was the first of Dickens's 'Christmas books' to be given the name solely because it was marketed at Christmas time.

The first copies of *The Cricket on the Hearth* were sold on 20 December 1845, and immediately theatres began working on pirated productions. Over a dozen plays based on the book were recorded that winter, even though Dickens had agreed to only one being produced. Theatres continually ignored any claims of copyright, eager to adapt the latest work by the author whose name had become synonymous with Christmas.

On Christmas Day 1845, the *Morning Chronicle* published an article about *The Cricket on the Hearth* and on the general effect that Charles Dickens had had on the celebrating of the festive season:

'Anybody who walked the streets yesterday, on one of the finest and most cheerful days of London weather, could not but remark what a hilarious air the town wore – how jolly and rosy people's faces looked in the foggy sunshine – how wonderfully pink and happy the little boys' countenances were who are come home for the holidays – and observe many other pleasant Christmas phenomena. To see the butchers' and poulterers' shops was quite a pleasure – the most obese geese, turkeys, and gigantic pantomime joints of beef hung in those hospitable warehouses – under the mistletoe boughs – reasoning with yourself, you asked why should those comestibles be fatter now at Christmas than at any other time? Fortnum and Mason's, in Piccadilly, is always a beautiful and astonishing shop ... Yesterday it was a perfect fairy-palace ... the theatres break out into pantomimes; the booksellers' windows glitter with gilt picture-books; and more charming to some well-regulated minds even than the Fortnum and Mason sugar-candy elysium, are Mr Nickisson's library tables in Regent-street, blazing with a hundred new Christmas volumes, in beautiful bindings, with beautiful pictures.... But for three years past the great monopoliser has been MR DICKENS. He has been elected as chief literary master of the ceremonies for Christmas. It is he who best understands the kindness and joviality and withal the pathos of the season. Many thousand copies of the "Cricket on the Hearth" have been sold, and it is not a week old. You hear talk of it in every company ... Going into the city on Tuesday, the writer of this beheld a bookseller's boy with a bag of "Crickets" over his shoulder, standing stock-still by the Royal Exchange, and reading one, sub Jove. On the very same day at dinner everybody had read it; everybody was talking about it; and the very clergyman who said grace confessed that he had been whimpering over it all the morning ... the general effect of the writing was of this heart-stirring, kindly character ... it is a good Christmas book, illuminated with extra gas, crammed with extra bon-bons, French plums and sweetnesses, like a certain Piccadilly palace before-mentioned ... As a Christmas pageant which you witness in the arm-chair – your private box by the fireside – the piece is excellent, uncomparably brilliant, and dexterous.'

The *Morning Chronicle* was also full of praise for Daniel Maclise's illustrations for *The Cricket on the Hearth*, describing them as 'one of the most brilliant specimens of the art which has appeared in the very best school of it'. The *Northern Star and Leeds General Advertiser* however was not happy with the lack of seasonal subject matter, although the critic goes on to claim that Dickens's third Christmas book is his favourite so far:

'The view we take of Mr Dickens's three Christmas offerings ... The first (the "Carol"), while exhibiting the crime and folly of grasping selfishness, at the same time teaches the great lesson, that the happiness of each individual is only to be ensured by each labouring to promote the happiness of all. This moral, illustrated by a story perfect in every sense, makes the "Carol" a model for *Christmas stories*; and, viewed as such, the "Carol" at present stands, and probably for ever will stand, unrivalled. The second (the "Chimes"), viewed politically, is the best of the author's works. As an exposition of the wrongs and sufferings endured by the man, and a vindication of their rights and claims to justice, – so regarded the "Chimes" is superior to the "Carol". Mr Dickens's present production, considered as a *Christmas story*, will not bear comparison with the "Carol"; indeed it might have been published at Midsummer instead of Christmas, as it contains nothing relating to Christmas, excepting a slight description of wintry weather, the time of the story being laid in the month of January. Viewed politically, the present story is not to be placed in competition with the "Chimes"; indeed it is a totally different story. Mr Dickens, in his "Cricket on the Hearth", has devoted himself wholly to the work of portraying home-scenes and home-feelings ... nevertheless, [it] has beauties of its own to which neither the "Carol" nor the "Chimes" can lay claim ... To Mr Dickens we return our heart-felt thanks for this new gift to his fellow creatures, assured as we are, that no one can become acquainted with its lessons of sympathy and goodness without becoming better and happier therefrom. We take our leave from this little book heartily recommending it to our readers, reminding each and all ... that "To have a cricket on the hearth is the luckiest thing in all the world!"'

With the publication of *The Cricket on the Hearth*, Dickens's reputation as the saviour and promoter of Christmas cheer was well and truly established. Three Christmas books in as many years had cemented his celebrity. On 27 December 1845, *The Examiner* newspaper commented:

'It is our strong belief that, in this largest and freest sense of benefit, very great public and private good has been done by the extraordinary popularity, the universal acceptance, of these Christmas Tales of Mr Dickens; much positive, earnest, and practical good. For they have carried to almost every fireside, with new enjoyment of the season, a new apprehension of its claims and duties ... they have brought within reach of the charities what seemed too remote for them to meddle with ... they have comforted the generous, rebuked the selfish, cured not a little folly.... Mere literary fame is a second-rate thing to this.'

'Old Christmas' by G. Linnaeus Banks

Hurrah! for old Christmas, the hearty and jolly,
Hurrah! for old Christmas the friend of us all,
Who laughs at the frowns of grim-faced melancholy,
And comes with a transport to great and to small.
Up, up! let us drink to the jocund old fellow,
Though wrinkled his brow, and his locks silver-grey,
Yet his footstep is light, and his heart it is mellow
As any that joins in our banquet to-day.
Then pluck from the mistletoe, pluck from the holly,
The red with the while in a chaplet appear.
While we banish dull care, which to cherish is folly,
And drink to old Christmas, the king of the year....

Printed in *Bentley's Miscellany*, 19 December 1846

Scrooge's Third Visitor by John Leech, 1843.
The image of the Ghost of Christmas Present, described as a 'jolly Giant', was inspired by ancient British traditions: that of the pagan Green Man and the old-style Father Christmas who appeared in mummers' dances.

Marley's Ghost by John Leech, 1843.
When the ghost of Jacob Marley appeared to warn his former business partner Ebenezer Scrooge to mend his ways, Dickens was hoping his readers would realise that they also needed to help those poorer than themselves.

The Last of the Spirits by John Leech, 1843.
The illustrator for *A Christmas Carol* was Dickens's great friend John Leech, who would become famous as one of the leading cartoonists for the satirical magazine *Punch*.

A depiction of a Christmas Choir practice.
From the 1840s onwards, the celebrating of Christmas started to become much more fashionable and 'old traditions' were revived. Singing carols, both in church and as travelling choirs, was very popular.

CHAPTER ELEVEN

The Battle of Life

By 1846, the literary world was in a fever of commissioning Christmas stories. Magazines and newspapers actively sought out seasonal short stories and Dickens's fellow authors quickly started to write their own. In December 1846, the year in which Dickens published his fourth Christmas story, *The Battle of Life*, the *Preston Chronicle* commented, 'This Christmas-custom of telling merry tales has been revived of late years by one or two of our most popular writers of prose fiction. Mr Dickens, we believe, began it, and his example has been worthily followed by (among others) Mr Thackeray.' After a good review of *The Battle of Life*, the paper went on to publish a long extract of Thackeray's new Christmas book, *Mrs Perkins's Ball*, which the journalist described as 'charming'.

Ironically, while everyone else was rushing to produce Christmas stories, Dickens struggled to write his fourth Christmas book. In the summer of 1846, the Dickens family were in Switzerland; Charles had wanted to return to Italy, but Catherine vetoed the idea, understandably jealous of an intense relationship that had grown between her husband and one of their friends, Madame Augusta de la Rue. Dickens found Switzerland enervating and distracting, because it was too orderly and silent. On 30 August he wrote to Forster that he was missing the 'magic lantern' of London:

'For a week or a fortnight I can write prodigiously in a retired place (such as Broadstairs), and a day in London sets me up again and starts me. But the toil and labour of writing, day after day, without

107

that magic lantern, is IMMENSE!! I don't say this, at all in low spirits, for we are perfectly comfortable here, and I like the place very much indeed, and the people are even more friendly and fond of me than they were in Genoa. I only mention it as a curious fact, which I have never had an opportunity of finding out before. My figures seem disposed to stagnate without crowds about them. I wrote very little in Genoa (only The Chimes), and fancied myself conscious of some such influence there – but Lord! I had two miles of streets at least, lighted at night, to walk about in; and a great theatre to repair to, every night …'

His writer's block was made worse by the pressure of knowing he had to write *The Battle of Life* as well as *Dombey and Son*, the serialisation of which was due to begin on 1 October. He wrote again to Forster in September:

'I really contemplated, at times, the total abandonment of the Christmas book this year, and the limitation of my labours to *Dombey and Son* … At length, thank Heaven, I nailed it all at once; and after going on comfortably up to yesterday, and working yesterday from half past nine to six, I was last night in such a state of enthusiasm about it that I think I was an inch or two taller.'

To Thomas Noon Talfourd he commented:

'I am horribly hard at work with my Christmas Book, which runs (rather inconveniently) in a Curricle just now, with "Dealings with the Firm of Dombey and Son".'

On 26 September, just a day after his letter to Talfourd, he wrote again to Forster, in a panic:

'I am going to write you a most startling piece of intelligence. I fear there may be NO CHRISTMAS BOOK! I would give the world to be on the spot to tell you this. Indeed I once thought of starting for London to-night. I have written nearly a third of it. It promises to be pretty; quite a new idea in the story, I hope; but to manage it without the supernatural agency now impossible of introduction, and yet to move it naturally within the required space, or with any shorter limit than a *Vicar of Wakefield*, I find a difficulty to be so perplexing …

that I am fearful of wearing myself out if I go on … If I had nothing but the Christmas book to do, I WOULD do it; but I get horrified and distressed beyond conception at the prospect of being jaded when I come back to the other, and making it a mere race against time. I have written the first part; I know the end and the upshot of the second; and the whole of the third (there are only three in all). I know the purport of each character, and the plain idea that each is to work out; and I have the principal effects sketched on paper. It cannot end *quite* happily, but will end cheerfully and pleasantly. But my soul sinks before the commencement of the second part – and longest – and the introduction of the under idea … I am now sure I could not have invented the *Carol* at the commencement of the *Chuzzelwit*, or gone to a new book from the *Chimes*. But this is certain. I am sick, giddy, and capriciously despondent. I have bad nights; am full of disquietude and anxiety, and am constantly haunted … I now resolve to make one effort more. I will go to Geneva to-morrow, and try … whether I can get in at all bravely, in the changed scene…'

The aptly named *The Battle of Life* tore at Dickens's peace of mind; he wrote to Forster four days after his previous letter:

'I have still not made up my mind as to what I CAN do with the Christmas book … On the other hand I am dreadfully averse to abandoning it, and am so torn between the two things that I know not what to do.'

A couple of days later, on 3 October, he wrote, 'I hope and trust, *now,* the Christmas book will come in due course! I have had three very good days' work at Geneva.'

As always, Dickens sent Forster the novella in parts, as he wrote them. Sending his friend the final episode he wrote, in a crisis of confidence:

'I really do not know what this story is worth. I am so floored: wanting sleep, and never having had my head free of it for this month past. I think there are some places in this last part which I may bring better together in the proof, and where a touch or two may be of service … What do you think of the concluding paragraph? Would you leave it for happiness? It is merely experimental.'

DICKENS AND CHRISTMAS

On 20 October he wrote yet another anguished letter to Forster:

> 'I dreamed all last week that the *Battle of Life* was a series of chambers impossible to be got to rights or got out of, through which I wandered drearily all night. On Saturday night I don't think I slept an hour. I was perpetually roaming through the story, and endeavouring to dovetail the revolution here into the plot. The mental distress, quite horrible.'

Despite the agonies of its creation, *The Battle of Life* was published on 19 December 1846 and was an immediate success. The Dickens family were spending the winter in Paris, but Dickens returned to London for eight days to publicise the book. He was also relieved to escape from a very cold Parisian winter:

> 'Cold intense. The water in the bed-room jugs freezes into solid masses from top to bottom, bursts the jugs with reports like small cannon, and rolls out on the table and washstands hard as granite. I stick to the shower-bath, but have been most hopelessly out of sorts.'

From Forster's home, Dickens penned a note to Catherine, 'Christmas Book published today – 23,000 copies already gone!!!'

The Battle of Life tells the story of two sisters, Grace and Marion Jeddler, who Dickens describes as 'very beautiful to look upon. Two better faces ... never made a fireside bright and sacred'. Marion, the younger sister, is engaged to her childhood sweetheart, Alfred Heathfield. As they are now adults and Alfred has finished his studies, the long-anticipated wedding is being planned. Then Marion disappears. It is rumoured she has eloped with Michael Warden, who is described as 'a man of about thirty, or that time of life, negligently dressed, and somewhat haggard in the face, but well-made, well-attired, and well-looking, who sat in the armchair of state, with one hand in his breast, and the other in his dishevelled hair, pondering moodily.' Michael is a brooding, Romantic hero – with a bad reputation. He had told people he was in love with Marion and wanted her to break her engagement and, because Michael leaves on the same day Marion disappears, the community mourns her as 'lost', meaning she is a 'fallen woman'.

In their sorrow, Grace and Alfred grow close and, in the third and final part of the story, Grace and Alfred are married and have a daughter, whom they have named Marion. After six years, the missing Marion returns – not as a fallen woman, but as a virtuous and selfless one. It transpires she had realised her sister was in love with Alfred. As Marion knew she was not truly in love with her fiancé, she decided to disappear and let Alfred and Grace discover real love together. Marion has spent the intervening years living with her aunt Martha and has no knowledge of where Michael Warden went to.

At the same time that Marion and her aunt return to the village, the broken-hearted Michael also returns. He has been travelling the world, convinced Marion had married Alfred, as they were expected to do on the day he left. Michael has returned only to sell his house and sort out his financial affairs, after which he plans to 'quit this place forever'. Instead, he discovers Marion is unmarried and in love with him. The story ends with the words:

> 'Michael Warden never went away again, and never sold his house, but opened it afresh, maintained a golden means of hospitality, and had a wife, the pride and honour of that countryside, whose name was Marion.'

In common with *The Cricket on the Hearth*, Dickens's fourth Christmas story is not a Christmas-themed book. There is a brief mention of Christmas when Dickens wants to explain how time has passed, 'The wounded trees had long ago made Christmas logs, and blazed and roared away' and again when Alfred returns from his studies, which happens at Christmas:

> 'The day arrived. A raging winter day, that shook the old house, sometimes, as if it shivered in the blast … All his old friends should congregate about him. He should not miss a face that he had known and liked. No! They should every one be there!
>
> 'So, guests were bidden, and musicians were engaged, and tables spread, and floors prepared for active feet, and bountiful provision made, of every hospitable kind. Because it was the Christmas season, and his eyes were all unused to English holly and its sturdy green, the dancing-room was garlanded and hung with it; and the red berries gleamed an English welcome to him, peeping from among the leaves.'

The rest of the story makes no reference to the season. To publish books at Christmas time made excellent business sense, but Dickens had no desire to write about Christmas in every story.

One of the main reasons Dickens returned to London from Paris was to see the authorised stage version of *The Battle of Life*, which he had given his friend Arthur Smith permission to stage at the Lyceum Theatre. Giving his blessing to an authorised version still didn't prevent pirated versions of his book from being performed all over the country. He arrived back in Paris just in time to celebrate Christmas, thrilled with his new book's success. Between Christmas and New Year, he wrote an emotional letter to Forster, who had been so supportive of his Christmas books:

'Amen, amen. Many merry Christmases, many happy new years, unbroken friendship, great accumulation of cheerful recollections, affection on earth, and heaven at last, for all of us.'

CHAPTER TWELVE

The Haunted Man

'The Christmas music he had heard before, began to play. He listened to it at first, as he had listened in the church-yard; but presently – it playing still, and being borne towards him on the night air, in a low, sweet, melancholy strain – he rose, and stood stretching his hands about him, as if there were some friend approaching within his reach, on whom his desolate touch might rest, yet do no harm. As he did this, his face became less fixed and wondering; a gentle trembling came upon him; and at last his eyes filled with tears, and he put his hands before them, and bowed down his head.'

Charles Dickens, *The Haunted Man, and the Ghost's Bargain* (1848)

Throughout the 1840s, the fashion for celebrating Christmas continued to expand, boosted by Dickens and his fellow authors' publications, by sentimental Christmas poetry published in newspapers and magazines, and by the activities of the royal household's Christmases being described in the newspapers. Spawned by the astounding success of *A Christmas Carol*, the season of Christmas was even bigger business than before, and people on the poorer end of the financial scale started saving for Christmas by joining clubs; these allowed people to make regular payments on account, which could then be redeemed at Christmas, spreading the cost of a Christmas meal over several weeks or months. Many newspapers published a report in December of 1846:

'Experienced salesmen at Leadenhall-market state that the demand for Christmas geese has this year exceeded that of any previous season, and that the establishment of clubs has, within the last few days, brought upwards of 20,000 geese into the market. In some parts of the metropolis, "plum pudding clubs" have been established.'

The lessons expressed in *A Christmas Carol* were beginning to affect the lives of the Victorian public. On 19 December 1846, three years since *A Christmas Carol*'s publication day, the *Hereford Times* reported:

'We notice that at Ross and other towns, Saturday next, as it intervenes between Christmas-day and Sunday, will be observed as a holiday; and a declaration to that effect is now being generally subscribed by the respectable tradesmen of this city, who have agreed to suspend business on that day.'

The *Liverpool Mail* reported:

'In Manchester, and many other towns of the kingdom, it is intended to suspend business on the Saturday following Christmas Day, (which falls on Friday) in order that parties visiting their friends may have the opportunity of absenting themselves from the toils and cares of this work-a day world, from Thursday night till Monday morning.'

No one, it seems, wanted to be compared to Bob Cratchit's employer.

Starting new Christmas traditions, and revamping old traditions, was becoming very fashionable as people rushed to embrace the new spirit of the season. As the fashion for celebrating Twelfth Night was dwindling, so too was the need for bakers to create elaborate Twelfth Cakes, so many had started to produce Christmas cakes instead. Newspapers in Manchester reported on a 'Monster Christmas Cake' that had caused a stir of excitement in the town. It had been sold in sections, and every purchaser hoped they would have bought a part that contained a hidden ring. On 1 January 1847, the *Manchester Times* reported:

'Four purchasers of parts of this cake have each acknowledged to be the lucky discoverers of a ring. The other eleven rings are yet to be found, as there were fifteen in before it was cut. If there be no magic in the rings, there will be mirth in finding them.'

'Of the "high days of the Calendar", Christmas was always the one which held the chief place in England, where it was celebrated in a manner so different from what was customary in other countries, as to excite the astonishment of foreigners. As soon as the Christmas holidays had arrived, work and care were universally thrown aside; and, instead of devotional practice, by which other countries commemorated the sacred occasion, England rang from one end to the other with mirth and joviality. Christmas Carols were trailed in every street; masquerades and plays took possession of houses and churches indifferently; a lord of misrule, whose reign lasted from All Hallow Eve till the day after the Feast of Pentecost, was elected in every noble household to preside over the sports and fooleries of the inmates, while each member prepared himself either to enact some strange character, or to devise some new stroke of mirth. The towns, on those occasions, assumed a sylvan appearance; the houses were dressed with branches of ivy and holly; the churches were converted into leafy tabernacles; and standards bedecked with evergreens were set up in the streets, while the young of both sexes danced around them.'

From 'Bringing in Christmas', the *Illustrated London News*,
20 December 1845

In the autumn of 1847, Dickens decided not to write a Christmas book. He was still struggling with *Dombey and Son*, and he had no desire to relive the stress of the previous year. By the time Christmas arrived, he had also embarked on a new venture – but, this time, it was not a literary one. He began a joint philanthropic venture with Angela Burdett-Coutts, the heiress to her grandfather Thomas Coutts's banking fortune. While Burdett-Coutts provided the necessary finances, Charles Dickens did the majority of the planning and practical work and in November 1847, they opened Urania Cottage, a home and refuge for 'fallen women'. Dickens and Burdett-Coutts believed passionately that women's prisons were full of innocent victims, both philanthropists were of the opinion that society and its double-standards forced women to turn to crime, usually thieving and prostitution, in order to feed themselves and their children. Urania Cottage offered a type of halfway house for women wanting to start a new life.

Perhaps relieved by the lessening of his workload by not producing a new Christmas book, Dickens was in a very jovial mood, writing to Angela Burdett-Coutts on Christmas Eve, 'A thousand thanks for the noble turkey. I thought it was an infant, sent here by mistake, when it was brought in. It looked so like a fine baby.' Gifts of food predominate in Dickens's Christmas letters; it was the custom to send food rather than the more elaborate Christmas gifts that people expected by the start of the twentieth century. People living in the countryside often packed up special Christmas food parcels to send to relatives and friends living in towns.

Dickens also sent similar gifts of food or drink to friends, such as the 'bottle of sweet wine of rare perfection, made from the Muscatelle Grape. Drunk with ice, or ice pudding, you will find it most delicious – with a generous and fragrant smack of the bright sun in it, that I have very seldom tasted' which he sent to John Forster in 1852, the 'half a dozen of an old liqueur brandy not easy to get' that he sent to Thomas Beard in 1859, and the 'big turkey and ham' that was sent to his editor and friend William Henry Wills in 1860. In the same year, Dickens wrote to the poet (and stockbroker) Samuel Collinson, 'I beg to thank you cordially for the superb Pork Pie which graces the side-board here to-day. Let me send you in return all the good wishes of the blessed season and time of year' and in 1863 Joseph Ellis was being thanked for 'the Paté. It arrived in the finest condition, and was received with rapture by a crowded house.' In 1866, he arranged with the landlord of his local pub, the Sir John Falstaff Inn, to send a Christmas gift to Mrs Marsh, the wife of Dickens's groom, '2 dozen pints of bottled stout' and at the start of 1870, Dickens wrote to Percy Fitzgerald and his wife thanking them for their gift of 'some delicious birds'.

The non-edible presents that Dickens wrote to thank people for were usually very simple gifts, for example a cigar case from his friend Mary Boyle. It was also common for friends and family members to give one other home-made gifts, such as pen wipers and handkerchiefs. In 1854, Dickens wrote to Angela Burdett-Coutts, who had thanked him and his family for their gift, to which Dickens responded, 'I am glad you like the baskets. May they help to make you tidy!' A couple of years later Burdett-Coutts sent Dickens a present of 'letter weights'. The over-commercialisation and expensive gift-buying now associated with Christmas had not yet happened. The royal family might have been renowned for giving each other expensive gifts, such as the jewels that Queen Victoria grew accustomed to her husband tying to her Christmas tree, but this was not common practice. The changes happened quite steadily throughout the nineteenth century until, by the 1880s, the pastime of 'Christmas shopping' had become well established for around six weeks before Christmas. It had also become fashionable for shops to create special 'Christmas windows'. In 1881, the *Lady's Pictorial* magazine described how shops decorated themselves for the festive season:

'Christmas cards in almost every window, in the companionship of the attractions of the toy-seller, the wares of the draper, the irresistible temptations of the milliner, and of their more legitimate comrades in the show-cases of the stationer – from everywhere have these pretty little tokens of goodwill and kindly thoughts been peering out and seeking the attention of the passer-by.'

In 1885, a traveller to America compared its Christmas preparations with those in Britain:

'The presentation of 'boxes' and souvenirs is the same in America as in England ... everybody expects to give and receive. A month before the event the fancy stores are crowded all day long with old and young in search of suitable souvenirs, and every object is purchased, from the costliest gems to the tawdriest babiole that may get into the market. If the weather should be fine, the principal streets are thronged with ladies shopping in sleighs ... laden with parcels of painted toys, instruments of mock music and septuagenarian dread, from a penny trumpet to a sheepskin drum.' (Howard Paul *Christmas in America,* 1885)

After taking a break from Christmas writing in 1847, Dickens was planning a new idea for the following year, but the start of 1848 was not a propitious one. After Christmas, Charles and Catherine Dickens were in Scotland and they had planned to travel home via York, where they would meet up with Charles's younger brother, Alfred. He was a talented and inventive engineer, who advised the government on sanitary reform and was working in the railways. Alfred had expected to spend New Year's Eve of 1847 with his brother and sister-in-law, but they did not arrive and on New Year's Day, Charles wrote apologetically to explain that while they were on a train to Glasgow, poor Catherine had suffered a very public miscarriage.

Charles and Catherine were back in London on time to celebrate their traditional Twelfth Night party for Charley's birthday; Dickens wrote to Frank Stone on 4 January 1848, 'There will be some children of both small and large growth, here on Thursday (Twelfth Night) and some dancing of Sir Roger de Coverley. Kate hopes you'll come, and so so [do?] I.' Catherine was unable to join in the festivities and energetic dancing; as Dickens wrote to Angela Burdett-Coutts, 'I am sorry to say, [Catherine] is in her own room, and likely to be there for two or three days.'

It was the beginning of a difficult and sad year, in which Fanny Burnett's health, and that of her son Harry, deteriorated rapidly. That summer, Charles was frantic with worry about Fanny as well as worrying about Catherine, who was pregnant again and not well. On 5 July, Charles wrote to Forster, after a visit to his sister, that he was very alarmed by a sudden change in Fanny's health, even though just two nights earlier she had been planning for 'after Christmas'. Fanny died on 2 September and her brother was devastated. He sank into depression. He was also being plagued by constant calls to pay off his brother Fred's debts and was furious that Fred was planning to marry despite being in such straits.

On 5 December, the family gathered together for the marriage of Dickens's youngest sibling, Augustus, to Harriett Lovell. Charles was pleased about the wedding, but less happy when Fred's marriage took place in between Christmas and New Year. Fred's new wife was the 18-year-old Anna Weller. Charles distrusted Anna and was concerned that neither she nor his brother were serious about the marriage. Ten years later, the couple separated, after infidelity on both sides. In the ensuing court case, Anna was granted alimony, which Fred was unable to pay. He fled the country to avoid payment, and when he returned some months later, was sent to debtors' prison, the very fate Charles Dickens had always feared and tried so hard to prevent. Augustus's marriage also failed when he ran away to America with his pregnant mistress, Bertha Phillips, abandoning Harriett in London.

It was already being considered traditional for Dickens to give readings from *A Christmas Carol*, but after 1848, every time he gave a reading, he was reminded that the 'little Fan' of Scrooge's schooldays, based on his own sister Fanny, was lost to him and soon it was apparent that the original Tiny Tim would not survive. Throughout that Christmas of 1848, while Catherine and Charles were awaiting the birth of their eighth child, Fanny's son, Henry Dickens Burnett, was dying. On 19 January 1849, Catherine gave birth to a son, whom they named Henry Fielding Dickens. His was a very difficult and painful birth, during which Catherine was given a new wonder-drug, chloroform. Henry Burnett died ten days after the birth of his cousin. He was buried beside his mother at Highgate Cemetery. Dickens's letters suggest that he threw himself into his work that Christmas, chasing invoices that should have been paid and ensuring Urania Cottage was running smoothly, trying not to think about the fact that despite having paid numerous eminent doctors, he had been unable to save his sister or her child.

Unaware of the misery the author was experiencing, for Dickens's readers the Christmas of 1848 was enhanced by his final Christmas Book. Today, *The Haunted Man and the Ghost's Bargain* is one of his least-remembered works, yet on the day it was published it sold around 18,000 copies. It saw a return to the Christmas-themed redemption story, which had been so popular in *A Christmas Carol*. The idea for the story had been growing in Dickens's imagination for some time, but he had put the idea aside to write *The Battle of Life*. From Switzerland, on 30 August 1846, Dickens had written to Forster, 'I have been dimly conceiving a very ghostly and wild idea, which I supposed I must now reserve for the *next* Christmas book. *Nous verrons.* It will mature in the streets of Paris by night, as well as in London.'

The newspapers were given a press release about the new book, which featured in papers all over the country – *The Haunted Man and the Ghost's Bargain*. A fancy for Christmas-time. Will be ready for sale on the 19th inst.' They were not, however, unanimous in their praise; in fact many were highly critical about the new book. *Bell's New Weekly Messenger* wrote, 'his new Christmas work ... we regret to say, is as unsatisfactory a thing, in a literary point of view, as Mr Dickens has ever written.' Yet again, in an attempt to eliminate the pirated versions of his work, Dickens gave Mark Lemon the rights to write a stage version of the story, but as always that did not stop pirated versions appearing.

The 'haunted man' of the book's title is Mr Redlaw, a chemistry teacher, haunted by sorrow over the death of his sister. At the start of his gothic story, Dickens describes where Redlaw lives and works:

'... his inner chamber, part library and part laboratory ... so solitary and vault-like, – an old, retired part of an ancient endowment for students, once a brave edifice, planted in an open place, but now the obsolete whim of forgotten architects; smoke-age-and-weather-darkened, squeezed on every side by the overgrowing of the great city, and choked, like an old well, with stones and bricks ... where no sun had straggled for a hundred years, but where, in compensation for the sun's neglect, the snow would lie for weeks when it lay nowhere else, and the black east wind would spin like a huge humming-top, when in all other places it was silent and still.'

When his servants, the Swidger family, bring him food and start to decorate the room with greenery for Christmas, Redlaw is despondent and wonders why they bother, saying, '"Another Christmas come, another year gone!" ... with a gloomy sigh.'

After being left alone Redlaw is visited by a phantom, who is also his doppelgänger or twin. 'Ghastly and cold, colourless in its leaden face and hands, but with his features, and his bright eyes, and his grizzled hair, and dressed in the gloomy shadow of his dress.' He offers Redlaw the chance to rid himself of his grief by having all painful memories erased from his mind. Eventually, Redlaw agrees. The phantom tells the chemist that 'the gift' he is giving him, he will be able to pass on to others.

The Haunted Man has many similarities with *A Christmas Carol*, including the visit by a spirit and the theme of a neglected, dangerous child ignored by society. Milly Swidger is renowned for taking in those in need, from poor people to injured animals, and soon after the phantom has erased his painful memories, Redlaw discovers a child hiding in the darkness, waiting for Milly:

'A bundle of tatters, held together by a hand, in size and form almost an infant's, but in its greedy, desperate little clutch, a bad old man's. A face rounded and smoothed by some half-dozen years, but pinched and twisted by the experiences of a life. Bright eyes, but not youthful. Naked feet, beautiful in their childish delicacy, – ugly in the blood and dirt that cracked upon them. A baby savage, a young monster, a child who had never been a child, a creature who might live to take the outward form of man, but who, within, would live and perish a mere beast.

'Used, already, to be worried and hunted like a beast, the boy crouched down as he was looked at, and looked back again, and interposed his arm to ward off the expected blow.

"I'll bite," he said, "if you hit me!"'

At the start of the story, Redlaw had shown compassion when told by Milly about a student, Edmund Denham, who is ill and too poor to afford to go home for the Christmas holidays and too poor to marry the woman he loves. After the phantom's visit, however, Redlaw shows no emotion about, and little interest in, the terrified and abused child. He is bemused about his own behaviour, but soon realises that anyone he touches, has the dubious 'gift' passed on to them. One by one the characters in the story start to lose their emotional capacity and their kindness. They become grumpy and short-tempered. In having allowed his memories to be erased, Redlaw has lost an integral part of his life, he has become incapable of feeling simple human emotions, such as sympathy, and has become 'a man turned to stone'. In forgetting the painful memories, he has not stopped feeling anger at the world – he just no longer knows why he feels that way and his bitterness starts to affect all those who know him. He tries to continue his previous behaviour, but his anger and bitterness taint his actions and Redlaw becomes aware not only of what he has lost, but that he is changing everyone around him as well. When Denham asks Redlaw what he has done and says, 'Give me back myself!' Redlaw responds:

'... like a madman. "I am infected! I am infectious! I am charged with poison for my own mind, and the minds of all mankind. Where I felt interest, compassion, sympathy, I am turning into stone. Selfishness and ingratitude spring up in my blighting footsteps. I am only so much less base than the wretches whom I make so, that in the moment of their transformation I can hate them."'

When the phantom returns, Redlaw asks him for help. He wants to go back to being the man he was before. He asks the phantom why the boy, who has been accompanying him on errands, is unaffected by Redlaw's ability to change people. The phantom tells him that the boy has no good memories to lose, so cannot be changed. He is a child destroyed by society, a 'desolate creature ... [a] barren wilderness' to whom no kindness or love has ever been shown. Just as he did with the child characters of Ignorance and Want in *A Christmas Carol*, Dickens berated his readers for allowing poor children to live in a world of such deprivation and cruelty.

The person who helps the professor and his unwitting victims recover is Milly Swidger. Although she is a bereaved mother, her grief has not stopped her from remembering the happy memories of her dead child. Milly spreads kindness. When she visits people who have been affected by Redlaw, they are cured, left only with a puzzlement about what had happened. By the end of the story, Redlaw has come to realise that he has to avoid becoming bitter. Like Ebenezer Scrooge, he is a changed man. Having always looked before on Milly only as his servant, he now sees her as a better person than himself 'as if their two positions were reversed'. The story ends with a magnificent Christmas dinner for everyone, from the poorest to the wealthiest.

'The purpose of Mr. Dickens in the Christmas tale he has produced this year, is conceived in the kindly spirit which has inspired many of his other writings. He strives to cultivate the unselfish properties of human nature; to develop the sympathies in greater force than the antipathies, to array love against hate, good against evil. He would show that the ills of life have their remedies, or their assuagement, and anguish its consolation ... To what class of literature this little book should be referred it would perhaps be difficult to decide, but Mr. Dickens has kindly spared of trouble of conjecture on that point, by endorsing his volume with a nomenclature of his own, as – "A Fancy". Fancies include all rules of criticism, and we shall not, therefore, consume time in a fruitless chase.'

The Morning Chronicle, 25 December 1848

Despite some critical reviews, the sales of *The Haunted Man, and the Ghost's Bargain*, were steadfast. In 1848, however, a new book by Charles Dickens was not the biggest Christmas news. For the young Queen Victoria, growing up in Kensington Palace with a German mother, a decorated tree was an essential part of Christmas. Her husband, Prince Albert, also came from Germany and they kept the tradition going. In 1841, Queen Victoria wrote in her journal, 'Today I have two children of my own to give presents to, who, they know not why, are full of happy wonder at the German Christmas tree and its radiant candles.' In December 1848, *The Illustrated London News* caused a sensation with its special Christmas supplement. It included a description of how the royal family would be spending the festive season, together with a drawing of the queen, the prince consort and their children gathered around a decorated Christmas tree.

'A Christmas tree is annually prepared, by her majesty's command, for the royal children. The tree employed for this festive purpose is a young fir, about eight feet high, and has six tiers of branches. On each tier or branch are arranged a dozen wax tapers. Pendent from the branches are elegant trays, baskets, *bonbonniers*, and other receptacles for sweetmeats of the most varied kind, and of all forms, colours, and degrees of beauty. Fancy cakes, gilt gingerbread, and eggs filled with sweetmeats, are also suspended by variously coloured ribands from the branches. The tree, which stands upon a table covered with white damask, is suported at the root of piles of sweets of a larger kind, and by toys and dolls of all description … On the summit of the tree stands the small figure of an angel, with outstretched wings, holding in each hand a wreath. Those trees are objects of much interest to all visitors at the Castle, from Christmas Eve, when they are first set up, until Twelfth night, when they are finally removed.'

Illustrated London News, 23 December 1848

Until this time, the custom of bringing a tree inside and decorating it had been confined to the royal household, the aristocracy and the immigrant German community. After the *Illustrated London News* article, however, the idea was being talked about all over the country and within a very few years, a Christmas tree had become fashionable in any household that could afford one. Prince Albert also helped to extend the tradition outside the royal household, by sending Christmas trees as presents to military barracks and local schools.

Queen Victoria was very proud of her Christmas trees, and commissioned artists and photographers to record them for posterity. In 1850, she commissioned the watercolour artists James Roberts to paint her Christmas at Windsor Castle. The painting shows the tree decorated with fake snow and wax candles; all around it are easels and tables displaying the family's gifts. The royal family did not have only one tree; the queen had her own tree, as did Prince Albert; the royal children had a tree to themselves; and the Duchess of Kent (Queen Victoria's mother) had another. In 1850, the queen wrote in her journal that 'My beloved Albert 1st took me to my tree & table, covered by such numberless gifts ... [the] children were then taken to their tree, jumping & shouting with joy over their toys & other presents.'

The new fashion of photography also helped to preserve an intimate glimpse into the royal family's Christmas decorations. A photograph, taken by Dr Ernst Becker on Christmas Eve 1857, shows a relatively small tree standing on top of a table, laden with ornaments and candles. All around it are presents including photographs, a richly decorated shawl, a small parasol, some small sculptures and sculpture busts and other trinkets. One of the presents that year was a set of eighteen photographs of Charles Kean, one of the queen's favourite actors, a Christmas presents from Prince Albert to Queen Victoria. By this date, the Christmas tree was already considered integral to the middle- and upper-class Christmas. In December 1855, *The Lady* magazine reported that 'natural fir trees [are] .... very popular'; it also recommended trying one of the newly fashionable artificial trees, such as a 'palm tree with leaves made from calico'. In the Museum of London's archives are the diaries of a young woman named Amelia Roper, who lived in Walthamstow, East London and in 1857 wrote to a friend that 'Miss Ward and I made a Christmas tree for Bobby and little Emily Roper they were highly delighted with it.' Amelia was a lower-middle-class girl who, at the time of writing her diary, was living with her parents who had an undertakers' business. She was preparing for her wedding to the local butcher. Her diary show how, in less than a decade since the *Illustrated London News* had published its drawing of the royal tree, people of all social classes had embraced the idea of a Christmas tree.

CHAPTER THIRTEEN

The New Fashion for the 'Christmas Story'

'A good time; a kind, forgiving, charitable time; the only time I
know of, in the long calendar of the year, when men and women
seem by one consent to open their shut-up hearts freely, and to think
of people below them as if they really were fellow passengers to
the grave, and not another race of creatures bound on other journeys.'

Charles Dickens, *A Christmas Carol* (1843)

In the late 1840s, Mark Lemon wrote a children's story entitled *The Enchanted Doll*, which he hoped would become popular as a Christmas present. The story is about a discontented doll maker named Jacob Pout, who is haunted by an enchanted doll who serves a similar purpose to the ghosts who haunt Ebenezer Scrooge. In 1848, Lemon wrote to Charles Dickens asking for permission to dedicate his story to Mamie and Katey Dickens, who were friends with his daughters. The book was published in 1849 and it includes a scene about a children's Christmas party, in which several of the Dickens children are named (although Sydney is changed to Sidney), as well as their dog Timber:

> 'As it is Christmas time there is a table loaded with good cheer, to which all comers are welcome; and those happy-looking folk crowding round the large sea-coal fire are drinking to the good Alderman's health in double ale ... Before the huge fire sits the turnspit, dozing and enjoying the warmth after the labours of the morning. Poor dog! he has to work hard at feast-times. He sits up (as

our little dog Timber does when he begs) … There go the fiddles! The Alderman and a buxom dame of forty lead off … Tony and Dorothy are in the middle of the set and dancing merrily …. What peals of laughter are heard every now and then as some blunder is made in the figure, when Charles, who should have turned to the right, wheels round to the left, and bumps against Mary, who nearly tumbles over Kate, who falls into the arms of Walter, whilst Frank, and Alfred, and Sidney clap their hands and declare that Kate did it on purpose. What a shout of laughter! Huzza!'

Another author who embraced the Christmas market was William Thackeray, whose first Christmas story, *Mrs Perkins' Ball* was published in 1847. He published six Christmas stories between 1847 and 1854, after which they were collated and published together as *The Christmas Books of Mr M.A. Titchmarsh*. The last of his Christmas stories, *The Rose and the Ring* (1854), is the best known of his Christmas works. It was subtitled 'A Fire-side Pantomime for Great and Small Children'. In the introduction, using his pseudonym of Mr M.A.Titchmarsh, Thackeray explains how his story was based upon Twelfth Night figures:

'It happened that the undersigned spent the last Christmas season in a foreign city where there were many English children.
   'In that city, if you wanted to give a child's party, you could not even get a magic-lantern or buy Twelfth-Night characters ... My friend Miss Bunch, who was governess of a large family ... begged me to draw a set of Twelfth-Night characters for the amusement of our young people. She is a lady of great fancy and droll imagination, and having looked at the characters, she and I composed a history about them, which was recited to the little folks at night, and served as our fire-side pantomime ... for a brief holiday, let us laugh and be as pleasant as we can. And you elder folk – a little joking, and dancing, and fooling will do even you no harm. The author wishes you a merry Christmas, and welcomes you to the Fire-side Pantomime.'

Not everyone was happy about how many authors were seen to be cashing in on the lucrative Christmas market, and many critics wrote scathing reviews, about the market being flooded by Christmas stories and books. On 5 January 1851, Thackeray felt compelled to add an introduction to his story,

THE NEW FASHION FOR THE 'CHRISTMAS STORY'

The Kickleburys on the Rhine, which had been published for Christmas 1850 and had borne the brunt of *The Times'* critic's ire about the preponderance of Christmas books. In his lengthy, introduction, Thackeray responded to the critic about why authors wrote Christmas stories:

> 'Any reader who may have a fancy to purchase a copy of this present edition of the "History of the Kickleburys Abroad", had best be warned in time, that the Times newspaper does not approve of the work, and has but a bad opinion both of the author and his readers ... It has been customary, of late years, for the purveyors of amusing literature – the popular authors of the day – to put forth certain opuscules, denominated "Christmas Books", ... "For the most part bearing the stamp of their origin in the vacuity of the writer's exchequer rather than in the fulness of his genius, they suggest by their feeble flavor the rinsings of a void brain after the more important concoctions of the expired year."... suppose you and I had to announce the important news that some writers published what are called Christmas books; that Christmas books are so called because they are published at Christmas: and that the purpose of the authors is to try and amuse people ... I protest, for my part, I had no idea what I was really about in writing and submitting my little book for sale, until my friend the critic, looking at the article, and examining it with the eyes of a connoisseur, pronounced that what I had fancied simply to be a book was in fact "an opuscule denominated so-and-so, and ostensibly intended to swell the tide of expansive emotion incident upon the inauguration of the new year." ... what can the Times' critic know about the vacuity of my exchequer? Did he ever lend me any money? Does he not himself write for money? ... Who are you? If you are the man I take you to be, it must have been you who asked the publisher for my book, and not I who sent it in, and begged a gratuity of your worship ...'

Ironically, in 1847 William Thackeray himself had written a disgruntled article about the number of Christmas stories that had appeared for sale since the publication of *A Christmas Carol*. Thackeray's article, 'A Grumble About the Christmas-books', was published in *Fraser's Magazine* and in it he complained about what he saw as a decline in the genre that year. One book he singled out for censure was *The Yule Log*, by Alexander Chamerovzow, which had been illustrated by Dickens's friend and illustrator George

Cruikshank. It was Chamerovzow's one attempt to capture the Christmas market; perhaps he was too daunted by Thackeray's condemnation of his work, as being formulaic and predictable, to try again. In the article, Thackeray lambasted the glut of Christmas stories published in 1847 as being 'streaky with benevolence, and larded with the most unctuous human kindness'.

The decision not to produce a Christmas story for 1849, seems to have made Dickens much happier than in the previous year. His letters are full of stories about parties and trips to the theatre, including a letter he wrote to Mark Lemon on Christmas Day, 'Merry Christmas and a happy new year, to you and all yours! Are you for a pankelmime on Thursday? If so, name your hour of dinner – anywhere – and I think I can bring Stanny with me.' Stanny was their friend, the artist Clarkson Stanfield RA.

The party for Charley's thirteenth birthday was fondly remembered in the family because, on 5 January 1850, Angela Burdett-Coutts sent her godson such a large Twelfth Cake, that the children danced an impromptu jig of delight around the cake as it waited on the table in preparation for the following day's party. In her memoir, *My Father As I Recall Him*, Mamie remembered:

'When "the boys" came home for the holidays there were constant rehearsals for the Christmas and New Year's parties; and more especially for the dance on Twelfth Night, the anniversary of my brother Charlie's birthday. Just before one of these celebrations my father insisted that my sister ... and I should teach the polka step to Mr. Leech and himself. My father was as much in earnest about learning to take that wonderful step correctly, as though there were nothing of greater importance in the world. Often he would practice gravely in a corner, without either partner or music, and I remember one cold winter's night his awakening with the fear that he had forgotten the step so strong upon him that, jumping out of bed, by the scant illumination of the old-fashioned rushlight, and to his own whistling, he diligently rehearsed its "one, two, three, one, two, three" until he was once more secure in his knowledge.'

By the end of the 1840s and the start of the 1850s, Charles Dickens was very heavily involved with trying to bring about social change. In addition to his and Angela Burdett-Coutts' Urania Cottage project, in 1849 he campaigned passionately for a change in the law that governed the death penalty. He was not campaigning against the death penalty itself, but against the practice of executions being carried out in public. He was sickened by the spectacle this presented, and the holiday atmosphere in which whole families would arrive as day-trippers to watch criminals being hanged. In *Oliver Twist*, at the start of his career, he had written a very compassionate account of Fagin's last night on earth. The chapter feels claustrophobic to read, as the reader gets sucked into the criminal's own counting down of the hours to his death, listening to the mob outside baying for him to be hanged. The letters that Dickens wrote to *The Times* in 1849, about public executions, in which the author queried what made the mob lusting after the spectacle of a hanging any better than the criminals being hanged, helped to sway public opinion and, ultimately, caused the law to be changed; public executions ended in Britain in 1868. From that time on, they were carried out only inside prisons where the public was unable to watch.

As the 1840s drew to a close, Dickens was thinking about making a change in the way he worked. He had been exhausted, both physically and emotionally, by the constant clamour from his public and his publishers about the desire for a new Christmas book every December and he knew he needed to change the way he was working. He also made a new business decision. He was tired of his work being edited and of seeing the money for the magazines which sold on the back of his works going into the pockets of others. So, he approached his publisher with an idea for setting up a magazine of his own. The new magazine was called *Household Words* and he used it to make a much-needed change in his Christmas publications. Dickens ran and edited *Household Words*, alongside his faithful colleague and editor William Henry Wills (better known by his initials, as W.H. Wills). Dickens had found the production of his five Christmas books exhausting. *A Christmas Carol* was different from the others. It had been a vocation, something he had felt called upon to write in an attempt to bring about social change. That desperate need to write it had made it the most straightforward and heartfelt of his Christmas books. With each successive year, however, he had found himself drained by the need to produce another Christmas book, or by the need to explain why he hadn't written one.

Although each of his five Christmas books was very popular in its time, the only one that has remained popular is *A Christmas Carol* and many people have no idea that Dickens wrote another four. With the beginning of *Household Words,* Dickens was able to start a new Christmas tradition, one that was less arduous and time-consuming than writing a new book every December. Instead of Christmas books, he began writing Christmas stories. He also commissioned other writers to do the same, including Wilkie Collins,

Elizabeth Gaskell and George Augustus Sala. *Household Words* continued until 1859, when Dickens replaced it with a new magazine, *All The Year Round*.

Both magazines became famous for their Christmas stories, which were published in a bumper Christmas edition – but the stories weren't necessarily about Christmas or New Year. By the time he became editor of *All The Year Round,* Dickens's commissioning instructions specified that he would be happy if their stories made no reference to the festive season, as is shown in this message sent by W.H. Wills 'To Contributors to *All The Year Round*' on 18 September 1862:

'In inviting you to contribute to our Christmas No. I beg to send you Mr Dickens's Memorandum of the range that may be taken this year. You will see that it is a wide one. The slight leading notion of the No. being devised with a view to placing as little restriction as possible on the fancies of my fellow-writers in it, there is again no limitation as to scene, or first person, or third person; nor is any reference to the season of the year essential.'

'Christmas goes out in fine style – with Twelfth Night. It is a finish worthy of the time. Christmas Day was the morning of the season: New Year's Day the middle of it, or noon; Twelfth Night is the night, brilliant with innumerable planets or Twelfth Cakes. The whole island keeps court; nay, all Christendom. All the world are kings and queens.'

Leigh Hunt, 1840

CHAPTER FOURTEEN

Christmas All the Year Round

'The custom of having illuminated trees at Christmas, laden with pretty little trifles, as mementoes to be presented to the guests of the Christmas party, is derived from Germany. A young fir is generally selected for the Christmas Tree, and little presents of various kinds are bound on the branches, as, crochet-purses, bonbons, preserved fruits, alum baskets, charms, dolls, toys in endless variety ... The whole is illuminated by numerous little wax tapers, which are lighted just before the guests are admitted to inspect the tree. Before the tapers are quite burnt out the guests all assemble around the tree, and the souvenirs are taken off and presented to the guests whose names have either been previously appended to them, or at the discretion of the distributor.'

Dictionary of Daily Wants 1858

In December 1850, Dickens had two important issues on his mind; one was his determination to get the queen to give a pension to an impoverished writer named John Poole. Dickens wrote personally to the Prime Minister, Lord John Russell, who had already provided some emergency funds, of the necessity of Poole receiving a regular pension:

'He is in a prematurely shattered state, and perfectly unable to write ... To the best of my belief, he has no relative whomsoever. He must either have starved, or gone to the workhouse (and I have little doubt that he would have done the former) but for the funds I have doled out to him, – which were exhausted before you generously assisted him from the Queen's Bounty. He has no resource of any kind.'

The prime minister agreed, and on Christmas Eve Dickens wrote a jubilant letter to Poole:

'My dear Poole, On the Sunday when I last saw you, I went straight to Lord John's with the letter you read ...To-day I got a letter from him, announcing that you have a pension of *a hundred a year*! of which I heartily wish you joy.'

The other issue commanding Dickens's attention, was the preparation and rehearsals for the family's Twelfth Night play. This year he had Dion Boucicault's play *Used Up*, and he threw himself into the production with great energy, helping his children learn their lines and commanding the operation of transforming the children's schoolroom at 1, Devonshire Terrace into a theatre. There were now nine children in the Dickens household, a third daughter, baby Dora, having been born in August. Several of the older children were taking part in the family theatrical, and there was great excitement over Charley's role as a tiger, for which a specially commissioned tiger suit was tailor-made.

For eighteen months, Dickens had been hard at work writing *David Copperfield* – which his children would later describe as their father's 'favourite child' – the novel which is usually considered his most autobiographical work. The novel was a great success and the final instalment was published in November of 1850, leaving its author free to enjoy himself at Christmas time. In *David Copperfield*, Dickens included a sad Christmas scene, evoking the feelings he remembered so well after being rejected by Maria Beadnell in the 1830s. In times of sadness, he still brooded on his lost love affair and his feelings for Maria had inspired the character of Dora Spenlow. While he is married to Dora, David comes to realise how unsuited they are, and finally understands – as the reader has long understood – that the right woman for him is Agnes Wickfield, his loyal friend since childhood, but whom David has only ever looked upon as a 'sister'. After Dora has died leaving David a sad young widower, he feels unable to tell Agnes that he loves her, believing she does not return his feelings. Convinced he is about to lose the woman he loves to an unknown rival, he finds the season one of misery:

'The year came round to Christmas-time, and I had been at home above two months ... It was – what lasting reason have I to remember it! – a cold, harsh, winter day. There had been snow, some hours before; and it lay, not deep, but hard-frozen on the ground. Out at sea, beyond my window, the wind blew ruggedly from the north. I had been thinking of it, sweeping over those mountain wastes of snow in Switzerland, then inaccessible to any human foot; and had been speculating which was the lonelier, those solitary regions, or a deserted ocean ... How well I recollect the wintry ride! The frozen particles of ice, brushed from the blades of grass by the wind, and borne across my face; the hard clatter of the horse's hoofs, beating a tune upon the ground; the stiff-tilled soil; the snowdrift, lightly eddying in the chalk-pit as the breeze ruffled it; the smoking team with the waggon of old hay, stopping to breathe on the hill-top, and shaking their bells musically; the whitened slopes and sweeps of Down-land lying against the dark sky, as if they were drawn on a huge slate!'

By contrast, over the Christmas of 1850, Dickens, having completed *David Copperfield*, was in a proud and excitable mood. On 19 December 1850, he wrote to his friend Lavinia Watson about his preparations for the family theatrical and joked about the despair allegedly felt by his manservant:

'I have closely overhauled the little Theatre, and the Carpenter and Painter. The whole has been entirely repainted (I mean the Proscenium and Scenery) for this especial purpose and it is extremely pretty ... It is as good as the Queen's little theatre at Windsor; raised stage excepted. I have had an alteration made, which will enable us to use the door. I am at present breaking my man's heart, by teaching him how to imitate the sounds of the smashing of the window, and the breaking of the balcony, in Used Up. In the event of his Death from grief, I have promised to do something for his Mother.'

It was a jubilant year for the family and the celebrations and play rehearsals continued throughout the twelve days of Christmas. Dickens wrote again to Lavinia Watson on New Year's Day:

'... we had a country dance last night (of nearly all my Amateur Company) which was of the wildest description, and the most appalling duration ... (I write this on my back on the floor.)"

DICKENS AND CHRISTMAS

Dickens's first Christmas story appeared in *Household Words* in 1850. Its title, *A Christmas Tree*, was very topical, once again capturing the zeitgeist:

> 'I have been looking on, this evening, at a merry company of children assembled round that pretty German toy, a Christmas Tree. The tree was planted in the middle of a great round table, and towered high above their heads. It was brilliantly lighted by a multitude of little tapers; and everywhere sparkled and glittered with bright objects. There were rosy-cheeked dolls, hiding behind the green leaves; and there were real watches (with movable hands, at least, and an endless capacity of being wound up) dangling from innumerable twigs; there were French-polished tables, chairs, bedsteads, wardrobes, eight-day clocks, and various other articles of domestic furniture (wonderfully made, in tin, at Wolverhampton), perched among the boughs, as if in preparation for some fairy housekeeping; there were jolly, broad-faced little men, much more agreeable in appearance than many real men – and no wonder, for their heads took off, and showed them to be full of sugar-plums; there were fiddles and drums; there were tambourines, books, work-boxes, paint-boxes, sweetmeat-boxes, peep-show boxes, and all kinds of boxes; there were trinkets for the elder girls, far brighter than any grown-up gold and jewels; there were baskets and pincushions in all devices; there were guns, swords, and banners; there were witches standing in enchanted rings of pasteboard, to tell fortunes; there were teetotums, humming-tops, needle-cases, pen-wipers, smelling-bottles, conversation-cards, bouquet-holders; real fruit, made artificially dazzling with gold leaf; imitation apples, pears, and walnuts, crammed with surprises ...' ('A Christmas Tree', *Household Words*, 21 December 1850)

From this year onwards, instead of waiting for a new Christmas book, Dickens's fans eagerly awaited a magazine filled with Christmas stories. In common with other publications, *Household Words* produced a special Christmas edition, and the planning of it took up much of Dickens's and Wills's time from late summer until the end of the year.

For both Charles and Catherine Dickens 1851 was a very sad year, in which they both suffered from depression. In March, the family was shocked by the death of John Dickens, and just two weeks later, baby Dora Dickens died. Since birth, she had not been a healthy baby and her father described her death as having been caused by 'something like congestion of the brain'. Charles and Catherine's marriage was already starting to feel the strain of his celebrity and the death of their daughter pushed them further apart. Both of them needed other things to focus on and as Dickens threw himself into his writing, editing and amateur theatricals, Catherine began working on a book of her own.

Under the pseudonym of Lady Maria Clutterbuck, a role she had played when they performed the play *Used Up* at Rockingham Castle, the home of their friends Richard and Lavinia Watson and the inspiration for Chesney Wold in *Bleak House,* Rockingham Castle, Catherine wrote a cookbook, *What Shall We Have for Dinner?* The book came out a few weeks before Christmas, well timed to be published for the season. It was subtitled 'A Guide for Young Wives' and contained menus for dinners and dinner parties for between two and eighteen people. It was popular and went into several editions over the next couple of years. For some reason, several academics have striven over the years to claim the book was actually written by Charles Dickens, even though it is well documented as having been written by Catherine, who was an excellent cook. The book reveals an interesting side to Dickens family life, as well as about the large number of courses and dishes expected at even a simple Victorian dinner party. One of Charles Dickens's favourite dishes, often served for the Savoury course at the end of a meal, was 'toasted cheese'. This recipe appears multiple times in the book's menus. Surprisingly, there are no special Christmas menus in the book.

Just before Christmas of 1851, the Dickens family left 1, Devonshire Terrace and moved to Tavistock House, on the edge of Tavistock Square, in the heart of London's Bloomsbury. This was a large house divided into two family homes. Their neighbours were their friends, Frank Stone and his family. Frank Stone was one of Dickens's illustrators and his eldest son, Marcus, was training to be an artist, as was Katey Dickens. In later years, after his father's death, Marcus Stone would also become one of Dickens's illustrators.

The Dickens family's side of the house, which was made up of eighteen rooms, was big enough to let them celebrate Christmas in grand style, but the builders took so long to complete the renovations that Charles and Catherine started to despair of it ever being ready in time. In October, Dickens wrote despairingly to Thomas Beard:

'I am wild to begin a new book – and can't, until I am settled – and have all manner of workmen, scooping, grooving, chiseling, sawing, planing, dabbing, puttying, clinking, hammering and going up ladders apparently with no earthly object but that of staying there until dinner time, every day.'

His brother-in-law Henry Austin, husband of his younger sister Letitia, was an architect who helped them with the renovations. A surviving sketch drawn by Dickens and sent to Henry Austin is of a modern-looking 'warm bath' – a bathtub with a shower above it, surrounded by 'waterproof curtains' – which he wanted to be installed in Tavistock House.

The Danish author Hans Christian Andersen visited Dickens at Tavistock House and some time later wrote down his memories of the family home:

'In Tavistock Square stands Tavistock House. This and the strip of garden in front of it are shut out from the thoroughfare by an iron railing. A large garden ... stretches behind the house, and gives it a countrified look in the midst of this coal and gas steaming London ... On the first floor was a rich library, with a fireplace and a writing-table, looking out on the garden; and here it was that in winter Dickens and his friends acted plays to the satisfaction of all parties. The kitchen was underground, and at the top of the house were the bedrooms.'

In November 1851, the house was finally ready for the family to move in, yet Dickens still had trouble in settling down to work. He wrote to Wills, 'I can't begin the Xmas article – and am going out to walk, after vain trials.' The article he was trying to write was 'Showing what Christmas is to Everybody'. He was battling with decisions about the format of Christmas editions *Household Words* should follow. Over the next couple of decades, Dickens's Christmas writing would evolve from short stories through to novellas written by a group of writers. He was never able to recreate the magical formula he had hit upon with *A Christmas Carol*, but his contemporary readers seldom cared – as long as there was a new story by Charles Dickens for the Christmas season, they would buy it. By the 1850s, the Dickensian Christmas story had become as integral a part of the season as mince pies, carol singing and the new fashion for Christmas trees.

One of Dickens's new recruits on *Household Words*, Henry Morley, was invited to a party at Tavistock House in December 1851, and he left a description of Catherine Dickens:

'Dickens has evidently made a comfortable choice. Mrs Dickens is stout, with a round, very round, rather pretty, very pleasant face, and ringlets on each side of it. One sees in five minutes that she loves her husband and her children, and has a warm heart for anybody who won't be satirical, but meet her on her own good-natured footing. We were capital friends at once, and had abundant talk together. She meant to know me, and once, after a little talk when she went to receive a new guest, she came back to find me ... I liked her, and felt that she liked me, and that we could be good friends.'

Another visitor to the new family home was a young law student named Wilkie Collins, with whom Dickens had recently become friends. Wilkie Collins, who would go on to become as famous a novelist as his friend, was someone to whom Dickens could reveal the less conventional sides to his personality. Over the coming years, the two men often took off on trips together and collaborated on a writing projects, including the *Lazy Tour of Two Idle Apprentices* and the play *The Frozen Deep*.

The Dickens family celebrated their first Twelfth Night at Tavistock House with friends, who had been invited to see the family theatrical of *Guy Fawkes*, a burlesque written by Albert Smith and performed jointly by the Dickens and Lemon children. On the day after the party, Dickens wrote to his brother-in-law Henry Austin:

'I am floored today; having, besides my cold, a Bilious attack which has robbed me of my appetite – set the dull knobs of two rusty pokers in my head instead of eyes – and generally enfeebled discomfited and perplexed me.'

The publication of *Bleak House* in 1852 was a great success for Dickens – although the book makes scant mention of Christmas and has no affecting Christmas scenes. He spent part of the year writing letters to the Royal Literary Fund on behalf of two impoverished writers, Maria Goodluck and Charles Whitehead, and was very pleased that the charity helped both of them. The Autumn of 1852 was depressingly cold and grey and Dickens wrote to his friend William de Cerjat in Switzerland:

'For two months it has been incessantly raining. At last, however, we have had a noble afternoon; and now the stars are shining brightly out of a clear blue sky ... I hope you will see the Xmas No. of Household Words, which has some very pretty stories in it – the first two, mine.'

Dickens's Christmas plans received a setback by a sudden illness that afflicted W.H. Wills. Rather dramatically, Wills suddenly 'went blind', although it turned out to be a temporary condition. As a result, Dickens's workload on *Household Words* doubled and on 23 December, he wrote to Wilkie Collins:

'I am suddenly laid by the heels in consequence of Wills having gone blind without any notice ... This obliges me to be at the office all day to-day, and to resume my attendance there tomorrow. But if you will come there tomorrow afternoon – say, at about 3 o'Clock – I think we may forage pleasantly for a dinner in the city, and then go and look at Christmas Eve in Whitechapel – which is always a curious thing.'

That Christmas, there were once again nine Dickens children in Tavistock House. Catherine and Charles's last baby, a son named Edward (but always known by his nickname of Plorn) had been born in March. In contrast to baby Dora, whose health had been a concern all through her brief life, Plorn was a robust and healthy baby. His father wrote adoring letters about him to his friends, and had a friendly rivalry with Angela Burdett-Coutts, who had recently become the aunt of a new nephew, about which house the world's best baby lived in. In the year in which the last Dickens baby was born, the author published a book for his children. It was called *A Child's History of England* and was dedicated 'To my own dear children whom I hope it may help, bye and bye, to read with interest larger and better books on the same subject.' *A Child's History of England* was under many families' Christmas trees that year.

A couple of days after Christmas Dickens went to see a pantomime with a group of male friends. Although today pantomimes are aimed at children and young families, in the nineteenth century the audience was expected to be made up of all ages. At home, the Dickens children were preparing for their Twelfth Night performance of *William Tell*, by Robert Brough. Charles Dickens had also decided that, in the following year, he would embark on a series of public readings.

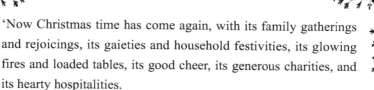

'Now Christmas time has come again, with its family gatherings and rejoicings, its gaieties and household festivities, its glowing fires and loaded tables, its good cheer, its generous charities, and its hearty hospitalities.

'Now the green holly bedecks many windows, the mistletoe is hung up for merry youths to sport under, and the old for a time forget the seriousness and the toils of life.

Now little children are in the highest glee, and look forward to their Christmas dinner, with its plum pudding and snapdragon, followed by romps and games, as the grandest festival of the year.... Now the young look forward, and the aged look back; the youth contemplating with joy the Christmas to come, the old looking back, perhaps, with saddened pleasure at the Christmases that have passed....

'Christmas is the saturnalia of minors; when guardians, natural and appointed, are thrust from their authority, and must see to obey the behests of their young charges.... We must quit our solemn trifles, and address ourselves earnestly to the office of ministering to the mirth and enjoyment of our little lords and ladies paramount. Mammas must turn their thoughts from the formal prescriptions of domestic cookery to the wild regions of flammery, tartlets, syllabubs, and whipt cream; papas must sweep away all preoccupations of office, desk, and ledger, into the lumber-rooms of their brains, rub up their reminiscences of schoolboy pranks, and rack their fancies for new conundrums.... Commend us ever to the to the frank and genial pleasures of innocent games ... 'Hot Cockles', 'Blindman's Buff' and 'Hunt the Slipper'.... The Lottery, or Tombola is quite a modern introduction, and is generally found productive of much fun.'

Belfast News Letter 26 December 1853

Ever since the publication of *A Christmas Carol*, newspapers took delight in reporting Scrooge-like conversations in their columns. They sought out heart-warming Christmas stories and gleefully reported them. In 1853, the *Lincolnshire Chronicle* reported on a story which they titled *A Good Example*:

> 'Messrs. Clayton, Shuttleworth and Co., iron-founders of this city, have presented a 20-stone sack of flour and a goose to each of the foremen in their extensive foundry as a Christmas treat. The leading workmen were also entertained at the Globe inn on Saturday night, when a splendid supper was provided on the occasion.'

The reporter also wrote about a special Christmas tea party held for around 300 children:

> 'The rooms were tastefully ornamented with evergreens and artificial roses, including mottoes and illustrations emblematical of the season. There was a most ample supply of excellent plum bread and tea, to which ample justice was done by the happy juveniles. After singing hymns, the children repaired to the boys' school-room, where a Christmas tree was fixed, loaded with every variety of fruit, & c., enabling every child to possess a sample. The children were addressed in a very feeling and useful manner by the Rev. G. Rigg, and after playing some good old Christmas games, retired highly delighted.... The cost of this treat was defrayed entirely by subscription.'

Dickens spent much of 1853 preparing for his new series of Christmas readings. His performances of *A Christmas Carol* and *The Cricket on the Hearth* were performed in Birmingham, in aid of the new Birmingham and Midland Institute. On New Year's Eve he wrote to John Forster that the Birmingham readings had attracted 'nearly six thousand people'. Dickens had specified to the organisers that he wanted the tickets to be available to as many 'working people' as possible and on 2 January he wrote to Angela Burdett-Coutts, 'If you could have seen the two thousand five hundred workpeople on Friday night, I think you would have been delighted.'

He was back in London on time for the Twelfth Night family theatrical. This year he was not only the production's manager, he was also an actor. The Dickens and Lemon families were performing *Tom Thumb* in the converted Tavistock House schoolroom, which Dickens had named the smallest theatre in the world. Both Charles Dickens and Mark Lemon acted alongside the children and this began a new tradition of bringing in adult friends to take starring roles in the plays. In *Tom Thumb*, Dickens played the ghost of Gaffer Thumb, Lemon played the Giantess Glumdalca and Henry Fielding Dickens, aged four, played Tom Thumb. As Henry's diction was very indistinct, the audience was given a printed copy of his words, so they could follow what he was meant to be saying.

A record of what it was like to perform in these plays was left by Alfred Ainger, a schoolfriend of the Dickens boys and a regular actor at the Tavistock House performances. At the end of 1870, he published an article entitled 'Mr Dickens's Amateur Theatricals' in *Macmillan's Magazine*.

'What evenings were those at Tavistock house, when the best wit and fancy and culture of the day met within its hospitable walls! ... In one sense our theatricals began and ended in the school-room. To the last that apartment served us for stage and auditorium and all. But in another sense we got promotion from the children's domain by degrees. Our earliest efforts were confined to the children of the family and their equals in age, though always aided and abetted by the good-natured manager ... Another year found us more ambitious, and with stronger resources, for Mr. Dickens himself and Mr. Mark Lemon joined our acting staff, though, with kindly consideration for their young brethren, they chose subordinate parts.... What fun it was, both on and off the stage! The gorgeous dresses from the eminent costumier of the Theatres Royal; our heads bewigged and our cheeks rouged by the hands of Mr. Clarkson himself; the properties from the Adelphi; the unflagging humour and suggestive resources of our manager, who took upon him the charge of everything, from the writing of the playbills to the composition of the punch, brewed for our refreshment between the acts, but "craftily qualified", as Michael Cassio would have said, to suit the capacities of the childish brain; for Dickens never forgot the *maxima reverentia* due to children, and some of us were of a *very* tender age; ... Nonsense, it may be said, all this; but the nonsense of a great genius has always something of genius in it.'

The following year, there was once again great excitement about the special Christmas edition of *Household Words*. Dickens wrote to his friend in Switzerland:

'My Dear Cerjat, When your Christmas letter did not arrive according to custom, I felt as if a bit of Christmas had fallen out and there was no supplying the piece. However, it was soon supplied by yourself, and the bowl became round and round again ... The Christmas No. of Household Words, I suppose will reach Lausanne about Midsummer. The first ten pages or so ... are written by me; and I hope you will find, in the story of the Soldier which they contain, something that may move you a little. It moved me not a little in the writing, and I believe has touched a vast number of people. We have sold 80,000 of it ... The whole nine [children] are well and happy. Ditto Mrs Dickens. Ditto Georgina ... They are all agog now about a great Fairy-play, which is to come off here next Monday.'

The 1854 Christmas story in *Household Words* was 'The Seven Poor Travellers'. Until this time, the magazine's Christmas issue had been filled with a selection of short stories by different writers. This year, Dickens had tried a new structure; still commissioning stories by different writers but fitting them into an overarching storyline, of which he wrote the beginning and the ending. *The Seven Poor Travellers* is set in Rochester, in Kent, on Christmas Eve, and was inspired by an historic building Dickens remembered from his childhood. The building was a hospice which provided a night's free lodging and food for any travellers passing through the town. In the story, there were six poor travellers staying in the hospice, and the narrator who becomes the seventh traveller of the title. He asks the landlady if he can meet the six other travellers, at which she first refuses until he persuades her:

'I urged to the good lady that this was Christmas-eve; that Christmas comes but once a year – which is unhappily too true, for when it begins to stay with us the whole year round we shall make this earth a very different place; that I was possessed by the desire to treat the Travellers to a supper and a temperate glass of hot Wassail ... In the end I prevailed, to my great joy. It was settled that at nine o'clock that night a Turkey and a piece of Roast Beef should smoke upon the board; and that I ... should preside as the Christmas-supper host of the six Poor Travellers.'

At the dinner, each of the travellers was encouraged to tell a story (these were written by Charles Dickens, George Augustus Sala, Wilkie Collins, Eliza Lynn and Adelaide Anne Procter). The critics were not entirely happy with this new format of the Christmas story and the critic for the *Kentish Advertiser* was particularly unhappy:

> Mr Dickens appears to labour under a sort of delusion that it is incumbent upon him to publish annually something apropos to the pleasant season of Christmas, which shall add to the enjoyment of our good cheer … His last Christmas tale was a dead failure; but still he is unwilling to confess himself beaten.'

The thing that seemed to annoy the Kentish reviewer most was that Dickens had played with historic fact to produce a work of fiction. Although other reviewers were also lukewarm about the story, the public loved the Christmas edition of *Household Words*. Dickens had hit upon a winning formula.

In between Christmas and the start of 1855, Dickens was on tour once again. He wrote to Catherine from Bradford, in Yorkshire, 'The hall is enormous. They expect to seat tonight, 3,700 *people*!' He was back in time for New Year's Eve, where they held a party 'to see the Old Year out'. They also invited friends for Twelfth Night, 'to see the children's Fairy-play. As Charley's birthday falls on a Saturday, we mean to keep it on Monday the 8th when will be presented Fortunio and his seven gifted Servants, by the entire strength of the Company.' As the Dickens children grew up and provided an even bigger cast for the family theatricals, each Twelfth Night play became more elaborate and Dickens threw himself into each one with great enthusiasm. On 4 January 1855, he postponed a planned business dinner because 'Dress rehearsal of the young Company demands the managerial presence!'

After the excitement of the Christmas season was over, Dickens became restless and depressed. Once again, he decided to leave London and try living abroad. His marriage was in serious trouble and it is possible that he and Catherine imagined that removal to a new city, might help. In reality, it seemed to make Dickens more restless and the gulf between them became even more apparent.

The second half of 1855 was spent in preparation for moving to Paris for a year. It was a very busy year for the French capital, as the city was hosting the *Exposition Universelle*, a response to the Great Exhibition in London of 1851. The family spent the summer in Boulogne, one of their favourite holiday destinations, and in the autumn, Charles and his sister-in-law Georgina, travelled to Paris to find suitable accommodation for the winter. On 6 October 1855, Dickens wrote to his wife:

'My Dearest Catherine,
We have had the most awful job to find a place that would in the least suit us, for Paris is perfectly full, and there is nothing to be got at any sane price. However, we have found two apartments – an entresol and a first floor – with a kitchen and servants' rooms at the top of the house – at No. 49 Avenue des champs Elysées
     You must be prepared for a regular continental abode. There is only one window in each room, but the front apartments all look upon the main street of the champs Elysées, and the view is delightfully cheerful. There are also plenty of rooms. They are not over and above well-furnished, but by changing furniture from rooms we don't care for, to rooms we do care for, we shall be able to make them comfortable and presentable. I think the situation itself, almost the finest in Paris; and the children will have a window from which to look on the busy life outside.'

He wrote to Wilkie Collins that their Parisian home was 'a regular little pack of closets with the ordinary queer staircase &c, but the most wonderful and amusing view from the windows, ever beheld.' Whilst in Paris, Dickens was courted by society hostesses and besieged by people asking him for money. He was also invited to sit for his portrait at the studio of two of the most famous portrait painters in Paris, the brothers Ary and Henri Scheffer. He took his daughter Katey, an aspiring portrait painter, to the studio, so she could observe how the brothers worked. It was not easy for Dickens to take time out from his work during the 'busiest time of my year' and the pressure became so intense that he was forced to postpone one sitting because 'the approach of Christmas brings me so many Proof sheets from England and involves me in so much correspondence (in addition to my regular occupation with my new book).' At the start of December he complained to John Forster:

'You may faintly imagine what I have suffered from sitting to Scheffer every day since I came back. He is a most noble fellow, and I have the greatest pleasure in his society ... but I can scarcely express how uneasy and unsettled it makes me to have to sit, sit, sit with *Little Dorrit* on my mind, and the Christmas business too.'

He was also disconcerted to discover that the Scheffers had invited around sixty people to come to the studio and hear him read *The Cricket on the Hearth*.

Throughout the second half of November, Dickens wrote a flurry of letters to W.H. Wills about the Christmas magazine, and about the fact he was worrying about his latest novel, confessing that he was 'Not working very well at Little Dorrit, since I went back to her from the Xmas No.' As a solution, Wills travelled to Paris so they could work on the proofs of the magazine's Christmas issue together. Dickens was excited to see him and took him to dinner at his favourite restaurant, the Trois Frères, and to the theatre.

Just as he had done from Genoa, Dickens travelled back to London for business meetings, but it was so much easier from Paris that he wrote to his friend Emile de la Rue mentioning that he was able to go 'backwards and forwards to London once a month or so'. In the middle of December, he was back in England to do readings in Peterborough and Sheffield. He also visited his now-widowed friend Lavinia Watson and her children at Rockingham Castle.

The Christmas story for 1855 was *The Holly Tree Inn*, once again a collection of stories written by Dickens and others. It tells the story of a traveller, who believes he has been rejected by the woman he loves and decides to emigrate to America. On Christmas Eve, he is the only guest at the Holly Tree Inn, where he and the staff are snowed in. The traveller whiles away the time writing down the stories the staff tell him; this gave Dickens the chance to include his own story *The Boots at the Holly Tree Inn*, which would go on to become one of his favourite Christmas readings once he started on his public reading tours. Other stories were written by Wilkie Collins, Adelaide Anne Proctor, William Howitt and Harriet Parr. At the end of the story, when the snow has gone and the roads are passable, the young man discovers that his love is requited, and, instead of emigrating, he travels back to London and gets married. Dickens found the task of trying to incorporate other people's writing into his framework a very difficult task, and the story and its editing preoccupied him for months. By the time it was published, he was sick of what he described to Wilkie Collins as a 'prodigious ... botheration'.

He arrived back in Paris on Christmas Eve after a very rough journey across the English Channel. Although Mamie, Katey and baby Edward were living with their parents in the Parisian flat already, when the school holidays began, all the Dickens boys arrived in Paris, making the tiny apartment even more of a tight squeeze. Charley arrived on Boxing Day. Dickens sent a jokey warning against having a large family to his friend Edmund Yates, whose wife had recently given birth to twin boys, 'I had seven sons in the Banquet Hall of this apartment – which would not make a very large warm bath...'

DICKENS AND CHRISTMAS

Over the pantomime season, Dickens became homesick for London, possibly caused by a bout of very bad Parisian weather. He wrote to Mark Lemon to ask what theatre shows he had been to and what the pantomime was like:

'I miss you, my dear old boy, at the play, woefully, and miss the walk home, and the partings at the corner of Tavistock Square … We are up to our knees in mud here. Literally in vehement despair, I walked down the avenue outside the Barrière de l'Etoile here yesterday, and went straight on among the trees. I came back with the top-boots of mud on. Nothing will cleanse the streets. Numbers of men and women are forever scooping in them, and they are always one lake of yellow mud. All my trousers go to the tailor's every day, and are ravelled out at the heels every night. Washing is awful.'

The following day he wrote to Mary Boyle:

'It is clear to me that climates are gradually assimilating over a great part of the world, and that in the most miserable time of our year, there is very little to choose between London and Paris – except that London is not so muddy. I have never seen dirtier or worse weather than we have had here ever since I returned [from England].'

The whole family was cheered in their muddy home by the arrival, on time for Charley's birthday and Twelfth Night, of a 'noble cake' sent by Angela Burdett-Coutts. Just as she had managed to do while they were living in Italy, she had secured safe passage for a highly decorated cake which had, somehow, survived the journey intact.

Throughout 1856, Dickens worked closely with Wilkie Collins on a play that Wilkie had promised to have finished on time for the next Twelfth Night. This was a new style of Christmas theatrical for Dickens. Not only was it not an adaptation of a well-known play or fairy tale, it was also a tragedy. The play was called *The Frozen Deep*, and it was to cause shock waves in the Dickens family and amongst his fans.

Dickens was also working on his new Christmas story, *The Wreck of the Golden Mary* which was advertised grandly in the November and December issues of *Household Words*:

'Early in December will be published, price Threepence,
or stamped Fourpence,
THE WRECK OF THE GOLDEN MARY;
Being the CAPTAIN'S ACCOUNT of the GREAT
DELIVERANCE OF HER PEOPLE IN AN OPEN
BOAT AT SEA: forming
THE CHRISTMAS NUMBER
Of HOUSEHOLD WORDS; and containing the amount
of One regular Number and a Half.'

The story caused great excitement. Dickens's stories were habitually read aloud and it had become a Christmas Day tradition for families to sit together and listen as the latest story was read out. *The Wreck of the Golden Mary* is narrated by the captain, William George Ravender. It tells the story of the ship being wrecked by an iceberg as it tries to navigate to California at the height of the Gold Rush. The story is set in 1856, but relates an accident that happened five years earlier; the stories told by the sailors and passengers, as they are bobbed around in a lifeboat, allowed Dickens, once again, to commission a stable of writers to write the Christmas story collaboratively.

The Wreck of the Golden Mary was superseded, however, by Dickens's fervour for *The Frozen Deep*. Throughout the autumn and into the Christmas season, Dickens's letters were full of stories about 'the play' and its rehearsals. Dickens's friend, the artist Clarkson Stanfield, who was a very well respected Royal Academician, had agreed to paint the scenery and backdrop, and Dickens hired a policeman whose role on Twelfth Night was to stand at the front door and check people's invitations. The evening was a triumph. A couple of years later, when reminiscing about the play, Dickens wrote to his friend Captain Cavendish Spencer Boyle:

'It would be as easy to find a Pelican in London, as a decent Stage-Carpenter while the Pantomimes are on. All the good men in that wise are so engaged, that when I brought out the Frozen Deep at Christmas time, I was obliged (though the Pantomimes were above a week old, and in good working order), to make my own stage-carpenters out of my own private materials.'

Dickens threw himself into his role of tragic hero Richard Wardour and used the experience to help formulate his ideas for *A Tale of Two Cities*, which focuses on the same theme as the play, that of two men being in love with the same woman and one of them sacrificing himself. On 19 January 1857, when the performances were over, Dickens wrote to his friend W F de Cerjat in Switzerland:

'...workmen are now battering and smashing down my Theatre here, where we have just been acting a new plat of great merit, done in what I may call (modestly speaking of the getting-up, and not the acting), an unprecedented way. I believe that any thing so complete, has never been seen. We had an act at the North Pole, where the slightest and greatest thing the eye beheld, were equally taken from the books of the Polar Voyagers ... It has been the talk of all London for these three weeks. And now it is a mere chaos of scaffolding, ladders, beams, canvass, paint pots, sawdust, artificial snow, gas pipes, and ghastliness. I have taken such pains with it for these ten weeks in all my leisure hours, that I feel, now, shipwrecked – as if I had never been without a Play on my hands, before.'

CHAPTER FIFTEEN

Empty Chairs

On Christmas-eve, grandmamma is always in excellent spirits, and after employing all the children, during the day, in stoning the plums, and all that, insists, regularly every year, on uncle George coming down into the kitchen, taking off his coat, and stirring the pudding for half an hour or so, which uncle George good-humouredly does, to the vociferous delight of the children and servants. The evening concludes with a glorious game of blind-man's-buff, in an early stage of which grandpapa takes great care to be caught, in order that he may have an opportunity of displaying his dexterity.

'On the following morning, the old couple, with as many of the children as the pew will hold, go to church in great state: leaving aunt George at home dusting decanters and filling casters, and uncle George carrying bottles into the dining-parlour, and calling for corkscrews, and getting into everybody's way.'

Charles Dickens, *Christmas Festivities* (1835)

In the summer of 1857, buoyed by the success of their Twelfth Night play and longing to perform on stage again, Dickens and Wilkie Collins reprised *The Frozen Deep* at a public theatre in London. They staged the play as a charity or 'benefit performance', starring their friends and family members, to raise money for the bereaved family of their friend, the playwright Douglas Jerrold. It proved such a success, that they decided to take the play on tour to Manchester. Because they would be performing in a very large and public theatre, they needed to hire professional actresses to perform the roles previously played by Dickens's daughters and sister-in-law. Through a theatrical friend, they were introduced to a family of actresses, Mrs Ternan and her daughters. Dickens hired the mother and two of her daughters for the tour. By the end of the summer, the 45-year-old Charles Dickens had fallen in love with the youngest actress, Ellen Ternan. She was 18 years old, the same age as his daughter Katey.

It was a miserable Christmas in the Dickens household that December. Not only were the older children aware of what was happening to their mother and father's marriage, but it was the first Christmas without Walter, who had gone to India, as a cadet in the East India Company. Charles wrote to a friend that his son 'likes the country and the life, of all things, and is quite happy', but Walter was only sixteen years old when he left his family. Catherine, who had not wanted him to go, missed him dreadfully.

Dickens was influenced by Walter's experiences to write, together with Wilkie Collins, a Christmas story entitled *The Perils of Certain English Prisoners*. The story is set in South America in 1744, but was very obviously inspired by the events of what was known at the time in England as 'the Indian Mutiny', which had taken place just a few months previously. Contemporary reviewers were divided, with the *Hampshire Advertiser* describing it as a 'thrilling and exquisite narrative' and the *Morning Chronicle* advertising the very first theatrical production based on it, while the *Daily Telegraph* reviewer was disappointed:

> 'The tale in the Christmas number of *Household Words* might as well have been published at mid-summer for any reference it has to Christmas. It looks, too, as if the author was "up" to some transatlantic "dodges" to make his story sell well … it is not as a story suited to the season to be placed by the side of the *Christmas Carol*. Will Dickens ever again give the public such another story so well adapted to the Yule log, the jollity and the humanity of Christmas?'

Around the country, the Christmas fervour was in full swing, with people trying to emulate the kind of seasonal cheer they had learnt about from the books of Charles Dickens. The London correspondent for the *Suffolk and Essex Free Press*, sent in his report of how the holiday was being celebrated in the capital:

> 'Just on the eve of Christmas, there is little said or done in London, not connected with this most festive season. Politics are disregarded

altogether. Housewives are looking to the condiments most in repute at such times; while the Lords of Creation amuse themselves with the Christmas number of the *Illustrated London News*, or Dickens's *Perils of Certain English Prisoners* ... London, left to itself for the time, makes gigantic preparations for the great event. Not to observe Christmas, is here looked upon as a sin ... In a word – Christmas, 1857, will be like all others which have passed away, a season of festivity for rich and poor. People may *say* the season is not kept as it was formerly; but these are generally old and grumbling people ...'

Ironically, in the Dickens household, the Christmas season was very subdued, and the situation was only going to get worse. Within a few months, Charles had applied for a legal separation from a very unhappy Catherine and the family had been split in half. It was the end of the Dickens family Christmases. From now on, the younger children had to celebrate Christmas without their mother and Charley Dickens, who chose to live with Catherine. At the time Charles and Catherine Dickens separated, the law was entirely favourable to men. Mothers had no legal rights over their children at all; in the eyes of the law a child was the legal property of its father. When Charley chose to live with his mother, he was only 20 years old, a year under the age of majority; legally, he could have been forced to stay in his father's house until his twenty-first birthday.

Dickens strove very hard to keep the real reason for the breakdown of his marriage a deep secret, with the result that his legions of fans believed him when he wrote unpleasant articles claiming the fault was Catherine's. He wanted people to believe Catherine was difficult and not a loving mother. He could not allow people to see that the Charles Dickens who was already being credited with 'inventing' Christmas, was not a benign Father Christmas-like figure always dispensing joy, but a man as deeply flawed as other human beings, with a very dark side to him. In December 1897, many years after her father's death, Katey wrote a long letter to her friend, George Bernard Shaw, which she ended with the postscript:

'If you could make the public understand that my father was not a joyous, jocose gentleman walking about the world with a plum pudding & a bowl of punch you would greatly oblige me.'

Trying to ignore the chaos that his extramarital love affair had created, throughout 1858 Dickens threw himself into a reinvention of his image. His taste of adulation on the stage in *The Frozen Deep* had rekindled his youthful desire to be an actor and he began a new phase in his career. In 1858, he started what would become his world-famous public reading tours. He went all over the British Isles with his public readings, and eventually to America. He started the Christmas season early, with a reading of *A Christmas Carol* in Glasgow on 8 October, determined that giving the public what they wanted would save his public image.

Now that Ellen was in his life, Dickens's interest in all things theatrical was even more heightened. He wrote to Forster in astonishment about a pantomime he had seen:

'I ... went to the Strand Theatre: having taken a stall beforehand, for it is always crammed ... to see the Maid and the Magpie burlesque there. There is the strangest thing in it that I have ever seen on the stage. The boy, Pippo, by Miss Wilton. While it is astonishingly impudent ... it is so stupendously like a boy, and unlike a woman, that it is perfectly free from offence. I have never seen such a thing ... I call her the cleverest girl I have ever seen on the stage in my time, and the most singularly original.'

In all the years that the family had lived in London, Dickens had never owned his own home. In 1856 he had finally bought a house, Gad's Hill Place in Kent, the county where he had spent his happiest times in childhood. The house is on the road between the towns of Rochester and Higham, and Dickens was very proud that Gad's Hill was mentioned in Shakespeare's Henriad trilogy. When he bought the house, he and Catherine had decided to use it as a summer home. Now his marriage was over, he decided to make it the family's main residence.

For the Dickens children, the Christmas of 1858 was a very strange time. Controversially, 'Aunty Georgy' had sided with her brother-in-law against her sister and had remained living with the family as housekeeper, assisted by Mamie. At Christmas, the children missed their mother, Charley and Walter. Christmas was made sadder still by the fact that Dickens and Georgina were being shunned by their Hogarth relatives, which meant that all the children living with him were unable to see that side of their family.

For Dickens's public, the Christmas of 1858 was enhanced by one of the most popular Christmas stories in *Household Words*, *A House to Let*. It was written by Dickens, Elizabeth Gaskell, Wilkie Collins and Adelaide Anne Procter. It is the story is of an elderly woman, named Sophonisba, who rents a house in London and becomes fascinated by the empty house across the road. The house is supposed to be derelict, but Sophonisba is sure she can detect signs of life inside it. The story is full of intrigue and mystery, until she discovers that a child has been hidden away in the house, unloved by his grandfather and robbed of his rightful inheritance. Sophonisba, who loves children and was unable to have her own, adopts the boy as her grandchild. There is little mention of Christmas in the story, but towards the end Sophibisba muses, 'That very night, as I sat thinking of the poor child, and of another poor child who is never to be thought about enough at Christmas-time, the idea came into my mind which I have lived to execute, and in the realisation of which I am the happiest of women this day.' She had decided to buy the once-sinister house and turn it into a children's hospital. This was a topical subject, as since 1852, Charles Dickens had been closely involved with the setting up of Great Ormond Street Hospital, London's first hospital for children. In 1858, the year in which *A House to Let* was published, he had raised thousands of pounds so the hospital could be expanded.

Although this story was more similar to Dickens's earlier works than his most recent Christmas stories had been, the reviews were not all complimentary, perhaps because many of the newspaper editors were aware of the true nature of his marriage breakdown. The literary review of *The Era* wrote scathingly:

'Mr. Dickens's annual literary present for 1859 ... has fewer of the faults and eccentricities of this deservedly popular writer than we have seen in any completed work of the same author for some considerable time. But though in saying it has fewer blemishes than some of its predecessors the praise is nearly a negative one, for we regret to add that the beauties, that should complete the sentence as an antithesis, are either not at all present or only in such limited number as to make the general absence more manifest. As usual of late with Mr. Dickens's Christmas tales ... Surely Christmas might suggest something more relative and congenial than such slip-shod substitute as "A House to Let" ...'

The *Marylebone Mercury* was even more blunt:

'Mr. Dickens is now at the head of eccentric literature. He endeavours after the success of *Punch* in the spirit of Thackeray, but fails at both.'

Although most of the reading public were unaware of the problems assailing the Dickens family, rumours were abounding in the worlds of literature and journalism. People took sides, with many wanting to believe that Catherine was entirely in the wrong, because they could not cope with the idea of their heroic idol falling so far. Others, however, felt sympathy for Catherine, including the poet Elizabeth Barrett-Browning, who wrote to a friend, 'What is this sad story about Dickens and his wife? Incompatibility of temper after twenty-three years of married life? What a plea! ... Poor woman! She must suffer bitterly – that is sure.' The knowledge that people were talking about his marriage and speculating over the causes of the breakdown incensed and stressed Dickens. He retreated into a furious self-righteousness, refusing to discuss it and berating anyone who breathed a word about Ellen or the true causes of his decision to separate from Catherine. It was not only Catherine whom Dickens cut out of his life. After the separation, he seems to have suffered from a mental breakdown and instigated furious rows with many of his formerly closest friends, including William Thackeray and Mark Lemon. He also fell out with his publishers, when they refused to publish the unpleasant public letter he had written, about his decision to end the marriage. In a fit of fury, considering his publishers were siding with his estranged wife, he left Bradbury and Evans and went back to Chapman and Hall. This decision also had yet more personal repercussions, because Charley was engaged to Bessie Evans, his childhood sweetheart and the daughter of the man who was now Charles Dickens's former publisher. The author did not go to his son's wedding.

'If [Dickens] had appeared twenty years later, when the new Puritanism of the industrial age had run its course, the popular enjoyments of Christmas might have become refined merely by becoming rare. Art critics might be talking about the exquisite proportions of a plum-pudding as of an Etruscan pot; and cultured persons might be hanging stockings on their bed-posts as gravely as they hung Morris curtains on their walls. But coming when he did, Dickens could appeal to a living tradition and not to a lost art. He was able to save the thing from dying, instead of trying to raise it from the dead … "A Christmas Carol" is perhaps the most genial and fanciful of all his stories. "Hard Times " is perhaps the most grim and realistic. But in both cases the moral beauty is perhaps greater than the artistic beauty; and both stand higher in any study of the man than of the writer … in both cases the author is fighting for the same cause. He is fighting an old miser named Scrooge, and a new miser named Gradgrind … Scrooge is a utilitarian and an individualist; that is, he is a miser in theory as well as in practise. He utters all the sophistries by which the age of machinery has tried to turn the virtue of charity into a vice. Indeed this is something of an understatement. Scrooge is not only as modern as Gradgrind but more modern than Gradgrind. He belongs not only to the hard times of the middle of the nineteenth century, but to the harder times of the beginning of the twentieth century; the yet harder times in which we live. Many amiable sociologists will say, as he said, "Let them die and decrease the surplus population." The improved proposal is that they should die before they are born … The answer to anyone who talks about the surplus population is to ask him whether he is the surplus population; or if he is not, how he knows he is not. That is the answer which the Spirit of Christmas gives to Scrooge; and there is more than one fine element of irony involved in it. There is this very mordant moral truth, among others; that Scrooge is exactly the sort of man who would really talk of the superfluous poor as of something dim and distant; and yet he is also exactly the kind of man whom others might regard as sufficiently dim, not to say dingy, to be himself superfluous.... We have all seen the most sedentary of scholars proving on paper that none should survive save the victors of aggressive war and the physical struggle for life; we have all heard the idle rich explaining why the idle poor deserve to be left to die of hunger. In all this the spirit of Scrooge survives...'

G.K. Chesterton in his Introduction to *A Christmas Carol* in 1922

155

DICKENS AND CHRISTMAS

In January 1859, the celebration of Twelfth Night in the Dickens household was a muted and sad celebration in comparison to those the children had enjoyed before. Charley was not with them for his birthday as he was living with Catherine, which meant that, of course, the usual Twelfth Cake for Charley's birthday did not arrive from Angela Burdett-Coutts. The philanthropist, who was known affectionately by the children as 'Miss Toots' and always considered a kind of fairy godmother, was furious with the way Catherine had been treated and a casualty of the cooling of her friendship with Charles Dickens was the charity Urania Cottage. Although Dickens and Burdett-Coutts did resume a friendship, they would never again be as close as they had been in the past and Burdett-Coutts remained a good friend to Catherine.

For the last year of the decade, trying to ignore any negative publicity and trying to keep his public happy, Dickens made sure he was kept fully occupied by his writing and his reading tours. He also set up another magazine. Because he had left Bradbury and Evans, the publication of *Household Words* came to an end and the Christmas story for 1859 was published in *All The Year Round* (published by Chapman and Hall). The title of *The Haunted House* – whose fellow authors included Wilkie Collins, Hesba Stratton, George Augustus Sala, Adelaide Anne Proctor and Elizabeth Gaskell – promised sensation and melodrama. The book is composed of eight stories, of which Dickens wrote three and the others wrote one each. *The Haunted House* was the Dickens Christmas story reviewers had been waiting for. This was what his audience wanted: a story about ghosts set at Christmas time.

The narrator, John, has been told to move temporarily to the countryside, for the sake of his health. Together with his sister Patty, he moves into a badly neglected eighteenth century manor house, which is allegedly haunted. After his servants complain of being terrorised by ghostly sounds, John and Patty decide to send away the servants, except for one man named Bottles, who is deaf. Then the siblings invite friends for the Christmas season and each is placed in a different room to see if they can withstand the ghosts:

'The understanding was established, that any one who heard unusual noises in the night, and who wished to trace them, should knock at my door; lastly, that on Twelfth Night, the last night of holy Christmas, all our individual experiences since that then present hour of our coming together in the haunted house, should be brought to light for the good of all; and that we would hold our peace on the subject till then, unless on some remarkable provocation to break silence.'

In Dickens's chapter *The Ghost in Master B's Room* the author wrote, 'Ah me; ah me! no other ghost has haunted the boys' room, my friends, since I have occupied it, than the ghost of my own childhood, the ghost of my own innocence, the ghost of my own airy belief.' Just as the ghost of Jacob Marley had shown Scrooge the ghosts from his past, the events of the 1850s had made Dickens look back at the ghosts of his childhood and how far he had come. When Ellen told him stories of her impoverished childhood and adolescence, Dickens could understand, because he had lived through the same frightening times. With the start of a new decade, Dickens had to cope with the consequences of the public ending of his marriage, his desperate desire to prevent the public from learning about Ellen and his need to keep pleasing his readers. For the last decade of his life he struggled to keep up with the never-ending clamour for yet another Christmas story.

'The burlesque ... is preceded by one of the inevitable Dickens Christmas dramas, which is about as unlike the Christmas story and as depressing as these Dickens' plays usually are. I wish dramatic authors would leave Dickens alone. It is a cruel thing to take the popular author and tear him to pieces; and this is now constantly done.'

Illustrated Times December 1870

CHAPTER SIXTEEN

'Heaven at Last, For All of Us'

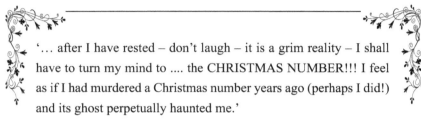

'... after I have rested – don't laugh – it is a grim reality – I shall have to turn my mind to .... the CHRISTMAS NUMBER!!! I feel as if I had murdered a Christmas number years ago (perhaps I did!) and its ghost perpetually haunted me.'

Letter from Charles Dickens to Charles Fechter, 8 March 1868

By the 1860s, the celebrating of Christmas had become a national obsession. Christmas trees could be seen in homes and public spaces all over the British Isles, Christmas cards were an expected part of the season and shops were enjoying the start of the new fashion for Christmas shopping. The invention of the Christmas cracker was also perfected in the 1860s. The idea had begun two decades earlier, when an enterprising young confectioner named Tom Smith took a trip to Paris. There, he had bought sugared almonds, or 'bonbons', wrapped up in twists of paper. He recreated the idea in London, where his customers flocked to buy them. Over the next few years, he developed his idea as a Christmas fashion, starting with the idea of putting little mottos inside the paper casing, so that when they were unwrapped, as well as finding the sugared almonds, the customer would have a surprise to read, usually something sentimental and loving. By the end of the 1840s, Smith had patented the idea and introduced a rod of stiff paper that gave a satisfying crackle when pulled apart; by the 1860s the 'crack' of the cracker had been perfected by the use of salpetre and the almonds had been replaced with little toys, or gifts for adults.

Another Christmas craze reached Britain from Germany in the 1860s, when shops began to sell glass baubles to decorate Christmas trees; people had also started to copy the German tradition of placing the figure of an angel at the top of the tree. The traditions of sending food parcels from the country had now been refined into the luxurious Christmas hampers and newspaper columns were filled with advertisements placed by businesses that sold them.

Dickens began the new decade in London, writing to Georgina in Kent, 'I don't feel quite so well today.... I went to Drury Lane again last night ... and did not get to bed until half past one!' In the summer, he sold the lease of Tavistock House to new tenants and made Gad's Hill Place his permanent home. In the coming years, he would rent houses in fashionable parts of the city for a couple of months, so his children could enjoy the 'London Season', but he was not an ideal tenant. Landlords who had been so excited to have such an eminent 'name' living in their house were shocked when he left by the damage that had been inflicted upon their home by the pack of Dickens family dogs.

The oldest Dickens children had been entering adulthood when their parents separated. At the start of the new decade, Charley Dickens travelled to Hong Kong, to learn about the tea trade; Mamie became her father's housekeeper (similarly to Esther Summerson in *Bleak House*); Katey Dickens married the Pre-Raphaelite artist Charles Allston Collins (the younger brother of Wilkie Collins); and Walter remained in India, although he managed to meet up with Charley during his travels in Asia, and prevailed upon his elder brother to pay off his debts. At the age of thirteen, Sydney Dickens left school and embarked on his chosen career, joining the Royal Navy as a cadet on the training ship HMS *Britannia*.

It had become common for Charles Dickens to spend around half of each year thinking about, planning, editing and writing the Christmas edition of *All The Year Round*. In 1860, he commissioned a short story from Elizabeth Gaskell, but decided it was too long to fit, so instead he gave the pride of place to a story written by his new son-in-law Charlie Collins. At the same time as he was producing the Christmas edition of the magazine, Dickens was working on his new novel, *Great Expectations*.

That winter, England suffered through the coldest Christmas that had been recorded for fifty years. It was so cold that Dickens's beard froze while he was out walking. He wrote:

'It was so intensely cold that in our warm dining-room on Christmas Day we could hardly sit at the table. In my study that morning, long after a great fire of coal and wood had been lighted, the thermometer was I don't know where below freezing. The bath froze, and all the pipes froze, and remained in a stony state for five or six weeks. The water in the bedroom jugs froze, and was imperfectly removed with axes. My beard froze as I walked about, and I couldn't detach my cravat and coat from it until I was thawed at the fire.'

He escaped Kent for London where he stayed in his magazine office and wrote to Georgina, 'It is certainly less cold here than at Gad's Hill, and the pipes are not frozen – which is a great comfort.' He celebrated the start of 1861 with Wilkie Collins, spending New Year's Eve watching 'Buckley's Serenaders' at St James's Hall.

'I pass my time here (I am staying here alone) in working, taking physic, and taking a Stall at a Theatre every night. On Boxing night, I was at Covent Garden. A dull pantomime was "worked" (as we say) better than I ever saw a heavy piece worked on a first night, until suddenly and without a moment's warning, every scene on that immense stage fell over on its face and disclosed Chaos by Gaslight, behind! There never was such a business – about sixty people who were on the stage, being extinguished in the most remarkable manner. Not a soul was hurt. In the uproar, some moon-calf rescued a porter pot, six feet high (out of which the clown had been drinking when the accident happened), and stood it on the cushion of the lowest Proscenium Box P.S. [prompt side] beside a lady and gentleman who were dreadfully ashamed of it. The moment the House knew that nobody was injured, they directed their whole attention to this gigantic porter pot in its genteel position (the lady and gentleman trying to hide behind it) and roared with laughter. When a modest footman came from behind the Curtain to clear it, and took it up in his arms, like a Brobdingnagian Baby, we all laughed more than we had ever laughed in our lives. I don't know why.

'We have had a fire here, but our people put it out before the Parish Engine arrived, like a drivelling Perambulator – with *the Beadle in it* – like an Imbecile Baby. Popular opinionm disappointed in the fire having been put out, Snow-balled the Beadle. God bless it!'

Charles Dickens, letter to Mary Boyle, 28 December 1860

By 3 January he was back in Kent and writing a bonhomous letter to his friend Captain E.E. Morgan:

'I am heartily obliged to you for your seasonable and welcome remembrance. It came to the office (when I was there) in the pleasantest manner, brought by two seafaring men, as if they had swum across with it. Never were such fine apples, or in such admirable preservation! And the Cigars came so opportunely, that I had just four and twenty of my Morgans – that's the name I give them – left.... I hope you will have seen the Christmas No. of All The Year Round? Here and there, in the description of the sea-going Hero [Captain Jorgan], I have given a touch or two of remembrance of Somebody you know; very heartily desiring that thousands of people may have some faint reflection of the pleasure I have for many years derived from the contemplation of a most amiable nature and most remarkable man.'

The Christmas stories were not immune to the plagiarism his Christmas books had suffered from and Dickens started 1861 by taking out an injunction to prevent an unauthorised performance of a play based on his and Wilkie Collins's story *A Message from the Sea*. He tried to counteract the plagiarism by writing a letter to the Editor of *The Times*,

'Sir,
I shall feel greatly obliged to you if you will allow me to make known to theatrical managers, through your columns, that I believe it is in the power of any English writer of fiction legally to prevent any work of his from being dramatized or adapted for the stage without his consent, and that I have taken measures for the assertion of this right in my own case, and intend to try it with whomsoever may violate it.

It happened but yesterday that I had, in conjunction with Mr Wilkie Collins, very unwillingly to assert this principle in defence of a joint production of ours against the proprietor of the Britannia Theatre. In a most frank and honest manner he immediately withdrew an announced piece on the night of its intended first representation, and when his audience were assembled. As I had no earlier opportunity of giving him notice of my intention to uphold the rights of authors, and as I inconvenienced a gentleman for whom I have a respect, with great reluctance, and should be exceedingly sorry to do the like in any other case, perhaps you will find space for this letter.

Faithfully yours
Charles Dickens' (8 January 1861)

In 1861, *The Book of Household Management* by Mrs Isabella Beeton contained what is believed to be the first recipe published in Britain for a Christmas Cake. This added an extra emphasis towards the shift to celebrate on Christmas Day instead of Twelfth Night.

'Mrs Beeton's recipe for Christmas Cake
'Ingredients – 5 teacupfuls of flour, 1 teacupful of melted butter, 1 teacupful of cream, 1 teacupful of treacle, 1 teacupful of moist sugar, 2 eggs, ½ oz. of powdered ginger, ½ lb of raisins. 1 teaspoonful of carbonate of soda, 1 tablespoonful of vinegar.
    'Mode – Make the butter sufficiently warm to melt it, but do not allow it to oil; put the flour in to a basin: add to it the sugar, ginger and raisins, which should be stoned and cut into small pieces. When these dry ingredients are thoroughly mixed, stir in the butter, cream, treacle and well-whisked eggs, and beat the mixture for a few minutes. Dissolve the soda in the vinegar, add it to the dough, and be particular that these latter ingredients are well incorporated with the others; put the cake into a buttered mould or tin, place it in a moderate oven immediately, and bake it from 1¾ to 2¼ hours.
    'Time – 1¾ to 2¼ hours. Average cost, 1s 6d.'

The Christmas cake added to an already groaning table of sweet Christmas foods, including plum pudding, which would soon become better known as Christmas pudding, and mince pies. In the past, the filling in the pies was made from minced meat, but by the nineteenth century, it was much more common for the "mincemeat" to be made of fruits, nuts, sugar and brandy. The change from savoury to sweet had begun in the eighteenth century, when sugar became much more plentiful, due to Britain's connections with the slave trade. In the first half of the nineteenth century, the pies were sometimes made from a combination of meat and fruits, although the fashion was changing. Both Eliza Acton's 1845 cookbook and Mrs Beeton's 1861 *Book of Household Management* include recipes for mince pies which contain minced meat (in Acton's recipe the pies are filled with 'minced ox-tongue'), but both describe these as 'traditional' mince pies, while seeming to recommend instead the more modern versions of mincemeat which contain only fruit, brandy, spices and sugar (although still bound together with beef suet). Eliza Acton calls her meat-free recipe her 'superlative mincemeat', and Mrs Beeton's is named 'excellent mincemeat'.

In June 1861, Dickens was already thinking about the next Christmas issue of his magazine, inviting Wilkie Collins, with whom he was co-writing regularly, to come and 'arrange our Xmas No. please God, under the shade of the Oak Trees.' A few weeks later he wrote a commissioning letter to Rev G.R. Gleig:

> It is our custom here at this time of year to invite all our contributors to write for the Extra Christmas No. … Any story would weave into the design; whether narrated in the first person, or the third; whether referring to time present, or time past; whether ghostly or otherwise. No reference to the Christmas season is in the least necessary, on the contrary, such reference is not desired.'

In the late autumn, Dickens set off on a reading tour, of over fifty events, throughout the country, a tour blighted by the very recent loss of his reading tour manager, Arthur Smith, who died in October. Mamie went to join her father in Carlisle, on his way back home from working in Edinburgh. Dickens, who always missed his dogs when travelling, asked his daughter to bring her Pomeranian, Mrs Bouncer, to the hotel, writing 'She shall be received with open arms.'

W.H. Wills worked on the magazine all through Dickens's absence, sending him proof copies of the Christmas issue to read on the road. On 13 December, Dickens wrote to him from Preston, 'The news of the Xmas No. is indeed Glorious, and nothing can look brighter or better than the prospects of the Illustrious Publication..' The following day, however, everything had to change after the country learnt about the death of Prince Albert. As the queen went into mourning, the country was expected to do so as well. Dickens wrote to his sister Letitia, 'I left Liverpool, confusedly and hastily: having postponed my readings there, because of the Prince's death.'

There was no Sydney at the Christmas table that year, as he had joined a new ship. Dickens wrote to Thomas Beard on Boxing Day:

'This is merely to return your Christmas greetings with hearty cordiality ... Sydney got appointed to the *Orlando* (a ship that every one in the service seemed to be trying for), and has sailed for Halifax. He looked very very small when he went away with a chest in which he could easily have stowed himself and a wife and family of his own proportions.'

By New Year, Dickens was back on his reading tour and away from his family once again. On 2 January, he wrote a heartfelt letter to W.H. Wills, composed while he was 'stranded' at Birmingham Station, on his way from Leamington, where he had been working, to Cheltenham, where he was going to stay with his old friend William Charles Macready:

'Firstly to reciprocate all your cordial and affectionate wishes for the New Year, and to express my earnest hope that we may go on through the years to come, as we have gone through many years that are gone. And I think we can say that we doubt whether any two men can have gone on more happily and smoothly, or with greater trust and confidence in one another ... Birmingham is in a very depressed state, with very few of its trades at work. Nevertheless we did extremely well here. At Leamington yesterday, immense. Copperfield in the morning absolutely stunned the people: and at Nickleby and the Trial at night, they roared and roared until I think they must have shaken all the air in Warwickshire.'

He continued his reading tour, now in the South coast of England, all through the remaining Christmas season. There was no chance for a Twelfth Night party with his children this year. As the 1860s continued, Dickens's Christmas work became even more pressing. His letters suggest he was working for at least six months of the year in preparation for Christmas. Ironically, the man who had encouraged his readers to celebrate in style with family and friends had turned his own Christmases into a season of hard work and not enough time with the people he loved.

On 25 August 1862, he wrote to John Forster, 'I am trying to coerce my thoughts into hammering out the Christmas number' and on 14 September he wrote to Wills, 'You will be a little surprised (and not disagreeably) to learn that I have done the opening and end of the Xmas No. (!) and that I mean soon to be at work on a pretty story for it.' Once again, Dickens had decided to spend time in Paris, writing to Thomas Beard in November:

'Mary, Georgina, and I, are here until just before Christmas Day. I am going to ask you a rather startling, staggering question. Hold up, therefore! If I were to decide to go and read in Australia, how stand your inclination and spirits for going with me? Outside term of absence, a year.'

The proposed Australian reading tour preoccupied Dickens's mind all over Christmas and well into the new year, although it was never brought to fruition.

In Paris, he continued to work solidly on the Christmas edition of *All The Year Round*, writing to his sister Letitia, on 7 November:

'I should have written to you from here sooner, but for having been constantly occupied. The Christmas No. obliges me to go over such an astonishing quantity of Proofs at this of the year (besides writing myself), that when I have done my day's work, which involves a pretty large correspondence too, I am glad to get up and go out. Moreover – this is a secret – I am again deliberating whether I will or will not go away for a whole year, and read in Australia; and there are so many reasons for and against, and I am so unwilling to go, that it causes me great uneasiness of mind in trying to do right and to decide for the best ... I came over to France before Georgina and Mary ... We have a pretty apartment here, but house rent is too awful to mention. Georgina keeps wonderfully better, and Mary is very well, and they send love. Mrs Bouncer (muzzled by the Parisian Police) is also here, and is a wonderful spectacle to behold in the streets, restrained like a raging Lion.'

Throughout December, Dickens wrote letters from Paris organising a flurry of social events for his time back in England, inviting family members to stay at Gad's Hill Place and asking friends to visit the pantomime, but although Christmas and New Year were to be spent in Kent, he was already arranging to return to Paris in January to do a charity reading at the British embassy.

On his return to Gad's Hill Place he was excited about enjoying a family Christmas. Mamie and Georgina delighted in getting the house decorated and taking out the special Christmas china, including a special brightly coloured dish for the Christmas pudding. In her memoirs, Mamie described a Christmas in the Dickens household:

'I think that our Christmas and New Year's tides at Gad's Hill were the happiest of all. Our house was always filled with guests, while a cottage in the village was reserved for the use of the bachelor members of our holiday party. My father himself, always deserted work for the week, and that was almost our greatest treat. He was the fun and life of Christmas gatherings for he loved to emphasise Christmas in every way and considered that the great festival should be fragrant with the love we should bear one another. Long walks with him were daily treats to be remembered. Games passed our evenings merrily. "Dumb Crambo" was a favourite and one in which my father's great imitative ability showed finely. I remember one evening his dumb showing of the word "frog" was so extremely laughable that even the memory of it convulsed Marcus Stone, the clever artist, when he tried to mention it.'

Many years later, Henry Fielding Dickens also recalled a game they had played at Christmas, it was a word-association game and Charles Dickens suddenly said the phrase, 'Warren's Blacking, 30, Strand.' Henry recalled, 'He gave this with an odd twinkle in his eye and a strange inflection in his voice which at once forcibly arrested my attention and left a vivid impression on my mind for some time afterwards. Why, I could not, for the life of me, understand.'

In the Christmas of 1862, Katey and her husband Charlie Collins joined the family party, and Dickens was hoping for a visit from his son Charley and his wife, the rift between them now healed, and their daughter, Mary Angela. Writing to a friend, Dickens said, 'Think of the unmitigated nonsense of an inimitable grandfather!' Despite the wording of this letter, Dickens was a very doting grandfather, although he didn't like to accept that he was old enough to be one, and refused to let the word be used. Instead he taught Mary Angela to call him 'Venerables', and joked constantly in letters that the 'relationship [is] never permitted to be hinted at'.

As the commercialisation of Christmas had grown, so too had the concept of Christmas outings. In addition to the pantomime, it was now popular for families to visit museums and other attractions on Boxing Day. On 26 December 1868, Henry Cole, by this time director of the new South Kensington museum, recorded in his diary, 'More than 20,000 came during this day, the greatest numbers ever attending on Boxing Day.'

This new fashion meant that Dickens's life was being arranged around Christmases. The season now dominated everything else in his working life.

'HEAVEN AT LAST, FOR ALL OF US'

By 30 August 1863 he was writing to John Forster:

'The Christmas number has come round again – it seems only yesterday that I did the last – but I am full of notions besides for the new twenty numbers. When I can clear the Christmas stone out of the road, I think I can dash into it on the grander journey.'

The Christmas story for 1863 was *Mrs Lirriper's Lodgings*, whose co-authors included Elizabeth Gaskell. The story was hailed as a masterpiece of Dickensian humour, with Mrs Lirriper fondly recalled as being reminiscent of the indomitable Betsy Trotwood in *David Copperfield*. The story, about the happy adoption of an orphan boy, was exactly what the public wanted to read at Christmas.

The end to the year was a very sober one. Never again would a family Christmas welcome Elizabeth Dickens and her mocked 'juvenile cap'. She died in September 1863. While the rest of the country was getting ready for Christmas with their families, the Dickens family was planning another sad goodbye, this one to Frank, who had been found a job with the Bengal Mounted Police and was preparing to travel out to India, joining Walter. Then, on Christmas Eve, the family heard the terrible news that William Thackeray had died very suddenly. After the breakdown of his marriage, Dickens had raged through an emotional, angry, guilt-ridden fury and had ended his friendship with Thackeray, accusing him of spreading rumours about Ellen Ternan. The two men had not spoken for almost five years and the rift had only recently been healed, just before Thackeray's unexpected death. Henry Cole, in whose household Christmas of 1863 was effectively cancelled, recorded in his diary on Christmas Eve that his son told him of his friend's death. 'News brought by Harry of Thackeray's death ... Went to see his daughters and to search for his will. None found.' As his daughters would soon discover, Thackeray had drafted his will, but had not signed it. Katey and Charlie Collins, close friends of the Thackeray daughters, rushed to be with them and invited them and Thackeray's grieving mother to stay in their tiny home. The artist John Everett Millais wrote to his wife Effie:

'I am sure you will be dreadfully shocked, as I was, at the death of Thackeray. I imagine, and hope truly, you will have heard of it before this reaches you. He was found dead by his servant in the morning, and of course the whole house is in a state of the utmost confusion and pain. They first sent to Charlie Collins and his wife, who went

167

immediately, and have been almost constantly there ever since. I sent this morning to know how the mother and girls were, and called myself this afternoon; and they are suffering terribly, as you might expect. He was found lying back, with his arms over his head, as though in great pain … Everyone I meet is affected by his death. Nothing else is spoken of.'

The Times journalist William Howard Russell, a friend of Thackeray's, wrote in his diary after the funeral, 'Such a scene! Such a gathering! Dickens, thin and worn...'

Another, even closer, tragedy was also in lying in wait for the Dickens family. At New Year, a house party was gathered at Gad's Hill Place, where they celebrated New Year's Eve and spent New Year's Day walking in the countryside and visiting the ruins of Rochester Castle. All the time they were enjoying themselves they had no idea that, far away in Calcutta, Walter Dickens was dying. He had been very ill and was in the military hospital waiting for a ship to take him home to his family, none of whom had seen him since he had left home aged sixteen. Walter died on New Year's Eve 1863, at the age of 22. Letters from India took weeks to arrive, so Dickens opened the news of his son's death on 7 February 1864; it had been delivered with the post for his fifty-second birthday. Angela Burdett-Coutts sent a letter of condolence and Dickens responded with a letter showing how superstitious he could be about death and funerals:

'On the last night of the old Year I was acting in charades with all the children. I had made something to carry, as the Goddess of Discord; and it came into my head as it stood against the wall while I was dressing, that it was like the dismal things carried at Funerals. I took a pair of scissors and cut away a quantity of black calico that was upon it, to remove this likeness. But while I was using it, I noticed that its shadow on the wall still had that resemblance, through the thing itself had not. And when I went to bed, it was in my bedroom, and still looked to like, that I took it to pieces before I went to sleep. All this would have been exactly same, if poor Walter had not died that night.'

Katey wrote to her friend Anny Thackeray about her brother's death, 'I don't believe he is dead – I feel as if he must be coming home. Oh I think he might have been allowed to live just to see home once more.' The family was now living in fear about what Frank's fate might be in India. No one had been able to contact him on board his ship, so he arrived in India expecting his brother to be there to greet him. He stayed in India for six more years, returning to England in 1870. He then moved to Canada, where he became an officer in the Royal Canadian Mounted Police.

The serialisation of *Our Mutual Friend* was begun in May 1864, and continued for eighteen months, but by July of 1864 Dickens was once more writing to Forster about his Christmas work:

'Although I have not been wanting in industry, I have been wanting in invention, and have fallen back with the book. Looming large before me is the Christmas work, and I can hardly hope to do it without losing a number of *Our Friend*. I have very nearly lost one already, and two would take half of my whole advance. This week I have been very unwell; am still out of sorts; and, as I know from two days' slow experience, have a very mountain to climb before I shall see the open country of my work.'

The Christmas story for 1864 was a reprise of the previous year's success, *Mrs Lirriper's Legacy*. Dickens had been thinking about the story for months, writing to W.H. Wills in June, 'It has occurred to me that Mrs Lirriper might have a mixing in it of Paris and London – she and the Major, and the boy, all working out the story in two places.' In the story, when Mrs Lirriper's adopted son, young Jemmy, returns home from school, he joins his mother and the Major on an adventure in France, searching for a mysterious benefactor. *Mrs Lirriper's Legacy* was an immediate success.

At the end of November, Dickens returned to Gad's Hill from London and was thrilled by the arrival of an early Christmas present from W.H. Wills: a new carriage. He wrote to Wills with glee:

'I found the beautiful and perfect Brougham awaiting me in triumph at the station when I came down yesterday afternoon; – Georgina and Marsh both highly mortified that it had fallen dark, and the beauties of the carriage were obscured. But of course I had it out in the yard the first thing this morning, and got in and out at both the doors, and let down and pulled up the windows, and checked an imaginary coachman, and leaned back in a state of placid contemplation. It is the lightest and prettiest and best carriage of the class, ever made. But you know that I value it for higher reasons than these. It will always be dear to me – far dearer than anything on wheels could ever be for its own sake – as a proof of your ever generous friendship and appreciation, and a memorial of a happy intercourse and a perfect confidence that have never had a break, and that surely never can have any break now (after all these years) but one.'

Another unusual Christmas present was given by a friend on Christmas Eve 1864. While welcoming guests to the usual Christmas house party at a snowy Gad's Hill Place, Dickens was alerted to a large number of parcels addressed to him that had arrived for him. It was a Swiss Chalet, in ninety-four pieces, ready to be constructed, his Christmas present from the actor Charles Fechter. The men of the house party – which included Fechter – attempted to build the chalet, together with one of Fechter's servants who was said to be an expert, although Dickens was not convinced. Dickens owned a field across the road from Gad's Hill Place and the chalet was constructed there. It became his favourite writing place in the summer. He didn't even need to cross over the public road in public to get to it, as he had commissioned a tunnel to be built under the road and was able to walk straight from his garden to the chalet. He wrote to Forster on 7 January:

'The chalet is going on excellently, though the ornamental part is more slowly put together than the substantial. It will really be a very pretty thing; and in the summer (supposing it not to be blown away in the spring), the upper room will make a charming study. It is much higher than we supposed.'

In his biography of Dickens, John Forster commented:

'Once up, it did really become a great resource in the summer months, and much of Dickens's work was done there. "I have put five mirrors in the chalet where I write," he told an American friend, "and they reflect and refract, in all kinds of ways, the leaves that are quivering at the windows, and the great fields of waving corn, and the sail-dotted river. My room is up among the branches of the trees; and the birds and the butterflies fly in and out, and the green branches shoot in at the open windows, and the lights and shadows of the clouds come and go with the rest of the company. The scent of the flowers, and indeed of everything that is growing for miles and miles, is most delicious."'

In the chalet, he composed a new Christmas character that would become one of his most popular. He wrote to Forster in the autumn of 1865:

'I do hope that in the beginning and end of this Christmas number you will find something that will strike you as being fresh, forcible, and full of spirits. Tired with *Our Mutual*, I sat down to cast about for an idea, with a depressing notion that I was, for the moment, overworked. Suddenly, the little character that you will see, and all belonging to it, came flashing up in the most cheerful manner, and I had only to look on and leisurely describe it.'

Doctor Marigold's Prescriptions is an unusual story, about a man whose wife beats their child and then, when the child dies from a fever, is so wracked with guilt she commits suicide. Marigold is also filled with guilt for not having protected his child, so when he sees a young deaf girl being beaten by her stepfather, her rescues and adopts her. Together they develop a special sign language. He re-names the girl Sophy, which was the name of his deceased daughter. When Sophy grows up and goes to a school for 'deaf and dumb' students, she falls in love with a fellow student and they marry. The story ends with Doctor Marigold discovering that their child, whom he considers his grandchild, is able to hear. It was a very unusual and quite brave subject matter for an author of that time. Discussion of disability, and having disabled heroes and heroines in books were almost unheard in Victorian Britain. Dickens had long been interested in the work being done by the pioneering doctor Prospere Ménière in Paris. In 1855, when he lived in Paris, Dickens visited the city's Deaf and Dumb Institution, and when for some unknown reason Walter Dickens, at the age of 14, went temporarily deaf, he was treated for three months at the institution by Ménière himself.

The new Christmas story was advertised in *All The Year Round* in November 1865:

'On the 7th of December will be published THE EXTRA
CHRISTMAS DOUBLE NUMBER, entitled
DOCTOR MARIGOLD'S
PRESCRIPTIONS.
I. TO BE TAKEN IMMEDIATELY.
II. NOT TO BE TAKEN AT BED-TIME.
III. TO BE TAKEN AT THE DINNER-TABLE.
IV. NOT TO BE TAKEN FOR GRANTED.

V. TO BE TAKEN IN WATER.
VI. TO BE TAKEN WITH A GRAIN OF SALT.
VII. TO BE TAKEN AND TRIED.
VIII. TO BE TAKEN FOR LIFE.
Price Fourpence, stitched in a cover.'

It was an immediate success; according to Dickens's letters it sold over 200,000 copies within a few weeks of publication. On New Year's Eve he wrote to his friend Edward Bulwer Lytton, 'I received your letter in praise of Dr. Marigold, and read and re-read all your generous words, fifty times over, and with inexpressible delight. I cannot tell you how they gratified and affected me.'

The success of his new story was much-needed, as Dickens had experienced a very harrowing accident. On 9 June, he had been returning from France with Ellen Ternan and her mother. They travelled by boat from Boulogne to Folkestone, where they caught the train – and were lucky not to have been killed. The Staplehurst Crash, as it became known, was reported in the *Kentish Gazette* on Tuesday 13 June 1865:

'DREADFUL RAILWAY ACCIDENT AT STAPLEHURST
TEN PERSONS KILLED – UPWARDS OF TWENTY WOUNDED
'The fast tidal train ... started as usual, with about 110 passengers, and proceeded nearly 30 miles on its journey, when, at Staplehurst, the accident occurred ... the railway crosses a stream which in winter is of formidable dimensions and of considerable depth, but in summer shrinks to the proportions of a rivulet. On the bridge itself a plate had been loosened by the platelayers, and the engine running over this was thrown off the rails. Though displaced from its proper track the locomotive adhered to the permanent way, but the train broke into two parts, and seven or eight of the carriages plunged into the stream, a fall of several feet. These vehicles were so crushed and shattered to pieces that together they did not occupy the space of two whole carriages ... of the occupants several were killed and many injured.... Mr Charles Dickens had a narrow escape. He was in the train, but, fortunately for himself and for the interests of literature, received no injuries whatever.'

As Dickens explained to a friend, in a very shaky version of his handwriting:

'I was in the only carriage which did not go over into the stream. It was caught upon the turn by some of the ruin of the bridge, and became suspended and balanced in an apparently impossible manner … I got out without the least notion of what had happened. Fortunately I got out with great caution, and stood upon the step. Looking down I saw the bridge gone, and nothing below me but the line of rail. Some people in the other two compartments were madly trying to plunge out at a window, and had no idea that there was an open, swampy field fifteen feet down below them, and nothing else. The two guards (one with his face cut) were running up and down on the down-track of the bridge (which was not torn up) quite wildly. I called out to them: "Look at me! Do stop an instant and look at me, and tell me whether you don't know me?" One of them answered: "We know you very well, Mr. Dickens." "Then," I said, "my good fellow, for God's sake, give me your key, and send one of those laborers here, and I'll empty this carriage." We did it quite safely, by means of a plank or two, and when it was done I saw all the rest of the train, except the two baggage vans, down the stream. I got into the carriage again for my brandy flask, took off my travelling hat for a basin, climbed down the brickwork, and filled my hat with water. Suddenly I came upon a staggering man, covered with blood (I think he must have been flung clean out of his carriage), with such a frightful cut across the skull that I couldn't bear to look at him. I poured some water over his face, and gave him some to drink, then gave him some brandy, and laid him down on the grass.'

The Staplehurst Crash affected Dickens's health for the rest of his life and the emotional scars affected his ability to enjoy travelling and performing on his reading tours.

Another new publication in the Christmas of 1865 was a private one, seen only by family and friends. The Dickens children had followed their father's example and begun a magazine, *The Gad's Hill Gazette*. On 30 December 1865, the magazine included its report of 'Christmas at Gad's Hill':

'During the past week, Gad's Hill has resounded with the sounds of festivity and merriment. As is usually the case, the house has been filled with the guests who have come to taste of Mr Dickens' hospitality. These consisted of Mr, Mad, and Master Fechter, Mr & Mrs Collins, Mr, Mrs and Master C. Dickens junr, Mr Morgan (who suddenly appeared on Christmas Day, having just returned from America) Mr M. Stone, Mr Chorley and Mr Dickenson.

'The latter gentleman has not yet entirely recovered from the effects of a most disastrous railway accident in which he was a sufferer, and had it not been for the courage and intrepidity of Mr Dickens, he would not now be spending his Christmas at Gad's Hill. A short time before the accident occurred, Mr Dickenson had a dispute with a French gentleman about the opening of the window when the former offered to change places, if the open window was disagreeable to his fellow traveller – this they did. –

'Then came the accident, accompanied by all its frightful incidents. The French gentleman was killed, Mr Dickenson was stunned and hurled with great violence under the debris of a carriage.

'Mr Dickens, who was in another compartment, managed to crawl out of the window and then, caring little for his own safety, busied himself in helping the wounded. Whilst engaged in doing this, he passed a carriage, underneath which he saw a gentleman (Mr Dickenson) lying perfectly still, and bleeding from the ears, eyes, nose and mouth.

'He was immediately taken to the town of Staplehurst where he so far recovered as to be able to return to London, that evening.

'Next morning he was suffering from a very severe concussion of the brain and was ill for many weeks – But to our subject.

'On Christmas Day, Mr, Mrs & Miss Malleson came to dinner. At about 9, and ex tempore dance began and was kept up till about 2 o'clock Tuesday morning. During the week, billiards has been much resorted to. (See next page)

All the visitors are still here, except Mr Fechter and family who left on December 26th, and Mr Morgan (who is to return on the 31st. Talking of Mr Fechter, our readers will be glad to hear that he has made a most decided success in his new piece entitled – The Master of Ravenswood...'

A week later, the *Gad's Hill Gazette* reported on the New Year celebrations:

New Year's Eve was celebrated at Gad's Hill, as usual, but it being Sunday, the entertainment was confined to amusements of a simpler description, such as the games called Buzz, Crambo, Spanish Merchant, & c. As the clock struck twelve, the usual formula was gone through, and Mr. John Thompson favoured the company with the chimes on the gong. At one o'clock the company separated for the night, in a good humour with themselves and with everybody.'

The following year, Dickens collaborated with a group of writers, including Hesba Stratton, and his son-in-law Charlie Collins, to produce a series of short stories known as *Mugby Junction*, published in the Christmas edition of *All The Year Round*. The most famous short story from *Mugby Junction*, is a ghost story, *The Signalman*, about a man haunted by a ghost, which appears to prophesy tragedies on the railway.

Mugby Junction was to prove a great success, but the writing of it was not easy. On 1 October 1866, Dickens wrote to W.H. Wills 'I am still unapproachable on the general subject of Xmas Nos. myself – am lame – ferocious – and dangerous.' Three days later he wrote to Wilkie Collins, 'This is a pretty state of things! – That I should be in Christmas Labour, while you are cruising about the world'. In the middle of October, he wrote to his American publisher James T. Fields, 'Although I perpetually see in the papers that I am coming out with a new Serial, I assure you I know no more of it at present. I am *not* writing (except for Christmas No. of All The Year Round), and am going to begin, in the middle of January, a series of 42 Readings. Those will probably occupy me until Easter.'

Dickens was also preoccupied with news he had heard from America. A few years earlier his youngest brother, Augustus, had run away to America with his pregnant mistress, abandoning his wife in London. Dickens immediately took on the financial responsibility for his sister-in-law, Harriett. Over the years, the family had heard little from or about Augustus, except on such occasions as when a stranger contacted Charles Dickens to ask him to repay his brother's debts. Then, in the winter of 1866, the news reached Dickens in a rather roundabout way that his youngest sibling had died. Dickens wrote to W.H. Wills, 'That news of Augustus, I think may be taken as true. It was very thoughtful of you – and like you – to send it. Poor fellow! A sad business altogether! My mind misgives me that it will bring a host of disagreeables from America.' Discovering that Augustus's lover Bertha Phillips had been left alone with three young children, Dickens sent her money, but this led to him worrying that Harriett would be offended.

The news of his estranged brother's death arrived at his busiest time of year and in this particular year, Dickens felt he had taken on too much. A letter to Mrs Cowden Clarke begins:

'This is written in the greatest haste and distraction, by reason of my being in the height of the business of the Xmas No. And as I have this year written half of it myself, the always difficult work of selecting from an immense heap of contributions is rendered twice as difficult as usual, by the contracted space available.'

His hard work was rewarded when *Mugby Junction* proved even more popular than *Doctor Marigold's Prescriptions*. On 13 December, Dickens wrote to his sister Letitia, 'The Xmas No to day is at the astonishing number of *40,000 ahead* of even Doctor Marigold at the same date.'

After all the stress, Dickens was planning to spend the full twelve days of Christmas at Gad's Hill Place and to host a special public sporting event on Boxing Day, in the field opposite his house. He wrote to Macready that *Mugby Junction* had now sold a quarter of a million copies and described the success of the sports day:

'You will be interested in knowing, that, encouraged by the success of Summer Cricket Matches, I got up a quantity of footraces and rustic sports in my field here on the 26th. Last past. As I have never yet had a case of drunkenness, the landlord of the Falstaff had a drinking booth on the ground. All the Prizes I gave were in money too. We had two thousand people here. Among the crowd were soldiers, navvies, and labourers of all kinds. Not a stake was pulled up, or a rope slackened, or one farthing's worth of damage done. To every competitor (only) a printed bill of general rules was given, with the concluding words: 'Mrs Dickens puts every man upon his honor [sic] to assist in preserving order'. There was not a dispute all day, and they went away at sunset rending the air with cheers, and leaving every flag on a 600 yards course, as neat as they found it when the gates were opened at 10 in the morning. Surely this is a bright sign in the neighbourhood of such a place as Chatham!'

Mamie estimated that there were between two and three thousand people on the field 'and by a kind of magical influence, my father seemed to rule every creature present to do his or her best to maintain order. The likelihood of things going wrong was anticipated, and despite the general prejudice of the neighbours against the undertaking, my father's belief and trust in his guests was not disappointed.' On New Year's Day Dickens wrote about it to John Forster:

'The great mass of the crowd were labouring men of all kinds, soldiers, sailors, and navvies ... The road between this and Chatham was like a Fair all day; and surely it is a fine thing to get such perfect behaviour out of a reckless seaport town. Among other oddities we had A Hurdle Race for Strangers. One man (he came in second) ran 120 yards and leaped over ten hurdles in twenty seconds, *with a pipe in his mouth, and smoking all the time.* "If it hadn't been for your pipe," I said to him at the winning-post, "you would have been the first". "I beg your pardon, sir," he answered, "but if it hadn't been for my pipe, I should have been nowhere."'

Despite Dickens's comments that he wanted to repeat the sports day the following year, he turned out to have very different plans for the winter of 1867. For months he vacillated over the idea of making a return trip to America, twenty-five years after he and Catherine had visited together, twenty-five years after his controversial publication of *American Notes*, and after the country had come through a civil war. He could not make up his mind whether or not to go, but just in case, he started work on the Christmas edition of *All The Year Round* in the summer. At the end of August, he wrote to his reading tour manager George Dolby, 'We have a Cricket Match here to day, and I am going to score ... I must go up to the office tomorrow to hold Xmas consultation with Wilkie.'

In September 1867, strange newspaper reports started to circulate claiming Dickens was suffering from failing health. His American publisher, James Fields, was worried, and Dickens wrote to reassure him, 'Charles Reade and Wilkie Collins are here; and the joke of the time is to feel my pulse when I appear at table...' The reports became so widespread, that Dickens felt compelled to write to *The Times* to explain he was quite well. He was still agonising over whether or not to go to America; one day he would send a letter saying he was going, then the next he would write that he had decided against it absolutely. Finally, on 30 September, he wrote to Georgina, 'I have made up my mind to see it out ... I am so nervous with travelling and anxiety to decide sensibly, that I can hardly write.' To his son Henry, at boarding school, he detailed his plans: 'I sail for America, from Liverpool, on Saturday the 9th of November. My Cunard Ship is the *Cuba*, and I have one of the officers' cabins on deck. I hope to return by the First Cunard ship in May. It will be a very fatiguing business....'

He promised James Fields that he would bring with him an early proof of the new Christmas issue of *All The Year Round*:

'I will bring you out the early proof of the Xmas No. We publish it here on the 12th of December. I am planning it out into a play for Wilkie Collins to manipulate after I sail, and have arranged for Fechter to go to the Adelphi Theatre and play a Swiss in it. It will be brought out, the day after Christmas Day.'

The Christmas story for 1867 was *No Thoroughfare*, a novella written jointly with Wilkie Collins. The story harked back to one of his earliest inspirations, the Foundling Hospital in London, which had inspired him while writing *Oliver Twist*. The story centres on two foundling children who are given the same name, Walter Wilding, and the confusion that results from the mother of the first Walter Wilding adopting the second child by mistake and leaving him a large inheritance. The story was adventurous and melodramatic, and very popular, but Dickens was concerned about the stage version and wrote to Wilkie from America that he was worried it would not be a success – he was wrong. It was performed at the Adelphi Theatre with Charles Fechter in one of the starring roles and was a great success. Dickens carefully stage-managed what should happen with the publication of *Household Words* in his five-months absence; amongst the instructions he gave to Wills was that no stories about America were to be published in the magazine while he was over there. The new, post-civil-war America seemed, finally, to have forgiven him for *American Notes* and Dickens was very wary of allowing any further controversy.

On 19 November, the *Cuba* landed in Boston. Charles Dickens and George Dolby had a full schedule ahead of them, and for Dickens this was to be an exhausting and quite depressing time. He had a couple of weeks until his first reading, on 2 December, which was intended to give him time to recover from the rigours of the journey and to prepare his performances, but the enforced idleness made him irritable and exacerbated his homesickness, a feeling that engulfed him throughout this second American trip. Americans were overjoyed to have the man who had 'invented' Christmas spend the festive season in their country and they worked very hard to make him feel welcome and adored; but for Dickens it was the most miserable Christmas of his adult life. He had been unable to take Ellen with him, having been persuaded by friends and colleagues that no one would believe she was just a family friend, and he missed her and his children. He also found the cold weather of an East Coast winter far more difficult to cope with than he had expected. His publisher James T. Fields and his wife Annie had befriended Dickens some years earlier and he had been invited to spend Thanksgiving at the home of Annie's sister, Mrs James Beal. When the day arrived, however, Dickens wrote to apologise that he was unable to make the party due to a sudden 'melancholy' that washed over him. He was unable, he said, to leave the fireside in his hotel bedroom. He needed solitude. This breaking of an engagement, especially on the day of the party itself, shows just how depressed Dickens was, as to do so was very out of character. In his memoir, *Dickens As I Knew Him*, George Dolby wrote, 'He held it as a maxim that "No man had a right to break an engagement with the public if he were able to be out of bed."'

On 1 December 1867 Dickens wrote to Mamie, from his hotel, the Parker House in Boston, about how exhausted he was:

'A horrible custom obtains in these parts of asking you to dinner somewhere at halfpast two, and to supper somewhere else about eight. I have run this gauntlet more than once, and its effect is that there is no day for any useful purpose, and that the length of the evening is multiplied by a hundred … The weather has been rather muggy and languid until yesterday, when there was the coldest wind blowing that I ever felt. In the night it froze very hard and to-day the sky is beautiful.'

His readings began the following day, at the Tremont Temple, in the middle of a snowstorm. The *New York Tribune* wrote of the 'line of carriages' thronging the streets as over two thousand ticket holders swarmed towards the venue, 'the gay, struggling, swarming multitude that was trying to get inside the doors, watched by the long-faced silent multitude that crowded round the doorways without tickets'.

Dickens was on a high when he continued writing Mamie's letter the day after his reading:

'Most magnificent reception last night, and most signal and complete success. Nothing could be more triumphant. The people will hear of nothing else and talk of nothing else.'

Two weeks later he wrote to Georgina, from New York:

'The excitement of the readings continues unabated, the tickets for readings are sold as soon as they are ready, and the public pay treble prices to the speculators who buy them up. They are a wonderfully fine audience … Dolby continues to be the most unpopular man in

America (mainly because he can't get four thousand people into a room that holds two thousand), and is reviled in print daily.'

In his book, *Charles Dickens As I Knew Him*, published in 1885, Dolby wrote a description of the start of the American reading tour:

'The Readings selected were, the "Christmas Carol" and the "Trial from Pickwick". The audience was of the most brilliant description, being composed of all the notables in Boston, literary and artistic, added to which New York had supplied its contingent from the same sources, and had further sent to Boston a staff of newspaper men to report, by telegraph, columns of description of the first Reading, so that, on Tuesday, December 3rd, not only had all the Boston papers a full account, but so had also the New York papers – a compliment that was highly appreciated by Mr Dickens … When everything was quiet, and the deafening cheers which had greeted his appearance had subsided, a terrible silence prevailed, and it seemed a relief to his hearers when he at last commenced the Reading. The effect of the first few words (without any prefatory remark): "A Christmas Carol in four staves. Stave one, Marley's Ghost" ... placed the reader and his audience on good terms with one another, the audience settling itself down in rapt attention for what was to follow; and by the time the first chapter was finished the success of the Readings, certainly as far as Boston was concerned, was an accomplished fact ... in all my experiences with him, I never knew him to read the description of the Cratchit's Christmas dinner with so much evident enjoyment to himself, and with so much relish to his audience. When at last the Reading of "The Carol" was finished, and the final words had been delivered, and "so, as Tiny Tim observed, God bless us every one," a dead silence seemed to prevail – a sort of public sigh as it were – only to be broken by cheers and calls, the most enthusiastic and uproarious, causing Mr Dickens to break through his rule, and again presenting himself before his audience, to bow his acknowledgments.'

Although it seems not every audience member was entranced. Dolby wrote about one very disappointed Dickens fan:

'During the progress of this Reading ['The Trial of Pickwick'], I was engaged in conversation with one of my staff as the foot of the stairs leading into the hall, when my attention was drawn to a gentleman coming down the stairs in a most excited state. Imagining him to be ill and wanting assistance, I said, "What's the matter with you?" From the accent of his reply, I concluded that he was a "reg'lar down Easter."

"Say, who's that man on the platform reading?"

"Mr Charles Dickens," I replied.

"But that aint the real Charles Dickens, the man as wrote all them books I've been reading all these years."

"The same."

After a moment's pause, as if for thought, he replied, "Wall [sic], all I've got to say about it then is, that he knows no more about Sam Weller 'n a cow does of pleatin' a shirt, at all events that ain't my idea of Sam Weller, anyhow."

After the delivery of this speech he clapped his hat upon his head, and left the building in a state of high dudgeon.'

Both he and Dickens were astounded by the number of fabricated stories printed in American newspapers, such as an alleged account of Dolby getting into a fight with 'an Irishman' and spending the night in a police cell. As Dickens wrote to Georgina, 'As a general rule, you may lay it down that whatever you see about me in the papers is not true.' In a buoyant mood, Dickens wrote to W.H. Wills from the Westminster Hotel in New York:

'No news, except that this house was on fire last Sunday night (a matter scarcely worth mentioning in New York), and that we turned out and packed up. But the fire was happily got under. The meeting of all the inmates, in the most extraordinary dresses, and with their most precious possessions under their arms or imperfectly crammed into their pockets, was very ridiculous. Everybody talked to everybody else, and it was on the whole convivial. Everything unchanged. Everybody sleighing. Everybody coming to the Readings. There were at least ten thousand sleighs in the Park last Sunday. Your illustrious chief – in a red sleigh covered with furs, and drawn by a pair of fine horses covered with bells, and tearing up 14 miles of snow an hour – made an imposing appearance.'

It was not, however, all as happy and carefree as he was making it sound. On 22 December, he wrote to Forster about the journey from New York back to

Boston, 'The railways are truly alarming. Much worse (because more worn I suppose) than when I was here before. We were beaten about yesterday, as if we had been aboard the Cuba.' Still trying to cope with the emotional trauma of the Staplehurst Crash, Dickens was finding the need to travel around America by train very stressful. He was also dreading spending Christmas away from his family and the closer it got to Christmas Day, the more miserable he became, all of which was exacerbated by him catching a bad cold and feeling wretched. He was also infuriated to discover how many stage versions of his works were being performed in America, for which he was receiving no royalties. He wrote to Wilkie Collins, 'They are doing Crickets, Oliver Twists, and all sorts of versions of me. Under these circumstances, they fence when they have to pay.'

When Dickens and Dolby reached Boston just before Christmas, however, there was a wonderful surprise waiting for them, as he told Georgy in a letter on 22 December:

'We found that Mrs. Fields had not only garnished the rooms with flowers, but also with holly (with real red berries) and festoons of moss dependent from looking-glasses and picture frames. She is one of the dearest little women in the world. The homely Christmas look of the place quite affected us. Yesterday we dined at her house, and there was a plum pudding, brought on blazing, and not to be surpassed in any house in England. There is a certain Captain Dolliver, belonging to the Boston Custom House, who came off in the little steamer that brought me ashore from the Cuba. He took it into his head that he would have a piece of English mistletoe brought out in this week's Cunard, which should be laid upon my breakfast-table. And there it was this morning. In such affectionate touches as this, these New England people are especially amiable ... I must leave-off, as I am going out for a walk in a bright sunlight and a complete break-up of the frost and snow. I am much better than I have been during the last week, but have a cold.'

Dickens's friendship with James and Annie Fields had already lasted for several years, but this trip to America made the friendship even closer. They cherished him and took care of him in a way that Dickens, always expected to take care of everyone else, needed very much. At the end of March, he wrote to Mamie that they were 'the most devoted friends, and never in the way and never out of it.'

'HEAVEN AT LAST, FOR ALL OF US'

Knowing that Dickens and Dolby would be spending Christmas Day on a train, James and Annie Fields arranged a special early Christmas dinner. As Dolby remembered:

'A most brilliant company had been invited to do honour to the occasion, and all the well-known features of an English Christmas dinner-table, in the shape of roast beef and turkey, were placed before us, even to the plum pudding, made in England, and sent over specially for this entertainment. All feeling of depression at being away from home at such a time was dissipated by the geniality of our host and hostess, and the guests invited to meet Mr Dickens; and there was universal regret when the hands of the clock pointed to the small hours in the morning, suggesting most painfully that the time for breaking up had arrived.'

On Christmas Eve Dickens wrote to W.H. Wills from Boston, 'Many many merry Christmases and Happy New Years to you and yours, and to all of us! *We* spend our Christmas Day this year on the Railway between this place and New York …My New York landlord makes me a drink melodiously called "a Rocky Mountain Sneezer".' The drink was composed of brandy, rum, and snow. Dolby recalled their Christmas Eve as being one of homesickness and introspection:

'It must be confessed that at our late dinner that evening we were less conversational and more thoughtful than the depressing effects produced by the Chief's influenza had made us for some days past. After dinner we sat round the fire and talked of nothing but home and the dear ones there, until the early hours in the morning, when we went to bed thoroughly worn out.'

On the morning of 25 December, a group of Dickens's friends, including James and Annie Fields, Henry Wadsworth Longfellow and Oliver Wendell Holmes, came to the train station in Boston to say goodbye and to wish Dickens and Dolby good luck on their journey. Dickens was already feeling so low that he found it very difficult not to cry and, as Dolby wrote, the kindly wishes ended in a perfect break-down of heart and speech to him who had done so much to keep Christmas green in the hearts of Englishmen'. Dickens was morose and silent on the train journey, very unlike the man who was being toasted all over the world as the father of the Christmas story. His readers would barely have recognised him as the man who had created the Cratchits and the Fezziwigs. During their journey, the train passengers had to cross a river by steam ferry, which must have reminded Dickens of the river at Staplehurst, into which his and Ellen's train had crashed. The steam ferry went past an American battleship whose captain had been told Charles Dickens would be on board the ferry. The captain had ordered the band to play *God Save the Queen* and for his men to raise the British flag and swags of holly as the ferry went past – but Dickens remained gracelessly unmoved by the honour, and Dolby recorded, 'Our fellow passengers knew the meaning of this tasteful tribute and set up a ringing cheer with "three times three and a little one thrown in" which had the effect of rather increasing the depression from which we were both suffering.'

Dickens was courted by theatre managers in New York, but he was reluctant to visit them, having declared himself unimpressed by the standard of acting in America – and allegedly shocked by how short the dancers' skirts were. They were surprised by how important New Year's Day was considered in New York, with everybody 'either paying calls or receiving visitors (as in Paris)', and at the level of drunkenness, as according to Dolby 'even the teetotallers' drank bourbon in New York on New Year's Day.

In advance of his visit, Dickens had written a series of short stories in a new style, but they were not for publication in *All The Year Round*. Instead they were written specially for the American children's magazine *Our Young Folks*. Although Dickens had written stories narrated by children before, such as Pip in *Great Expectations* and *David Copperfield*, they were stories intended to be read by adults. These four new stories, known collectively as *A Holiday Romance*, were written from the viewpoint of children and written for children. The first story purports to come 'from the pen of William Tinkling Esq (aged eight)' and begins with the words, 'This beginning-part is not made out of anybody's head, you know. It's real. You must believe this beginning-part more than what comes after, else you won't understand how what comes after came to be written. You must believe it all; but you must believe this most, please.' Two of the other child narrators are named as 'Lieut-Col. Robin Redforth (aged nine)' and 'Miss Nettie Ashford (aged half-past six)', but the most famous of the stories in *A Holiday Romance* is the second story, known as *The Magic Fishbone*, allegedly 'from the pen of Miss Alice Rainbird (aged seven)'. These stories were written in a similar style to that which Dickens used in a book he wrote for his own children, *The Life of Our Lord* which was kept firmly guarded in the Dickens family home and not allowed to be seen by anyone outside the family and not published until

1934, after all of that generation had died. The stories in *A Holiday Romance* were intended both to be read aloud and for children to read for themselves.

The Magic Fishbone has become an enduring fairytale. It tells the story of a king and queen and their nineteen children; the heroine of the story is the intelligent and practical eldest child, Princess Alicia. 'The king was, in his private profession, under government. The queen's father had been a medical man out of town. They had nineteen children, and were always having more. Seventeen of these children took care of the baby; and Alicia, the eldest, took care of them all.' The story begins with King Watkins The First in a melancholy mood because 'quarter-day was such a long way off, and several of the dear children were growing out of their clothes'. Quarter-day was the day when the rent and other bills were due and the king – in the manner of John Dickens – could never afford to pay the rent. On the way to his office he meets a mysterious old woman, the Fairy Grandmarina, who tells him that after the family have eaten their salmon for dinner, he will notice that Princess Alicia 'will leave a fish-bone on her plate. Tell her to dry it, and to rub it, and to polish it till it shines like mother-of-pearl, and to take care of it as a present from me.' This becomes the magic fishbone of the title, a talisman that the princess can use to get the family out of any bad situation. Princess Alicia understands much more than her father, and she confides in her best friend, a doll named The Duchess, who is all-knowing and wise. The king cannot understand why Alicia doesn't use the magic powers immediately, and he becomes frustrated at how many times Alicia ignores the magic present, instead using her own common sense and practical skills to sort out problems. The story is written in the style of a pantomime and ends, of course, happily:

> 'The Princess Alicia saw King Watkins the First, her father, standing in the doorway looking on, and he said, "What have you been doing, Alicia?"
> "Cooking and contriving, papa."
> "What else have you been doing, Alicia?"
> "Keeping the children light-hearted, papa."
> "Where is the magic fish-bone, Alicia?"
> "In my pocket, papa."
> "I thought you had lost it?"
> "O, no, papa!"
> "Or forgotten it?"
> "No, indeed, papa."
> The king then sighed so heavily, and seemed so low-spirited, and

sat down so miserably, leaning his head upon his hand, and his elbow upon the kitchen-table pushed away in the corner, that the seventeen princes and princesses crept softly out of the kitchen, and left him alone with the Princess Alicia and the angelic baby.

"What is the matter, papa?"

"I am dreadfully poor, my child."

"Have you no money at all, papa?"

"None, my child."

"Is there no way of getting any, papa?"

"No way," said the king. "I have tried very hard, and I have tried all ways."

When she heard those last words, the Princess Alicia began to put her hand into the pocket where she kept the magic fish-bone.

"Papa," said she, "when we have tried very hard, and tried all ways, we must have done our very, very best?"

"No doubt, Alicia."

"When we have done our very, very best, papa, and that is not enough, then I think the right time must have come for asking help of others." This was the very secret connected with the magic fish-bone, which she had found out for herself from the good Fairy Grandmarina's words, and which she had so often whispered to her beautiful and fashionable friend, the duchess.

'So she took out of her pocket the magic fish-bone, that had been dried and rubbed and polished till it shone like mother-of-pearl; and she gave it one little kiss, and wished it was quarter-day. And immediately it WAS quarter-day; and the king's quarter's salary came rattling down the chimney, and bounced into the middle of the floor.

'But this was not half of what happened, – no, not a quarter; for immediately afterwards the good Fairy Grandmarina came riding in, in a carriage and four (peacocks), with Mr. Pickles's boy up behind, dressed in silver and gold, with a cocked-hat, powdered-hair, pink silk stockings, a jewelled cane, and a nosegay. Down jumped Mr. Pickles's boy, with his cocked-hat in his hand, and wonderfully polite (being entirely changed by enchantment), and handed Grandmarina out; and there she stood, in her rich shot-silk smelling of dried lavender, fanning herself with a sparkling fan....'

Alicia marries Prince Certainpersonio, with the duchess as her bridesmaid, and the Fairy Grandmarina announces that 'in future there would be eight quarter-days in every year, except in leap-year, when there would be ten'. She also adds that Princess Alicia and Prince Certainpersonio will have more daughters than sons, that all their hair will 'curl naturally' and 'They will never have the measles, and will have recovered from the whooping-cough before being born.'

It is easy to see how much of Dickens's own life was encapsulated in *The Magic Fishbone*: a childhood longing for his father's financial worries to be at an end, a fairy godmother to make all things right, and the way in which Dickens doted on his daughters more than on his sons. He was a very good father, highly unusual for his era in refusing to allow his children to receive any physical punishment, and in allowing his children to reason with him if they wanted something, but he was always much more indulgent towards his daughters than he was to his sons. That Christmas, his writing and his reading performances were providing seasonal cheer for thousands of Americans, who queued for hours to buy tickets to see him and queued at newspaper stands to buy *A Holiday Romance*, but the author was pining for his family and his lover in England.

He wrote to Mamie, with evident homesickness, asking her to tell him everything about how Christmas had been at Gad's Hill Place, and saying how grateful he had been to receive a letter from Georgina:

'I got your aunt's last letter at Boston yesterday, Christmas Day morning, when I was starting at eleven o'clock to come back to this place. I wanted it very much, for I had a frightful cold (English colds are nothing to those of this country), and was exceedingly depressed and miserable. Not that I had any reason but illness for being so, since the Bostonians had been quite astounding in their demonstrations. I never saw anything like them on Christmas Eve. But it is a bad country to be unwell and travelling in; you are one of say a hundred people in a heated car, with a great stove in it, and all the little windows closed, and the hurrying and banging about are indescribable. The atmosphere is detestable and the motion often all but intolerable. However, we got our dinner here at eight o'clock, and plucked up a little, and I made some hot gin punch to drink a merry Christmas to all at home in. But it must be confessed that we were both very dull. I have been in bed all day until two o'clock, and here I am now (at three o'clock) a little better. But I am not fit to read, and I must read to-night.'

He managed to perform the reading, but a doctor was called to attend to him. To his friend Mrs Charles Eliot Norton, he wrote, 'Your kind note and pretty mark of remembrance brightened a very dull Christmas Day on the Railroad, and did me quite as much good as the Doctor.'

By the new year, Dickens had started to feel happier. He was thrilled that his readings of 'Doctor Marigold' had 'made really a tremendous hit', as had his readings from *Nicholas Nickleby* and 'Boots at the Holly Tree Inn'. The most popular reading, of course, was always *A Christmas Carol*. There is a well-known, although possibly apocryphal, story about a Scrooge-like conversion that happened after one of Dickens's readings. It was reported that a wealthy factory owner from Chicago had travelled specially to Boston to hear Dickens speak and was so affected by the reading of *A Christmas Carol*, that he realised he was far too much like Ebenezer Scrooge and needed to change the way he worked. According to the story, he returned to Chicago and promised his workers that they would always have Christmas Day as a holiday and gave a turkey to every family that worked for him. Whether or not the story is true, it has become part of Dickensian folklore and emphasises the way in which Charles Dickens was identified so strongly with the spirit of Christmas.

This tour was not only about spreading Christmas cheer, it was a gruelling five-month trip, that lasted until April 1868, and its main purpose was to make money. It did so abundantly and both Dickens and Dolby felt that the author had gone some way towards recouping some of the fortune that a lack of international copyright law had deemed would benefit publishing houses, but not the man who wrote the novels that sold so well all over the United States of America. Dickens wrote to Forster:

'... our last New York night bringing £500 English into the house, after making more than the necessary deduction for the present price of gold! The manager is always going about with an immense bundle that looks like a sofa-cushion, but is in reality paper-money, and it had risen to the proportions of a sofa on the morning he left for Philadelphia.'

Despite the adulation he was receiving and the money he was making, Dickens was perpetually homesick. He wrote to Wilkie Collins in January, 'I ... am always counting the days that lie between me and home' and on the same day to Georgina Hogarth he complained about the frequency with which he and his party had suffered from food poisoning and:

'... severity of the weather, and the heat of the intolerable furnaces, [they] dry the hair and break the nails of strangers... There is not a complete nail in the whole British suite, and my hair cracks again when I brush it. (I am losing my hair with great rapidity, and what I don't lose is getting very grey.)'

Dickens felt ill and depressed for much of his five months in America. When he sailed home in April 1868, he was only 56 years old, but he looked much, much older. He was much cheered by the narrow escape he and Dolby had from the American tax inspectors, who were chasing Dolby for their portion of Dickens's earnings over the past few months. Neither Dickens nor Dolby was disposed to pay tax in a country where many hundreds of thousands of pirated copies of Dickens's novels had made publishers wealthy but from which Dickens had not received a single cent. The sight of the tax inspectors on the harbour after their ship had already set sail cheered Dickens's soul.

After his return, Dickens spent a clandestine couple of weeks with Ellen before returning to his family in Kent. He arrived home to the news that Charley was in serious financial trouble; his business had failed, he was bankrupt and badly in debt, and he had five young children and a wife to support. This coincided with Wills having been injured in a hunting accident, so Dickens found a solution to both problems by hiring Charley to work on *All The Year Round*. That summer, Dickens was back in Paris where a French version of his and Wilkie's Christmas story, *No Thoroughfare*, entitled *L'Abîme*, was due to open, starring Charles Fechter.

By Christmas, Dickens was ready to celebrate in style with his family, but there was yet another of his children missing from the party. At the end of September, sixteen-year old Plorn had sailed off to Australia to join his brother Alfred. It is unknown why Dickens was so keen to send five of his seven sons overseas, and to such far-flung destinations as India and Australia. He wrote about crying as though his heart would break after saying goodbye to young Plorn, whom he described as his 'youngest and best-loved son', yet he had arranged for Plorn to leave and he knew, as he said goodbye, that he might never see him, or Alfred, again. A couple of years earlier, Dickens had been considering arranging a reading tour of Australia, but he had already decided against that before buying Plorn a ticket to sail to the other side of the world.

Another loss to the family was the death of Uncle Fred. The fun-loving and much-loved uncle of the Dickens children's childhood, who had taken care of them when Charles and Catherine spent their six months in North America, had become an alcoholic gambling addict, constantly in debt, in disgrace and in very poor health. He died in Darlington, County Durham, at the home of a retired pub landlord, Jonathan Ross Feetum. Dickens wrote to James and Annie Fields in America at the end of October, a few days after hearing of his brother's death:

'I ... have been so busy and so fatigued that my hands have been quite full. Here are Dolby and I again leading the kind of life that you know so well. We stop next week (except in London) for the month of November, on account of the elections, and then go on again, with a short holiday at Christmas … My reason for abandoning the Christmas No. was that I became weary of having my own writing swamped by that of other people.'

To another friend he explained, 'With the exception of a few days at Christmas, this has to go on through 103 Readings, at the rate of 4 a week!' Mamie often helped her father with his reading tour preparations. On Christmas Eve 1868, he was due to give a reading in London and he wrote to ask for her help:

'It occurs to me that my table at St. James' Hall might be appropriately ornamented with a little holly next Tuesday. If the two front legs were entwined with it, for instance, and a border of it ran round the top of the fringe in front, with a little sprig by way of bouquet at each corner, it would present a seasonable appearance. If you think of this and will have the materials ready in a little basket, I will call for you at the office and take you up to the hall where the table will be ready for you.'

Christmas of 1868 was spent at Gad's Hill Place, with Dickens making the most of everything he had missed the year before. George Dolby sent him a turkey and mistletoe for Christmas and the family was entranced by the arrival of a Newfoundland puppy, whom Dickens named Bumble, after the beadle in *Oliver Twist*, because, as he explained to John Forster, he had noticed in the puppy 'a peculiarly pompous and overbearing manner he had of appearing to mount guard over the yard when he was an absolute infant'. George Dolby also left his recollections of Bumble. 'Although well trained and obedient in every respect, he had a bad habit of returning from a long walk of eluding, if he could, his master's attention, and, when about two miles from home, would race there as fast as he could; whether to get his own dinner, and that of the other dogs as well, never could be ascertained.'

Much to the disappointment of his public, Dickens had decided against writing a new Christmas story for 1868. To appease the public the Special Christmas Number of *All The Year Round* was a compilation of his Christmas Stories.

The following winter saw a great deal of snow and Dickens's letters from the end of 1869 show that he was revelling in a traditional white Christmas. On the day after Boxing Day, he sent several letters, including penning a quick note to his friend Charles Kent in which he explained, 'The postman is waiting at the gate to tramp through the snow to Rochester, and is (unlawfully) drinking a glass of gin while I write this; consequently "this" is brief.' To Macready he wrote happily of having so many of his children, as well as his grandchild, Mary Angela, with him for Christmas:

'We send ... all conceivable good Christmas and New Year greetings. They come out of a deal of snow, but are warm enough to thaw every flake of it.... It needs no Christmas time, my dearest Macready, to bring the thought of you and of our long and close friendship round to my heart, for it is always there. God bless and preserve you!'

These letters are a poignant confirmation that Charles Dickens's very last Christmas was one of the happiest and most traditional that he had known for several years.

In the final months of his life, he was working on a new novel, partly inspired by the story of a real-life murder he had become fascinated by in America. He had heard about the 1850 murder of Dr George Parkman by Professor John Webster, and when he was in Boston, he had visited Harvard University, where Webster had been a professor of chemistry and where he had attempted to dispose of his victim's body. *The Mystery of Edwin Drood* was destined to remain the greatest mystery story ever written, as Dickens died while writing it. In common with *Great Expectations*, Dickens's last novel is brooding and gothic. It begins with a scene in an opium den, peopled by drug addicts. The Christmas spirit in *The Mystery of Edwin Drood* is also one of brooding mystery, rather than of happiness. The characters seem singularly lacking in Christmas cheer and, when the novel's heroine Rosa Bud asks her guardian, the lawyer Mr Grewgious, if they can have a business meeting on Christmas Day, he is happy to oblige, saying to her:

'"As a particularly Angular man, I do not fit smoothly into the social circle, and consequently I have no other engagement at Christmas-

191

time than to partake, on the twenty-fifth, of a boiled turkey and celery sauce with a – with a particularly Angular clerk I have the good fortune to possess, whose father, being a Norfolk farmer, sends him up (the turkey up), as a present to me, from the neighbourhood of Norwich. I should be quite proud of your wishing to see me, my dear. As a professional Receiver of rents, so very few people do wish to see me, that the novelty would be bracing."'

It is on Christmas Eve that Edwin Drood disappears and on Christmas Day that his disappearance is discovered – and assumed to be murder. As Dickens died without finishing the novel and left no clear notes behind as to his intentions, it is unknown whether he intended Edwin to be the victim of murder, or whether the hero would have returned later in the novel to reveal some of the many secrets hinted at throughout the early chapters. If Dickens did intend Edwin to be killed, it would have been ironic that the man credited with 'inventing' the way in which Christmas was celebrated in Victorian Britain, should have ended his life's work with a Christmas murder mystery.

'Christmas Eve in Cloisterham. A few strange faces in the streets; a few other faces, half strange and half familiar, once the faces of Cloisterham children, now the faces of men and women who come back from the outer world at long intervals to find the city wonderfully shrunken in size, as if it had not washed by any means well in the meanwhile. To these, the striking of the Cathedral clock, and the cawing of the rooks from the Cathedral tower, are like voices of their nursery time.... Seasonable tokens are about. Red berries shine here and there in the lattices of Minor Canon Corner; Mr. and Mrs. Tope are daintily sticking sprigs of holly into the carvings and sconces of the Cathedral stalls, as if they were sticking them into the coat- button-holes of the Dean and Chapter.... Public amusements are not wanting. The Wax-Work which made so deep an impression on the reflective mind of the Emperor of China is to be seen by particular desire during Christmas Week only, on the premises of the bankrupt livery-stable-keeper up the

lane; and a new grand comic Christmas pantomime is to be produced at
the Theatre: the latter heralded by the portrait of Signor Jacksonini the
clown, saying 'How do you do to-morrow?' quite as large as life, and
almost as miserably.'

Charles Dickens, The Mystery of Edwin Drood (1870)

Charles Dickens gave a series of Christmas readings at the end of 1869, but his
family were very worried about his health. His children noticed that his speech
was becoming slurred and that he was having particular trouble pronouncing
the word Pickwick. They begged him to stop the reading tours, because they
caused him such exertion – especially when he read Bill Sikes's murder of
Nancy from *Oliver Twist* – that they were worried he would die from the stress.
He agreed and arranged a farewell tour for the spring. Mamie Dickens wrote
about her father's final public reading on 15 March 1870 and that the programme
included a reading from *A Christmas Carol*. So many people turned up without
tickets that huge crowds had to be turned away from the door.

Dickens died on the fifth anniversary of the Staplehurst Crash. He was
58 years old. His death, on 9 June 1870, was considered a national disaster.
Many stories were told of the public's reaction to his death. His son, Henry
Fielding Dickens, was told by a friend that he had been in a tobacconist's
shop when a 'working man' came in, threw his money on the counter and
reportedly said, 'Charles Dickens is dead, we have lost our best friend.' The
poet Theodore Watts-Dunton famously recalled walking along Drury Lane
in London and hearing a young market girl say, when she heard Charles
Dickens had died, 'Then will Father Christmas die too?' For many, Dickens
was the man who represented the very spirit of Christmas. His fans had no
idea how much of a hardworking trial the festive season had come to
represent to the author in the last years of his life; for them, he was as integral
a part of Christmas as the Christmas Tree and John Leech's now-iconic
drawing of the Ghost of Christmas Present had become.

During Christmas of 1870, the newspapers mourned Dickens anew. *The
Daily Telegraph* professed itself disappointed with the latest Christmas
publications and suggested that their readers return to Dickens's works
instead of reading any new stories. It also recommended a volume newly
published by Charley Dickens, now the editor of *All The Year Round*:

'It would be ungracious and unjust to the memory of the great literary master-spirit of Christmas, if we did not warmly commend the idea of Mr. Charles Dickens in issuing in one volume the "Nine Christmas Numbers of All The Year Round." Those most delightful little blue brochures for which our teeth used to water as the December days drew on, and in which, though not all was Dickens, all was singularly, and almost magically "Dickensised," have ceased now for ever; but this volume will be a most welcome guest at many a fireside this Christmastide – welcome even while it renews the memory of a great loss and sorrow.'

Many newspapers and magazines offered Dickens souvenirs in their Christmas issues, such as *The Graphic*, which included Luke Fildes's drawing *The Empty Chair*, which depicted Web Order Reference: UB3GIT3T29X Order Date: 14 Jul 17 02:58 PM Dickens's study at Gad's Hill Place the day after he died. All over the country theatres staged performances of Dickens's novels and stories, with *A Christmas Carol* proving the most popular. The legacy of Dickens's Christmas Books remained stronger than that of his Christmas stories. In 1906, when a spectacular dolls house was being created for Queen Mary, a miniature set of Dickens's five Christmas books was commissioned. The tiny versions of the books are just five centimetres high, but they contain faithful reproductions of the original text and are bound in tooled leather with gilded edges to the pages. On 1 January 1871, *Lloyd's Weekly Newspaper* gave a summary of the previous year:

'The reminiscences of Dickens are welcome to all. Dickens is inseparably connected with Christmas. His inimitable "Christmas Carol" unites him with the merry season, and it is our belief that very few spent their Christmas-day without giving a tender, regretful thought to the kindly heart that has ceased to beat – to the great name that has become of the past since the opening of the disastrous year — 1870.'

Amid all the newspapers' commentary on Dickens is a short paragraph in the *Hackney and Kingsland Gazette*, published on Christmas Eve 1870:

The inscription engraved on the tomb of Charles Dickens in Westminster Abbey has lately been exposed to the view of the public. It consists only of the few plain and simple words which he desired in his will to mark his grave:– "Charles Dickens, born February 7, 1812; died the 9th of June, 1870.".'

'One morning – it was the last day of the year, I remember – while we were at breakfast at "Gad's Hill," my father suggested that we should celebrate the evening by a charade to be acted in pantomime. The suggestion was received with acclamation, and amid shouts and laughing we were then and there, guests and members of the family, allotted our respective parts. My father went about collecting "stage properties," rehearsals were "called" at least four times during the morning, and in all our excitement no thought was given to that necessary part of a charade, the audience, whose business it is to guess the pantomime. At luncheon someone asked suddenly: "But what about an audience?" "Why, bless my soul," said my father, "I'd forgotten all about that." Invitations were quickly dispatched to our neighbours, and additional preparations made for supper. In due time the audience came, and the charade was acted so successfully that the evening stands out in my memory as one of the merriest and happiest of the many merry and happy evenings in our dear old home. My father was so extremely funny in his part that the rest of us found it almost impossible to maintain sufficient control over ourselves to enable the charade to proceed as it was planned to do. It wound up with a country dance, which had been invented that morning and practised quite a dozen times through the day, and which was concluded at just a few moments before midnight. Then leading us all, characters and audience, out into the wide hall, and throwing wide open the door, my father, watch in hand, stood waiting to hear the bells ring in the New Year. All was hush and silence after the laughter and merriment! Suddenly the peal of bells sounded, and turning he said: "A happy New Year to us all! God bless us." Kisses, good wishes and shaking of hands brought us again back to the fun and gaiety of a few moments earlier. Supper was served, the hot mulled wine drunk in toasts, and the maddest and wildest of "Sir Roger de Coverlys" ended our evening and began our New Year.'

Mamie Dickens, *My Father As I Recall Him*

Bibliography

ACKROYD, Peter, *Dickens*, Sinclair-Stevenson, 1990.

ALLEN, Michael, *Charles Dickens' Childhood*, Macmillan, 1988.

ARMSTRONG, Neil, *Christmas in Nineteenth-Century England*, MUP, 2010.

CHAMBERS, Robert, *The Book of Days, a Miscellany of Popular Antiquities*, 1862.

COX, Helen, *Mr. and Mrs. Charles Dickens Entertain at Home*, Elsevier, 2014.

CROSSLEY, Alice and **SALMON, Richard** (eds), *Thackeray in Time: History, Memory, and Modernity*, Routledge, 2016.

DICKENS, Catherine (psuedonym Lady Maria Clutterbuck), *What Shall We Have for Dinner?*, Bradbury & Evans, 1852 [fascimile copy at Charles Dickens Museum].

DICKENS, Charles, *Christmas Books*, Chapman and Hall (undated).

DICKENS, Charles, *Christmas Stories from 'Household Words' and 'All The Year Round'*, Chapman and Hall (undated).

DICKENS, Mamie, *My Father As I Recall Him*, Roxburghe Press, 1897.

DOLBY, George, *Charles Dickens as I Knew Him*, T. Fisher Unwin, 1885.

FORSTER, John, *The Life of Charles Dickens: The Illustrated Edition*, Sterling Signature, 2011.

GREAVES, John, *Dickens at Doughty Street*, Elm Tree Books, 1975.

GREY, Elizabeth, Countess of Kent, *A True Gentlewoman's Delight: Wherein is contained all manner of cookery: together with preserving, conserving, drying and candying. Very necessary for all ladies and gentlewomen,* W.I.Gent, 1653.

HAHN, Daniel, *The Oxford Companion to Children's Literature*, OUP, 2015.

HAWKSLEY, Lucinda, *Katey: The Life and Loves of Dickens's Artist Daughter*, Doubleday, 2006.

HIBBERT, Christopher, *The Making of Charles Dickens*, Longmans, 1967.

JOHNES, Martin, *Christmas and the British: A Modern History*, Bloomsbury, 2016.

BIBLIOGRAPHY

JOHNSON, Edgar, *Charles Dickens, His Tragedy and Triumph*, Viking, 1977.

KAPLAN, Fred, *Dickens: A Biography*, Sceptre, 1988.

LAMB, Hubert H., *Climate, History and the Modern World*, Routledge, 1995.

LEACH, Helen, Browne, Mary & Inglis, Raelene, *The Twelve Cakes of Christmas*, Otago, 2011.

LANGTON, Robert, *The Childhood and Youth of Charles Dickens*, F.R. Hist. Soc., 1883.

PAGE, Norman, *A Dickens Chronology*, Springer, 1988.

Philological Society of London, *The European Magazine and London Review*, Vol 77, 1820.

SCHLICKE, Paul (ed.), *The Oxford Companion to Charles Dickens*, OUP, 2011.

SLATER, Michael, *Charles Dickens*, Yale, 2009.

WATERS, Catherine, *Dickens and the Politics of the Family*, CUP, 1997.

WEIGHTMAN, Gavin and **HUMPHRIES, Steve**, *Christmas Past*, Sidgwick and Jackson, 1987.

Henry Cole's diaries accessed via the V&A website.
William Thackeray's Christmas Books accessed via Online Literature.

Index

INDEX